Also by Frank Tannenbaum

The Labor Movement: Its Conservative Functions and Social Consequences (1921)

Wall Shadows: A Study in American Prisons (1922)

Darker Phases of the South (1924)

The Mexican Agrarian Revolution (1928)

Osborne of Sing Sing (1933)

Peace by Revolution: An Interpretation of Mexico (1933)

Whither Latin America? (1934)

Crime and the Community (1938)

Slave and Citizen: The Negro in the Americas (1947)

Mexico: The Struggle for Peace and Bread (1950)

A Philosophy of Labor (1951)

The American Tradition in Foreign Policy (1955)

Ten Keys to Latin America (1962)

The Balance of Power in Society (1969)

THE FUTURE
OF DEMOCRACY IN
LATIN AMERICA

THE FUTURE
OF DEMOCRACY IN
LATIN AMERICA

*Essays by FRANK
TANNENBAUM*

*Edited and with an Introduction
by* JOSEPH MAIER
and RICHARD W. WEATHERHEAD

ALFRED·A·KNOPF
New York 1974

THIS IS A BORZOI BOOK
PUBLISHED BY ALFRED A. KNOPF, INC.

Copyright © 1974 by Albert G. Redpath

LIBRARY OF CONGRESS CATALOGING IN PUBLICATION DATA
Tannenbaum, Frank, 1893–1969.   The future of democracy
in Latin America; essays.
    1. Latin America—History—20th century—Addresses,
essays, lectures. I. Title.
F1414.T36   320.9'8'003   74–7761
ISBN 0–394–49019–3

MANUFACTURED IN THE UNITED STATES OF AMERICA
FIRST EDITION

To Alice H. Maier,
*for her long and continuing association
with Frank Tannenbaum and the University
Seminars at Columbia*

Contents

Preface

The editors have taken few liberties with these essays on Latin America by Frank Tannenbaum. The unpublished manuscripts, six in all, have been revised in accord with what we felt to be the thinking and style of their author. The published pieces have been altered only to avoid repetition.

The following list shows the time and place of original publication, or the year in which the unpublished essays were written:

1. "The Future of Democracy in Latin America (I)." *Foreign Affairs*, April 1955.

2. "The Future of Democracy in Latin America (II)." Unpublished, 1968.

3. "Economic Efficiency and Social Justice: Toynbee on Revolution in Latin America." Unpublished, 1962.

4. "The Continuing Ferment in Latin America." *The Year Book of World Affairs*, vol. 10, 1956. Published under the auspices of the London Institute of World Affairs.

5. "Politics and Government in Latin America." First published in Spanish as "Política y administración pública en Latinoamérica," in *Foro Internacional*, vol. IV, October–December 1963, no. 2.

6. "The Spanish Conquest and *Forjando Patria*." Derived mostly from "Agrarismo, Indianismo y Nacionalismo" (published in

The Hispanic American Historical Review, vol. 23, no. 3, August 1943), along with material taken from "The Spanish Tradition and the Search for National Identity," an incomplete and unpublished essay written in 1968.

7. "An American Commonwealth of Nations." An essay taken from "An American Commonwealth of Nations" (*Foreign Affairs*, July 1944) and "The Future of the Inter-American System" (an address given for the Academy of Political Science, Columbia University, April 1945).

8. "Technology and Race in Mexico." *Political Science Quarterly*, vol. LXI, no. 3, September 1946.

9. "The Continuing Revolution." Unpublished. An abbreviated version of this essay was read at the Fourteenth Annual Conference on the Caribbean, held at the University of Florida, Gainesville, December 1963.

10. "Some Reflections on the Mexican Revolution." Published, in honor of Dr. Manuel Gamio, in *Estudios Antropológicos*, Mexico City, 1956.

11. "Spontaneity and Adaptation in the Mexican Revolution." *Journal of World History*, vol. IX, no. 1, 1965.

12. "Lázaro Cárdenas." Unpublished, 1960.

13. "Latin America as a Field of Study for the Social Scientist." Unpublished. A paper read at the European–Latin American Conference, sponsored by the Ford Foundation and held in Bellagio, Italy, October 1964.

For permission to publish the essays that have already appeared elsewhere, the editors wish to express their gratitude. For their generous advice, we are deeply indebted to Albert G. Redpath, John Herman Randall, Jr., James Gutmann, and Horace L. Friess, lifelong friends of Frank Tannenbaum; to Louis Tannenbaum and Estelle Tannenbaum Rothman; to

Richard Eells, Richard S. Childs, and Muriel Golden. Special appreciation must be expressed to Alice H. Maier, long-time assistant and friend of Frank Tannenbaum, for her help in producing this volume.

THE FUTURE
OF DEMOCRACY IN
LATIN AMERICA

Introduction
Frank Tannenbaum (1893–1969)

Frank Tannenbaum was not a conventional scholar. During his years at Columbia University (1935–69), as Professor of Latin American History and later as Director of the University Seminars, there used to hang on his office wall two pictures, one above the other. The upper one was a caricature of a scholar, wearing his academic raiments and mortarboard, with angular features and an aquiline nose, a figure obviously ascetic in tastes and pedantic in manner. The one below was an enlarged snapshot of Frank Tannenbaum, wearing a weather-beaten, dirty old hat, a pipe protruding from a broadly smiling mouth. The contrasting portraits suggested that Frank Tannenbaum saw himself as a maverick in the university and in the world.

Born in Brod, a small town in Austrian Galicia, in 1893, Tannenbaum was raised in meager circumstances and helped his parents do odd jobs on the land when he was not in the village school. In 1904 he journeyed with his parents and a younger brother and sister to America. They came for the usual reasons that attracted immigrants to the United States—to escape poverty and to seek out a better life. Some of the family's relatives had already established themselves in the New York area, so the New World was not altogether strange to them. Soon after arriving, the Tannenbaums heard of a 300-acre abandoned farm in the Berkshire hills near Great Barrington, Massachusetts. They purchased the land for a nominal price with money borrowed from relatives and friends and soon they settled on it.

Young Frank's first lessons in America came from farm life
and the sundry daily chores that everyone in the family had to
perform. Each morning he rose early to attend to the usual
round of farming duties and, when he had finished his share of
them, he would walk a mile and a half to the local schoolhouse.
As he was growing up, he learned to follow many of Poor
Richard's maxims, which reinforced at the same time the
family's Jewish heritage: the enduring ties of family, thrift, and
hard work, deeds above words, life as learning (and vice versa),
and compassion for the underdog. Almost immediately after
landing in New York, young Tannenbaum began to experience
the process of Americanization, identifying himself and these
American values, with the rural setting and the natural rhythms
of farm life.

The America he grew up in was also an America growing
up. The frontier may have closed in 1890, but it still possessed
its mystique; the first decade of the new century was the age of
Theodore Roosevelt and the great influx of immigrants. Americans viewed themselves as a moral people, beneficent and
powerful, destined to bring goodness and freedom to the world.
Here the burdens of Europe would be lifted by the special grace
of the New World. American history was a chronicle of
progress. The Horatio Alger heroes were prototypes of individual achievement; integrity and hard work would naturally be
rewarded by riches and success. Americans were not troubled
by an awareness of tragedy or presentiments of failure. Owen
Wister's *The Virginian* epitomized American uprightness,
simplicity, and self-reliance. The quick victory over Spain made
the United States a righteous guardian over lesser, "uncivilized"
peoples. American optimism, benevolence, missionary zeal, and
industrial might would soon make the world "safe for democracy." There was, however, another and darker side to this main
image of America. The muckrakers inveighed against the sins of
the city and the excesses of capitalism. But most Americans
thought that the aberrations were temporary and could be
corrected once they were recognized and once enough planning
and energy had been directed towards their solution.

In 1906, following a quarrel with his father about chores, Tannenbaum ran away from the farm and took the train down to New York City, where he went to his relatives and stayed for the next few years. The escape from Great Barrington turned out to be a relatively mild act of adolescent rebellion: it was a partial and temporary separation, and not a break, from the family. Frank went back to the farm regularly when an extra hand was needed. For all of his idealized reverence for rural ways, Tannenbaum was probably drawn to the city by the promise of new things and experiences.

While living with his relatives in New York City, Tannenbaum made his own way by doing odd jobs such as waiting table and operating an elevator. When he had the time, he attended night classes at the Ferrer School at 63 West 107th Street in Manhattan. It was "a laboratory in which new social theories are tested," as the school's president described it to a reporter of the *New York Times*, adding that it was "the first institution devoted to the constructive side of anarchism." Here anarchist intellectuals, radical labor leaders, and social activists met together and were able to talk to and learn from each other about the world as it was and how it could be. No doubt there was a millennial spirit dominating the school and a feeling that by proselytizing paradise could be re-created on earth. Emma Goldman, Lincoln Steffens, and Alexander Berkman ("Sasha") were among the faculty of the Ferrer School.

By the middle of the new century's second decade, Tannenbaum's interests in the problems of the poor working-man and the unemployed were focused on an attempt at solutions. He joined the "Wobblies," the Industrial Workers of the World, and soon became a local leader. For Thorstein Veblen, the I.W.W. was an "exuberant" and "untidy" van-guard of dissent. It was a radical labor group that sought to effect changes for the good of society by sporadic violence and strikes. The Wobblies aimed at improving the worker's lot by making specific demands such as reducing working hours, increasing wages, and bettering the conditions under which he toiled. As a movement, the I.W.W. grew out of conflicts in the West between lumberjacks and miners and company owners, and later carried its techniques of class warfare to the East Coast. Its principles were summarized in the preamble of the I.W.W. constitution:

> *The working class and the employing class have nothing in common. There can be no peace so long as hunger and want are found among millions of working people, and the few who make up the employing class have all the good things of life.*
>
> *Between these two classes a struggle must go on until all the toilers come together on the political as well as on the industrial field, and take and hold that which they produce by their labor, through an economic organization of the working class, without affiliation with any political party.*

In the winter of 1913–14, thousands of unemployed workers roamed the streets of New York in search of jobs without success—they were hungry and desperate and the I.W.W. message held out a promise of immediate relief. On March 1, 1914, Frank Tannenbaum led a group of 300 homeless poor into the First Presbyterian Church and demanded money for food and shelter. After some negotiation, he convinced the church leaders to provide each of the "sit-down strikers" with thirty cents. This technique worked and was to be repeated at different churches; Tannenbaum exhorted his followers to organize and demand an eight-hour workday and a minimum daily wage of $3.00, and to continue sitting down in churches until these basic demands were met. No church in the city could be sure that it would not be the next target.

In her autobiography, Emma Goldman recalled the special role Tannenbaum played during that winter of despair and hope:

> *Over a quarter of a million persons were out of work in New York, and other cities were stricken in no lesser degree.*

> *The suffering was augmented by the extraordinarily severe weather. The papers minimized the appalling state of affairs; the politicians and reformers remained lukewarm. . . .*
>
> *Then an unexpected thing happened, which gave the situation compelling publicity. Out of the ranks of starved and frozen humanity the slogan came to visit religious institutions. The unemployed, led by a vivid youth named Frank Tannenbaum, began a march on the churches of New York.*
>
> *We all had loved Frank for his wide-awakeness and his unassuming ways. He had spent much of his free time in our office, reading and helping in the work connected with* Mother Earth. *His fine qualities held out the hope that Frank would some day play an important part in the labor struggle. None of us had expected however that our studious, quiet friend would so quickly respond to the call of the hour.*
>
> *Whether out of fear or because of the realization of the significance of the march on the churches, several of them gave shelter, food, and money to the bands of unemployed. Emboldened by their success, one hundred and eighty-nine jobless men, with Frank at their head, went to one of the Catholic churches in the city. . . .*
>
> *Frank was condemned to serve a year in the penitentiary [on Blackwell's—now Welfare—Island]. . . . He made a splendid stand, his speech in his own defence being intelligent and defiant.*

The contemporary reports on Tannenbaum's activities in behalf of the poor received somewhat different interpretations in the *New York Times.* "Urges Workers on to Anarchy," screamed a front-page headline on March 3, 1914. For the entire month his radical activities received front-page attention and editorial-page scorn. The next day the *Times's* front page announced: "Tells Unemployed to Adopt Force—Tannenbaum, at Old St. Paul's, Urges Descent on Some Church Tonight—Says 'No Right but Might,' " while the editorial pages excoriated Tannenbaum, his "army of the unemployed," and the Wobblies. "All but a few of

Tannenbaum's followers are weak members of the hobo class," the editorial writer frowned. "They are not laboring men, they do not want employment. Immediate and decisive steps should be taken by the police to suppress this IWW pest, which is in effect nothing more than a cheap advertisement of the most abominable organization ever formed in this country, but might well lead to a violent outbreak."

On the fifth of March, the *Times*'s lead story was: "IWW Invaders Seized in Church—Tannenbaum Is Held in $5,000 Bail." The *Times*, apparently, was greatly relieved by such decisive action and on the following day's editorial page, a column entitled "The Hobo Riots Quelled" explained the situation in this fashion: "The crowds lately inflamed by Tannenbaum and his fellow orators in Rutgers Square have been increasing in size. Tannenbaum's threats are not to be lightly disregarded. He has an organization behind him which one of its precious literary friends suggested yesterday might use dynamite."

It is of interest here to examine some of the things Tannenbaum was saying and demanding at the time in order to determine the place of radical ideas in his conservative social philosophy. He once addressed his followers:

> *We are members of the working class. Everything in this city was created by our hands or the hands of our brothers and sisters. We have a right to a share in every house and in every man's loaf of bread. What's more we're going to make the city give it to us or take it by force. . . . We want work, but we will not work for 50¢ or a $1 a day. We want $3 a day for an eight hour day. We want union wages and union conditions and we will not work until we get them. We would rather go to jail. . . . The IWW is going to take over the whole earth. It is an organization only for workingmen and nobody else can belong. If capital doesn't want to work, let it get off the earth.*

Tannenbaum spoke about the specific purpose of the church "sit-ins":

Until a few days ago New York didn't have an
unemployed movement. Then we decided to show the city
what it meant. . . . Tonight we have 500 men. In two weeks
we will be 20,000 strong and when New York learns that
these men mean business it will hurry and scurry to do
something for us. There is no right but might. If such a thing
as justice could be had in this city, why, we wouldn't have to
go around this way to get something to eat.

Radicalism was essential to Tannenbaum's social philosophy;
violence was not. The experiences he had with radical reform
ideas, organized labor, arrest, and imprisonment became subjects
of intellectual inquiry. His radical thinking, although close in
some of its aspects to the socialism of Eugene Debs, never
developed or converted into a set ideology. The passion of his
radicalism, as seen in the speeches excerpted from the *Times*,
was in fact tempered by his experience with the Wobblies. He
did not abandon their goals of improving the worker's condition,
nor was his compassion for the underdog lessened. But he had
learned the distinction between reform and apocalypse and
had realized the complexities of human organization; law, he had
discovered, was both an instrument of and an obstacle to
progress.

Tannenbaum's activist role in labor developed into a
lifelong concern with the labor movement and the union.
Surprisingly, for a radical who ran afoul of the law, for an
ex-convict as he referred to himself on occasion, he did not have
a political ax to grind and his writings are free of venom and
invective. He looked upon his involvement reflectively. When
he wrote of labor, and of most other subjects, he wrote as a
historian with a sociological bent. The trade union, he believed,
had a special purpose in industrial society; it was an institution
with its own makeup and morale and mission, and, paradoxi-
cally, one of its major contributions was towards ensuring the
stability of society. In his first book, *The Labor Movement: Its
Conservative Functions and Social Consequences* (1921), which
was "humbly dedicated to John Dewey," Tannenbaum could

say: "It is the ideal aim of the labor movement to abolish revolutions. It aims to eliminate the cost of human sacrifice due to social change by making change a pragmatic and deliberate thing." Thirty years later, his interest in the labor movement was just as keen, but he viewed it more broadly. In *A Philosophy of Labor* (1951), he saw "the trade union movement as an unconscious rebellion against the atomization of industrial society." He still understood it as basically conservative, indeed counterrevolutionary, in the sense that it was

> *a repudiation of the individualism of the French Revolution and of the liberalism of the English utilitarian philosophers. It rests upon the group, upon the organized "society" forged by the mine, mill, and factory. Trade-unionism is a repudiation of Marxism because its ends are moral rather than economic. It is a social and ethical system, not merely an economic one. . . . The values implicit in trade-unionism are those of an older day . . . security, justice, freedom, and faith.*

Finally, "he who would understand the labor movement must look backward and see where it came from. The future direction is to be discerned in the institutional pattern resting on previously established rule, habit, and commitment."

None of his writings on labor was pure economic history or merely sociological interpretation. His analysis of labor was an alloy of these and more. Although his viewpoint became more and more detached, he never forgot his personal experiences as a labor leader. Any institution, he discovered, had its own "philosophy," whether it was the trade union, the prison, the family, the church, the state, the army, slavery, the *hacienda,* or the university. How did he define the "philosophy" of an institution? "Every institution tends to mold the character, the ideas and to determine the place in society of the individuals it dominates. . . . A major key to an understanding of a complex society is through a study of the role, claims and conflicts [of its] institutions."

When Frank Tannenbaum was arrested and imprisoned he was exposed to institutions, procedures, and people different from those he had known as a labor leader. His response to the abruptly changed situation was one of fascination and curiosity about the new environment and experience rather than one of personal resentment towards the world. It led him to write three books on the subjects of crime, prison, the criminal and society, and to request in early 1916 that he be voluntarily committed for a period of time at Sing Sing for the purpose of observing, participating in, studying, and living the life of the prison. Eventually, in 1932, he even served on the staff of the National Commission on Law Observance and Law Enforcement. From 1914 until 1922, all aspects of crime in society occupied much of his attention, while at the same time he was gathering his thoughts together about labor and experiencing new intellectual sensations at Columbia College. In 1920, one year before his graduation, he spent his summer vacation taking a trip across the United States in a Model T Ford to visit some seventy penal institutions.

When he wrote his first book on crime and society, *Wall Shadows: A Study in American Prisons* (1922), Tannenbaum was concerned with the complex nature of crime and community organization in prisons. The book describes what happens to the criminal after conviction and, although the focus may appear somewhat narrow, nonetheless Tannenbaum's attitude is that of a reformer who hoped that the book would "help some few to take up the cause of society against our medieval prisons." It was Thomas Mott Osborne, the reform-minded warden of Sing Sing, whose improvements in prison administration caught Tannenbaum's imagination and who contributed an introduction to the book. During his voluntary confinement at Sing Sing, Tannenbaum began a long and close friendship with Osborne, one result of which was *Osborne of Sing Sing* (1933), a book that not only applauded what Osborne had done and advocated while warden, but also represented a refinement of his own earlier analysis of penal institutions.

Frank Tannenbaum's most detailed study of the general problem was *Crime and the Community* (1938). Although he did not write it as a textbook, it soon became a basic source, widely adopted in criminology and sociology courses in colleges and universities throughout the United States; later, parts of the book were made required reading for the Chicago police. *Crime and the Community* is to the study of the organization of crime as *A Philosophy of Labor* is to the study of labor. Both were written after many years of direct experience and firsthand knowledge and represent a summing-up of Tannenbaum's studies, reflections, and, to a degree, predictions about these two different subjects. He believed that prisons could, with difficulty, be improved, but that crime itself was an inevitable problem permeating all levels of society.

> *There is no reason to assume that in dealing with the criminal we are dealing with something extraneous. We are really dealing with all of society even when we begin dealing with the problem of crime. What is true of the pattern of criminal life is true also of the various social and political agencies that have grown up around the attempt to deal with the problem of crime. They too are part of the whole, and an attempt to revise them involves by indirection an attempt to revise all the social and political agencies, because in one way or another they all affect the judicial and the penal institutions.*

If the criminal had to be understood in relation to society at large and to the institution of the prison in particular, he could not be seen as separate from the group or groups that molded him. It was the special traits of group activity—communal traits, if you will—that endowed the criminal with roles, and hence a social character.

> *The only way to reach the criminal is to reach his group. It is the group that sets the pattern, provides the stimulus, gives the rewards in glory and companionship, offers the protection and loyalty, and, most of all, gives the criminal life*

> *its ethical content without which it cannot persist. To offer to*
> *reform a criminal by tearing him out of his own value-giving*
> *environment . . . without making him part of another group*
> *which provides an equally genuine essential base of existence*
> *. . . is to attempt the impossible.*

Tannenbaum's experiences and studies in labor organization and in crime (as a necessary and natural aspect of society) taught him much about institutional structures, the habits people adopt and the roles they assume, the pressures on human personality by the group or groups within which an individual acts, and the difficulties that attend any effort to change radically any institution. He held that we live in an "intractable" and "recalcitrant" universe (words which would frequently recur among his writings), one in which he took the etymological meaning of "utopia"—"not a place"—at face value. "Until I went to school I thought there was only one way to accomplish an end," he once said. "Now I know that there are many ways. The study of history is dangerous to radicalism. One of the greatest blows I suffered in college was the realization that the world had a past as well as a present and a future."

Higher education came largely as a result of Tannenbaum's imprisonment. As already noted, he had achieved a good deal of fame or notoriety, depending upon one's viewpoint, prior to his jail sentence in 1914. One person, Grace Hatch Childs, had followed Tannenbaum's brief career as a labor leader, as reported in the *New York Times*. Grace Childs, who was the daughter of a distinguished Chicago lawyer, came to New York as a bride in 1912 and turned immediately to social work in the Charity Organization Society. Her husband, Richard Childs, still a prominent national figure in municipal government reform, recalls his wife's interest in the young Tannenbaum.

> *One day in her early years here she was struck by the*
> *sincerity and perceptiveness of the reported words of a young*
> *waiter on trial in court, words spoken on behalf of the*

> *neglected winter army of the unemployed. She sent to him in*
> *prison an invitation to come to her at the end of his term,*
> *found him to be a boy of character, eager above all else to get*
> *an education. She pledged him what money he needed to*
> *supplement his own earnings through four years of college.*

The invitation was carried to Tannenbaum by E. Stagg Whitin, Grace Childs' friend and the chairman of the Executive Council of the National Committee on Prisons and Prison Labor, located on the Columbia campus. Whitin was also a good friend of Thomas Mott Osborne, of Sing Sing, and Professor Carlton J. H. Hayes, at Columbia. It was through Whitin that Tannenbaum met both of these men and through them that he entered the university in the fall of 1916. Whitin had gone to Hayes and asked if it would be possible to admit Tannenbaum to Columbia even though he had no high school education or, for that matter, much in the way of formal schooling of any sort. Hayes said that he would discuss the matter with Dean Frederick P. Keppel. An interview was arranged; everything went smoothly and, after it was over, Keppel was heard to remark that it would be easier to get Tannenbaum in than to get him out. In the mid-thirties, Tannenbaum dedicated his *Whither Latin America?* to Keppel, "one-time dean of Columbia College, in appreciation."

Tannenbaum claimed to have read all of Plato's works before entering Columbia. Whether the claim was authentic or apocryphal is beside the point. There can be no question about his having been well read in many areas and that he was indeed obsessed with reading. For him it was a vital experience. He was said to have preferred the job of elevator operator over all the other menial jobs he held because, especially at night when few people used the car, he could sit in peace and read. Towards the end of his incarceration on Blackwell's Island, the *New York Times* editorially chided Tannenbaum, "our young anarchist friend," about his complaints against the warden for withholding certain books he had asked for:

> *For some reason Mr. Tannenbaum seems much excited because the warden excluded Goethe's* Faust *on the ground that it was immoral, and Buckle's* History of Civilization, Jevons's First Principles of Science, *Lecky's* History of European Morals, *Tate's* Essays and Lectures *and our respected weekly neighbor* The Nation *on the ground that they were too radical.*

Columbia College was a new and stimulating experience for Tannenbaum, and his attachment to the institution and its members continued to the end of his life. His first appetite for history was aroused by Carlton Hayes. His interest in economics developed from courses taken with Edwin R. A. Seligman, and his concern with education and the philosophy of experience grew from his friendship with John Dewey. He became good friends with these and other Columbia luminaries. An enduring anecdote has Tannenbaum visiting his professors before their lectures and advising them on what they should say in the classroom. A close friend of Tannenbaum's, John Herman Randall, remembers that "Dewey's own bent of mind—and patient tolerance—made him amenable to Frank's instruction, and together they gave a most suggestive course in institutional functional pluralism. This course is best known through Dewey's *The Public and Its Problems.*"

Conversation and comradeship as media for developing ideas were important elements in Tannenbaum's life and education. Early in his college days he was introduced to a fellow student, Albert Redpath, by Dean Keppel, who wanted Redpath to be helpful to Tannenbaum, and suggested that he and a small group of students meet regularly to talk about things important to them. Keppel arranged for them to gather at the Faculty Club each Thursday night for dinner. Redpath asked Horace Friess, James Gutmann, John Herman Randall, and Edward Gluck to join Tannenbaum and himself. It was decided that Bertrand Russell's *Why Men Fight* should be the first book to be discussed. With a one-year interruption during the war, these students met regularly while at Columbia, and the friendly group became an institution in itself, subsequently meeting every Friday for luncheon for more than fifty years. All of the group, with the exception of Edward Gluck and Albert Redpath, went on to become professors at Columbia.

Horace Friess recalls that at each group session, "Frank used to put us on the rack. He would ask each of us questions, if such and such a social conflict arose, what would you do?" And then Friess, summing up Tannenbaum's early Columbia experience and his way of seeing the world, continued:

> *Another aspect of Frank's manner of going at things was to try to interpret a situation with which he had come into contact. He had usually, after being immersed in something, a theory about it. Now, that involved a crusading element but also an observing element. Frank moved into new interests at Columbia and talked more about those. Both his interest in labor and in prison reform became generalized for him into a theory of human relations and society. And he thought that the labor movement was a good paradigm for the kind of society that he was interested in.*

Tannenbaum added the university to the collection of institutions that compelled his interest. While in college, he continued to think and write about the prison community and the labor movement. Of course, he led the full life of a student, attending classes, going to the library, participating in the founding of a new poetry magazine called *The Lyric*, and developing lasting friendships. He was a serious student, partly perhaps because he was several years the senior of his classmates, partly because he had originally thought of using his education as a tool of advancement in the labor movement. When he entered Columbia there was no labor leader with a formal college education and Tannenbaum probably felt that with such learning, he could be of greater aid to his comrades in the labor field. Columbia changed all that. He fell in love with it and with the idea and the experience of the university. And so Keppel's comment about Tannenbaum, that it would be easier to get him in than to get him out, proved accurate. Although he left Columbia in 1921 and did not return until 1935, when he succeeded W. R. Shepherd in the chair of Latin American History, he really was never absent from it in a spiritual and intellectual sense. When he graduated from Columbia, he did so with highest honors, a Phi Beta Kappa key, accolades from Carlton J. H. Hayes and Harry Carman as one of their best students ever, and a favorable write-up in the *New York Times*. In later years, Tannenbaum almost always wore his Phi Beta Kappa key as if were an insignia identifying him as belonging to a special order of men.

The University Seminars at Columbia, over which Tannenbaum presided as director for twenty-five years, may be seen as an outgrowth of his contacts with friends and professors at Columbia. Near the close of World War II, the administration of Columbia University asked the faculty, all of them individually, to make suggestions for improving the mind and relevance of the institution. It was in response to this canvass that Frank Tannenbaum came up with his suggestion of "University" (i.e., interdisciplinary) Seminars for faculty members and invited associates from outside the university, to concentrate on discussion of selected lasting problems. Looking back on the origins of this latest of his continuing concerns, Tannenbaum wrote in 1964:

> *Since my undergraduate days I have had a close friendship with Horace L. Friess, James Gutmann, John Herman Randall, Jr., professors of philosophy at Columbia, and Albert G. Redpath, who has been a university trustee. We have met for lunch once a week for over forty years and have talked about many things including the university and its needs. On March 4, 1944, during our regular luncheon I read a letter [later to become the founding charter of the University Seminars] I had written to Frank Fackenthal, Provost of the*

university. After much talk, my friends agreed that the letter ought to be sent and offered to join me in signing it. Altogether, eighteen professors, in addition to myself, put their names to this letter.

In part, the Seminars grew out of the experience that Tannenbaum had had with his regular lunch meetings with friends. Partly, too, they evolved from Tannenbaum's feeling that a classroom or traditional research situation had many obstacles to the free play of the intellect. And, finally, they developed out of Tannenbaum's conviction that "the world could not be divided into political science, economics, sociology or history. . . . The subtleties, complexities, and interlacing of the threads that tied life together and made it meaningful lay beyond the reach of the specialized disciplines."

The University Seminar "movement," as Tannenbaum conceived of it, was organic, capable of infinite growth, and benign because it had no established bureaucratic procedures; ultimately, it might possibly absorb the entire university, replacing it with a new and more useful institution. The "movement" was at the same time an institution:

> *Unconsciously, perhaps, the University Seminar movement has a theory of the integration of human experience, as well as its own notion of the structure of knowledge, that is different from that which underlies the organization of the University. . . . The University, in building a separate department for each unique discipline, and then grouping them in faculties or schools, becomes the depository of all knowledge without violating the essential separateness of each discipline.*
>
> *In contrast, the University Seminar movement sees society organized in many continuing institutions . . . [that] are separate professional orders, with a logic uniquely different, and shared only by the initiated in each separate order. [A] University Seminar reaches for membership into all*

disciplines and activities pertinent to the objective—the under-standing of the behavior of a going concern.

Consistent with his view of the world, Tannenbaum did not think of the Seminars as problem-solving devices; as he had written earlier, problems, human and social, did not go away and total amelioration was chimerical. The Seminars could, however, improve the human condition (as it existed within an institutional setting) insofar as they could provide better understanding, insights, and vantage points from which to analyze a particular concern. In short, if the Seminars had an ultimate purpose for their existence, it was that they should be useful to the members of the university and to their fellows outside the university's walls. He felt, as he said in one of his last conversations on this subject, that

> *I've done many things in my life, but this is the richest. It has occupied a very large part of my energies for the last twenty-five years. It has probably interfered with my writing. . . . What has it meant to me personally? It has meant responsibility and also a great deal of satisfaction. It has given me a great many friends. And it has given me what, temperamentally, I think, I have always needed, an opportunity to be useful. I have often thought of myself, that the only thing I have ever wanted in this world was to be useful.*

His last comments on the usefulness of the University Seminars and of his life in their service squared fully with his early lessons at home combining the Jewish and the Protestant ethics.

Not only was the University Seminar movement an attempt to break down the traditional barriers among the academic disciplines and faculties, but it also sought to bring other centers of knowledge and experience into contact with the university. Men and women from business, industry, finance, labor, government, museums, hospitals, and other universities, all sharing some common interest, would band together voluntarily and found a seminar around a "going concern." A "going concern" might be the problem of peace, religion, the state, the Renaissance, international communism, the Atlantic community, modern East Asia, to cite some of the sixty Seminars at the moment. The founders would then admit new associates by election. A bridge was effectively built between the worlds of town and gown. And the meetings were conducted in an atmosphere of good fellowship and conviviality. Conversation was the medium. Most of the Seminars met at dinner time. "Eating together," as Dr. Johnson would say, "promotes good will, sir; commensality is benevolent."

As Tannenbaum grew intellectually in the university, he sought to reform it. It may not be exaggerating to say that he was an educational revolutionary in the way that John Dewey— or perhaps, as John Herman Randall suggests, Hildebrand— was. Tannenbaum believed the Seminars added a fourth dimension to the university: "It can now accumulate, preserve, transmit, and *focus* knowledge. . . . The ability to focus involves a structural modification." The Seminars provided Columbia's inhabitants, and those outside it, with the tools for reshaping the university itself and for dealing with contemporary and persistent problems.

Tannenbaum was a revolutionary in a peculiar sense. His radical conservatism always served to restrain him from violent or destructive ideas or acts. He was radical in the sense that he looked at the essences or roots of institutions, conservative in that he thought institutions were not amenable to swift and thorough change. He sought to improve an institution, but he knew that it would take time and adjustment and that no amount of improving would lead to perfection. He also had a deep respect for institutions as such and especially for the university and its professors. "Like the Church," he wrote, "it must have a total dedication from its votaries. The academy has something of the quality we identify with 'holy,' 'sacred,' 'innocent,' 'disinterested.' " The statement is exaggerated in its claims, particularly in this day and age; but it does show

Tannenbaum's deep respect and love and awe of this special institution. It also reveals the zealous commitment to education that one often finds in those who have not had formal schooling. And, of course, Tannenbaum's radicalism was tempered by his recognition that universities, as all institutions, have "a peculiar logic to themselves," and that "the logic of the university creates a special order of men."

The normal consecutive four-year residence at Columbia College was broken for Tannenbaum by the intrusion of World War I. It would be well to remember here that the war was one of the great issues that dominated Tannenbaum's college years. Woodrow Wilson's domestic reforms and internationalism, the Mexican Revolution, and the continuing labor struggles were others. In fact, during the month of March 1914, Tannenbaum shared the front page of the *New York Times* with Pancho Villa. And these great issues were important and lasting experiences to live with. In the summer of 1918, he left Columbia to join the army and during his one-year stint he rose to the rank of sergeant. As usual, he wrote about the experience. Tannenbaum's army experience, however, inspired none of the fascination that led him to write so extensively about prison society, the labor movement, slavery, and the university—leaving aside Latin America for the moment.

In a brief critique, entitled "Life in an Army Training Camp" and published in *The Dial* of April 1919, Tannenbaum wrote about the stultifying aspects of day-to-day life in the army. In general, he found the consequences of army life destructive of the human personality: the social leveling, the monotony that "dresses all bodies in one cloth, and contracts all souls into one mood—irresponsibility," the boredom, gambling, and wanton sex. "Man," he wrote, "cannot live on obedience and submission alone." Why were the soldiers "irresponsible"? Tannenbaum believed that "the soldier has become a child. The camp is the place where this new child lives, and military discipline is the force which created him." He found that there was really no alternative to the present military system except to democratize the army, and that was impossible because it would "undermine the present function of all the military ideology and technique as it relates to the soldier." While describing the dreary aspects of army life—with a curious omission of any mention of heavy drinking and alcoholism—Tannenbaum still sought the inner logic of the army camp and was disappointed that his division was not sent to Europe to fight in the great war—that he and his soldiers were denied "the privilege of going across."

It is not possible to say exactly why Tannenbaum wrote so little about the army in comparison with his other writings on institutions. Perhaps he was not in it for a sufficiently long time to develop an abiding intellectual interest. Perhaps the restraints upon the free play of intellect repelled him; and certainly it is hard to imagine a man so comfortable in academic surroundings being at ease for long in the military. What is sure is that he maintained a respect, even fondness, for the military as an institution and for the soldier when he was a competent professional, when he had absorbed the logic of the institution, and when he expressed it in his actions. "This logic is strikingly indifferent to the particular political organization in which the army has its being. The essential features of the soldierly character tend to be the same in any society," Tannenbaum wrote thirty-five years after his return to civilian life.

Part of his service in the army was spent at Camp Sever in South Carolina, where Tannenbaum first noticed fundamental differences between the North and the South. Later he went to the South again to continue his writings on crime and prison life. As he traveled from state to state, he noted a quick-tempered penchant for violence, a geographic isolation from other sections of the country (and isolation of parts of the South from each other), and a crippling obsession with race. The five areas on which he focused in *Darker Phases of the South* (1924) to explain the violence, the isolation, and the obsession with race were the Ku Klux Klan, the cotton mill village, the prison system, the dominance of the single crop, and the consequences of slavery. If any or all of these matters were to be viewed as "problems," Tannenbaum would find no single satisfactory solution:

> *Yet solutions are not available for real problems; all that may be arrived at is attenuation, relief, a resetting of the strain, a removal of some of the friction. All that may be asked for is a change in the relative position of some of the factors, for the problem, as a problem, remains in a new form.*

To be more specific, he felt that

> *the race problem cannot be solved. There is no solution which can be devised that will do all of the things a solution would have to do: remove not only the difficulties but all the traces of it.* There is no solution for the race problem. And one might add that that is true of all fundamental social problems.

The mill village was a strange blend of forces for progress—industrialization—and for retardation: an isolated, autonomous, inbred, and paternalistic milieu. Tannenbaum's description of the mill village, written in the early twenties, anticipates his later treatment of the *hacienda* on much the same terms. Or it might have been that his slightly prior discovery of the Mexican *hacienda* as a unique institution prepared him to interpret the mill village as he did. As with the *hacienda*, he first established the concrete detail of its workings as a system and then proceeded to suggest broad generalizations or modifications. His attention was directed to the specific patterns of day-to-day chores, and the round of trivial but necessary activities that insidiously shape themselves into habits, because he felt these were the "intractable" and "recalcitrant" elements in any situation that probably could not be radically altered:

> *The mill village is a curious institution. . . . It has no life of its own. Its destinies are spun by the mill. . . . The houses are all the same. . . . It gives the impression of system.*

It is not a town. It is not an incorporated village. It is built upon private property. . . . The State may not enter in without a warrant. The school teacher is paid by the mill man, and the school is built by the mill man. So is the church. . . . The grocery-store, the moving-picture, the drug-store, the doctor, everything is in the hands of the mill man. . . . Even the policemen are paid by him. The people have no political life. They do not vote. They are not interested in politics. . . . They must go into debt for necessary supplies, and before they draw their first pay, their debt may be much more than the pay drawn will cover. . . . The mill population is in a world apart. It does not play with the community. It does not mix with it. It does not intermarry, it does not work with it. . . . This is so general a fact in the mill section of the South that it is recognized as a caste system.

Here, one could venture, was the *hacienda* in miniature; and not far from the mill village was to be found the persisting heritage of slavery. Tannenbaum found in the South what he had observed in Mexico and what he probably had seen as a child growing up in Austria—the ties of the land that held the typical peasant, mill worker, or *peón*. There are rural habits and expectations that prevent them from seeking change; their world is both too comfortable and too uncomfortable for them to leave it. The way of dress, the kinds of food and the manner of eating it, the friendships formed in and by the locality, the special flavor of the language, the webs of intimate knowledge and the superstitions of the outside world operate in such a fashion as to make anything beyond the immediate horizon impervious to the desires of the peasant, the mill hand, and the *peón*.

It was in 1922–23, as a journalist for *Century* magazine, and a year later for *Survey*, that Frank Tannenbaum first went to Mexico. His first piece on Mexico, an article in *Century* (August 1923) entitled "The Miracle School," describes a spontaneous and grassroots educational enterprise, learning by doing, in which "the children in the school have spread out into the community so that the community is becoming the school and the school is becoming the community. Soon it will be hard to tell which is which." The school itself was located in a slum section called *la colonia de la bolsa:* "a haven for the outcasts of Mexico City: the bums, tramps, thieves, pickpockets, burglars, and disreputable women . . . [and] the delinquent children. One half of all those of Mexico City came from that district." One would not have thought that such an environment—a thieves' market—would be fertile ground for the growth of any educational experiment. But the "miracle" did in fact occur. There was an outpouring of energy on the part of the people who lived in the *colonia,* in particular the children. There was self-reliance, self-government, cooperative organization for the solution of practical problems, and, as they learned about dealing with hygiene, crafts, planting vegetables, the people learned to read and write and, in the process, gained confidence and pride in themselves. The whole undertaking would have delighted John Dewey.

A previously disorganized community had, Tannenbaum reported, discovered itself through a natural, though complex, process of education and self-help. Nothing had been previously planned and all that existed before the "miracle school" took shape was good will on the part of the Mexican teacher who initiated it. The only thing he received from the Mexican government was its blessing—but that was enough to start the experiment. What impressed Tannenbaum about this school was its base in the spontaneous communal effort of these slum people and their ragamuffin children in their efforts to improve themselves. The climate that stimulated such growth was provided by the pre-Revolutionary experience. Indeed, the Mexican Revolution meant renaissance, as Tannenbaum observed in many other writings on Mexico. It provided a special atmosphere within which the creative impulses of the Mexicans were discovered, galvanized, and released, and in the process a new culture was forged and a new popular identity formed. For

Tannenbaum, the "miracle school" epitomized much of this spiritual renewal:

> *I have never seen brighter, more self-reliant and promising children anywhere in Mexico than in this outcast district. There is an obvious seriousness and joy of enterprise that if allowed to develop . . . will prove one of the greatest single influences for a better Mexico—and one of the most remarkable educational institutions anywhere in the world.*

Throughout his life, Frank Tannenbaum was as much a man of action as he was a scholar and philosopher; he always combined the maverick with the conventional. In the case at hand, he helped set up a Friends of Mexico Committee in 1924, whose purposes were to collect books for an English library in Mexico and "to seek better acquaintance between the peoples of Mexico and the United States." He recruited some important Americans to serve on the board, including Thomas Mott Osborne, its chairman, and Felix Adler, John Dewey, Samuel Gompers, Ernest Gruening, Samuel Guy Inman, Paul V. Kellogg, and George Foster Peabody. In its solicitations to the general public, the committee offered a free copy of Tannenbaum's *Century* article "The Miracle School" as "a splendid introduction of the people of Mexico to the people of the United States."

His knowledge of Mexico was to broaden with his assignment for *Survey* magazine to go to Mexico and persuade leading figures of the Revolution to write special articles on its different phases. *Survey*'s special issue on Mexico was to coincide with the reopening of diplomatic ties between the United States and Mexico. *Survey* had always been a publication with a social conscience. It began as *Charities* in January 1897, offering current information about social problems and ways of alleviating them through organized charitable giving. Within a few years the magazine had changed its name to *Survey*, reflecting a broader concern with an array of social issues, a more diverse reading public, and a more varied list of contributing writers. Liberal and reform-minded, *Survey* partook of the muckraking tradition and invited muckrakers to write for it. Its contents were as international as they were national; whole issues had been devoted to the Irish question, the Soviet Union, and the Negro question in America. And now, in May 1924, *Survey* came out with the issue on Mexico it had commissioned Frank Tannenbaum to prepare.

The nineteen articles he put together presented what we would call today an "overview" of the contemporary situation in Mexico, and most of the contributors were leading lights of the Revolution. Plutarco Elías Calles, Felipe Carrillo Puerta, Manuel Gamio, Dr. Atl, Pedro Henríquez Ureña, José Vasconcelos, Ramón de Negri, and Diego Rivera wrote articles dealing with such matters as educational reform, the persistence of revolution and the problem of political stability, the agrarian problem, communal agrarian associations, the relationship of church and state, and the artistic renaissance. Katherine Anne Porter interviewed Diego Rivera, collected all of the numerous art features for the issue, and found the *corridos* to be an enchanting popular art from.

> *In Mexico [she wrote] most of the birds, and all of the people, sing. . . . A race of singing people . . . used to sorrowful beginnings and tragic endings, in love with life, fiercely independent, a little desperate, but afraid of nothing. They see life as a flash of flame against a wall of darkness. Conscious players of vivid roles, they live and die well, and as they live and die, they sing.*

Tannenbaum's introductory piece was entitled "Mexico—A Promise." He found in the Revolution a promise of new social stability for Mexico and an augury of inevitable changes dramatically disruptive to the traditional setting in Latin America: ". . . in understanding the *meaning* of the Mexican revolution we can find patience and sympathetic good will for Latin America when the need for them arrives." And in a boxed insert quoting Haya de la Torre, then president of the Students Federation of Peru, and reinforcing the point, were the words: "Mexico is . . . the standard bearer of Latin America. . . . We are watching these labors of Mexico . . . with interest, with reverence and with hope, as though on the outcome of the great work of progress lay the fate of our common destiny."

This was Frank Tannenbaum's first general discussion on Mexico and in it he developed themes which were to recur in later writings on Mexico and Latin America. Mexico was a "strange" and "unknown" country with an indigenous culture that was unique. The culture and the people were difficult, perhaps in the end impossible, for the outsider to understand in any complete sense. Political life was marred by violence and by the intrusion of military chieftains into the "democratic" process. Constitutions were mocked by frequent abrogations, by military uprisings, or by revolution.

> *In good part, the revolutions were an attempt to square action with declaration, forgetting that true constitutions represent the habits rather than the dreams of the people. This constant attempt to achieve justice by revolution became a contributing factor to further revolution. Revolution itself became a habit.*

The promise of the Revolution lay in the possibilities it offered to achieve political stability for the first time since Independence and in releasing the potentialities of a gifted people. Specifically, Tannenbaum found the growing labor movement to be a principal force in "molding the Mexican community into new patterns and [it] is distributive of responsibility as well as of power." "The labor union," he continued, ". . . provides a new type of environment for the development of a new type of person . . . [and] the labor movement [is] the greatest source for social stability in Mexico—a fact that is recognized by Obregón and Calles." And the flowering of a new culture, though based upon the old indigenous values, was typified in the great intellectual and artistic leaders of Mexico, such as Diego Rivera and José Vasconcelos, and in the incorporation of the Indian into the nation's life.

Once again, Tannenbaum was attracted to the active as well as the reflective aspects of the enterprise in which he was involved. For him, the Indian question could be epitomized in two different individuals. One, Manuel Gamio, a student of Franz Boas', was a cultural anthropologist, largely responsible for the broad recognition and acceptance of the Indian as the base upon which contemporary culture in Mexico was to be identified. Henceforward, one would not speak of Mexico without including the Indian and one could even with good reason say that Mexico had at last recognized its true spiritual heritage and that its new identity derived in large part from all that existed before the Spanish Conquest. The other, Felipe Carrillo Puerta, was an activist political reformer in Yucatán, a Mayan Indian claiming descent from the last of the Mayan "kings," who organized the *Ligas de Resistencia*. These leagues were communal societies that sought more cohesive unification of the region, labor and social reforms, and greater dignity for the Indian peoples. Carrillo was murdered in 1923 by federal troops, while Gamio lived on to become a leading teacher for a generation of Mexican anthropologists.

Tannenbaum himself was playing the dual role of participant and observer. This particular issue of *Survey* was a first step in the process of informing the American people about Mexico at a significant point in the course of the Revolution; an implied purpose of his essay, and of all the other articles, was to make the period 1900–20 intelligible to the American public and to win sympathy for the Revolution and its leaders. Indeed, it is not excessive to say that he wrote as an apologist for Mexico and its Revolution. He had accepted much of its mythology and a good deal of its revisionist slant on Mexican history.

Here one should make a distinction between the work of an apologist and that of a propagandist. It is true that at this point in his career, as later, Frank Tannenbaum would view the

Revolution as an engine of progress—not always efficient in method, not always rational in function, not always beneficent in action, but nevertheless possessing a forward motion contributive to the common improvement of the Mexican people. His analysis of the promise and potential of the 1917 Constitution is instructive in this regard. The Constitution was, he said, "a broad formula which needs application—a promise which needs fulfillment. If the promise remains unfulfilled, it will again, as the constitutions in Mexico have before, become a good and legitimate excuse for revolution." The man who could say that the study of history is a blow to radicalism was not the sort of person to swallow whole any ideology.

In putting together this ensemble of articles, Tannenbaum had reinforced lessons of life and learning he had acquired earlier. For him, direct experience and personalities and friendship, rather than detached scholarly appraisal (although he did not disdain this as an intellectual activity), were the means by which understanding of a problem or a situation was obtained. He would say over and over that one had to understand the *ambiente*—something comparable to Carl Becker's "climate of opinion," or Max Weber's concept of *Verstehen*. How was one to do it? By traversing the land, by seeking out the unnotable people, by eating the local foods and enduring other hardships, and by making friends in a foreign locale. He always followed these rules in his friendships with Osborne, Gamio, Cárdenas, and Covarrubias. Indeed, one sees this essential rapport in many of the *Survey* articles. When one reads the appeal of Felipe Carrillo Puerta one almost feels as if it were Tannenbaum himself speaking.

Underlying all of Tannenbaum's works on Latin America was a concern with the processes and mechanisms by which a stable political system functions—legitimacy, transfer of power, political parties, constitutionality, local government, and political culture. He was intrigued by the British and American models of government, but he thought the British system to be the better example of continuing effective political stability. Indeed, among his posthumous papers is a long unfinished manuscript on the elements in the British system that allow it to operate with such uncommon smoothness.

Tannenbaum was as much concerned with the obstacles to political stability as he was with the conditions which facilitate it. In Latin America, as many of the essays in this book reveal, he saw several enduring sources of instability so ingrown in the history of the people and their institutions as to preclude the achievement of democracy as practiced in Great Britain or the United States. Perhaps fundamental to political instability in Latin America was the difficulty in finding a source and symbol of legitimacy after the crown had been violently removed. In Britain, monarchy prevailed while democracy flourished. In the United States, the president was endowed with great, not to say quasi-monarchical, attributes—only while in office—and there were historical and then constitutional limits placed upon a president's tenure. In Latin America, however, the monarchical symbols had been wiped away, the restraints upon presidential power and length of tenure were frail, and the long period of liberation from Spain had bred, or intensified, a penchant for solving matters by resort to violence. The habit of violence creates the expectancy that some form of violence will occur and the expectancy then becomes a self-fulfilling prophecy.

Other barriers to stability and democracy were studied by Tannenbaum. The webs of attachment created by *personalismo,* the faith in the authority or power of the *caudillo,* the casual resort to new constitutions as sure solutions, the tendency on the part of the military to intervene in the political process to save it, and the fustian language of most of the politicians—all of these added further impediments to the realization of stability and democracy. This is not to say that Tannenbaum saw no changes anywhere. In Mexico, the reverence and observance given to the 1917 Constitution, the rise of a middle class and a relatively independent labor movement, the absolute stricture against a president's reelection, the professional aloofness of the army, and the land-distribution programs were clear examples of progress. Nevertheless, progress and stability were achieved under the rule of a one-party system. Or, aga·n, in Puerto Rico, which he first visited in 1928–29 as a member of a survey staff for the Brookings Institute, he was to see over a period of time the development of stable political relationships, the expansion of education, and the growth of a middle class.

The game of politics, of course, is played within a cultural context and Tannenbaum attempted to immerse himself in it as far as he could. He preferred to interpret the stamp of Spain upon Latin America by studying the various meanings of Spanish character and history as he found them in *Don Quixote*. Formal political history of Spain or Portugal did not interest him, although he was familiar with it. To understand the setting within which Latin American politics takes place, he would read the novels of Rómulo Gallegos and Jorge Amado, for example, and he thought that the *ambiente* of life under the regime of Porfirio Díaz could be savored in *Los Bandidos del Río Frío*. A few interpretative works he considered to be of great value: Sarmiento's *Facundo*, Argüedas' *Pueblo Enfermo*, Basadre's *El pueblo, la ciudad y la gente*, Válcarcel's *La ruta cultural del Perú*, Octavio Paz's *El laberinto de la soledad*, and Gilberto Freyre's *Masters and Slaves*. But, mainly, Tannenbaum wanted to do his own interpreting. For instance, he would say that to understand Bolívar's thinking and his curious relationship with Santander and the other generals, he would sit down and read all of the collected letters and messages sent to and by Bolívar. He would do the same with the early chronicles and histories of Spain and Portugal in the Americas.

As previously noted, Tannenbaum could not write on a situation, problem, or country without some personal exposure to it. He had to see the lay of the land and react to it before he could organize his thinking about it. In fact, he always said that he couldn't know what he thought until he had talked about it. He was proud that he had spent two years traveling in the rural and remote areas of Mexico *"a lomo de mula."* In the company of five Indians, he went down the Amazon in a dugout; he rode horseback high in the Andes of Peru; he hiked from one end of Puerto Rico to the other for the better part of a year; and he was at one with W. H. Hudson in his appreciation of the Argentine pampas. Personal friendships allowed him other insights into a culture, and they made the strangeness of an alien environment easier to cope with, and ultimately easier to enjoy. Tannenbaum had many Latin American friends in all walks of life, but perhaps the most important of these friendships was the one he formed with Lázaro Cárdenas, whom Tannenbaum always addressed affectionately and respectfully as *"mi general."* It was a friendship that lasted over thirty years. They saw each other frequently during and after Cárdenas' presidential tenure. On many occasions, they would go to the countryside, visiting peasant villages and talking with the common people.

Curiously, Tannenbaum's spoken Spanish and Portuguese were nothing more than a patois. He was fluent but ungrammatical and his ideas often flowed too rapidly for any sense of grammar to come to the repair. He was aware of this and would often tell at his own expense an amusing anecdote taken from personal experience in rural Mexico. Once, when he was gathering data on education and population for the Mexican government in the late 1920s, he was called upon in some hamlet to give a speech on the value of education and how it could be brought to the little village. After speaking for half an hour or so, Tannenbaum stepped down from the improvised platform and was approached by an elderly Mexican, dressed in the peasant fashion and respectfully holding his hat in his hand. The Mexican congratulated Tannenbaum on his excellent talk, but apologetically added, *"Pero, dispense, señor profesor, no entendí lo que Ud. dijo porque yo no entiendo inglés."* ("Forgive me, Professor, but I did not understand what you said because I do not understand English.")

Mexico and its revolution continued to interest Tannenbaum for the rest of his life. He wrote three important books on various aspects of change in Mexico: *The Mexican Agrarian Revolution* (1928), *Peace by Revolution: An Interpretation of*

Mexico (1933), and *Mexico: The Struggle for Peace and Bread* (1950). The central theme in all of them is the course of revolution, but he also takes into account the history and the economic, social, racial, and cultural conditions of Mexico. In the first of these books, Tannenbaum examines closely the landholding patterns, especially the *hacienda,* as they changed under the impact of the Revolution. He felt that "the social revolution that has intermittently torn Mexico during the last twenty years [he was writing *Peace by Revolution*] may be best understood as an attempt to liquidate finally the consequences of the Spanish Conquest. This explanation of the Revolution is at the same time the best key to Mexican history." Tannenbaum was seeking out the dominant trends in the Mexican experience; he was not wedded, as he took pains to make clear, to a single or unitary explanation of historical or social phenomena. These three books continue to stand as highly reliable interpretations of the persistent elements in Mexican history as well as a valuable commentary upon topical issues and conditions at the time they were written. Anyone desirous of learning more about Mexico now, and probably for the next hundred years and more, should consult these texts as basic interpretations. They were written out of personal conviction and experience, and reflect learning gathered on the spot, in the stacks and archives, and derived from other places or institutions Tannenbaum had studied. His works on Mexico were widely translated and taken seriously for study and comment in Mexico, the United States, and elsewhere, whether or not his critical colleagues agreed with what the books advanced.

Three of Tannenbaum's fifteen books (only six of them were on Mexico and Latin America) dealt with the broad area of Latin America: *Whither Latin America?* (1934), *Slave and Citizen: The Negro in the Americas* (1947), and *Ten Keys to Latin America* (1962). The first of these titles, accompanied by the subtitle *An Introduction to Its Economic and Social Problems,* is Tannenbaum's most pedestrian effort. It is unlike most of his books in that it resembles a short textbook. He relies more upon available statistics than upon his own intuitive and intellectual abilities to interpret the area. Nonetheless, some of the points he develops are still valid in any consideration of Latin America. Tannenbaum thought that it would never be fertile ground for the growth of heavy industry because it lacked the necessary resources and an effective transportation system and was dependent upon the exports of raw materials for its capital accumulation. Consequently, Latin America's role in international affairs would never be of significance in influencing the great modern industrial states; it might, however, aspire to exert some moral and cultural influence upon them. If there is an underlying hypothesis to the book, it is Tannenbaum's recognition that change, unless it is sudden and revolutionary, comes painfully and slowly, and that progress can be merely illusory.

Ten Keys to Latin America, Tannenbaum thought, could only have been written after many years' association with the people it describes:

> *It is difficult, perhaps impossible, for anyone, especially an outsider, to understand and evaluate the major facets of a culture. This is a book about the totality of Latin America. The Ten Keys are merely ten different angles of vision. The whole is more complex than the sum of the parts.*

As a result of this book, and also in recognition of his many writings on Latin America, he was awarded the Bolton Prize in 1963. *Ten Keys* is a personal summing-up of his knowledge of the region and there are no footnotes or bibliography in it. The word "key" and the concept it represents recur throughout all of his works. Tannenbaum had defined it earlier by saying that a key to an understanding of a complex society was through a study of the role, claims, and conflicts of its institutions. And, now, after forty years of experience in and study of Latin America, he wrote primarily about its institutions. He discussed the church, the educational system, political parties, the *hacienda*, the *mestizo* and "the cosmic race," the place of the intellectual, the *caudillo*, and the military.

The book, of course, covered many other subjects, including the phenomenon of revolution. He saw a basic distinction between the Mexican and the Cuban revolutions. "Cuba is a commercial and industrial economy," he wrote, "whereas Mexico was a subsistence economy." He went on to generalize about the differences between the two revolutions:

> *If the Marxian concept of the class struggle has reality, it is to be found in a stratified agricultural society where the distance between the* hacendado *and the* peón *cannot be bridged, where there is no middle class, and where there is no built-in mechanism for social and economic change. In those societies social revolutions have occurred and may well occur again. But in no industrial and monetary society has all of Marxian theory produced a single truly proletarian uprising. A revolutionary uprising is simply not a viable means for social change in a monetary, commercial, and industrial society.*
>
> *The changes in Cuba were brought in the name of a future egalitarian society . . . the Mexican revolution had more modest ends. The changes that have followed in the wake of the Mexican upheaval have been the by-products of a popular movement whose leaders came from the bottom and had no fixed design to impose on the nation.*

The Mexican Revolution appealed to Tannenbaum because it was haphazard, unplanned, spontaneous, and because its leaders were for the most part free of binding ideological commitment. They could deal with a problem at hand in a practical way and they did not feel themselves obliged to consult an official ideology. Tannenbaum felt uncomfortable about the future of Cuba after Castro, not so much because of its communism, but because of the excessive zeal of the planners who would try to reshape Cuban society into an unattainable image. The Mexican Revolution dealt with the complexities and the subtleties of human life because no plan of progress was imposed upon the people. Solutions evolved or happened in Mexico; in Cuba, solutions were contrived beforehand in accordance with a theory or formula of social change. And, for Tannenbaum, the latter approach did not square with the reality of human life.

Perhaps Tannenbaum's most important book, for its impact on the scholarly world and American society, is *Slave and Citizen*. Three leading contemporary historians, Stanley M. Elkins, David Brion Davis, and Eugene Genovese, are in agreement that it is a "pioneering essay" in the historiography of Negro slavery. The book developed out of an interdisciplinary seminar on slavery held at Columbia in the late thirties and early forties in which this peculiar institution was looked at comparatively, bringing to bear upon a common theme the historical experience of different cultures. (It was, incidentally, the immediate forerunner of what were to become the University Seminars.) This is Tannenbaum's shortest book, but the most scholarly in appearance—it has hundreds of footnotes citing many different sources.

Branch Rickey, then general manager of the Brooklyn Dodgers, credited this book with having influenced him in his decision to bring Jackie Robinson into the major leagues to play baseball. It is possible that this particular statement of Tannenbaum's was especially compelling to Rickey:

> *The shadow of slavery is still cast ahead of us, and we behave toward the Negro as if the imputation of slavery had something of a slave by nature in it. The Emancipation may have legally freed the Negro, but it failed to free the white man, and by that failure it denied to the Negro the moral status requisite for effective legal freedom.*

In *Slave and Citizen*, Tannenbaum presented a threefold argument. Slavery was a moral as well as a legal relationship; where a society accepted the moral personality of the slave, the way to abolition would be relatively peaceful; the recognition of the slave's moral personality depended upon the religious, moral, and legal history of the white slaveholders, and their view of man's relationship to God. Eugene Genovese, a former student of Tannenbaum's, says that "we may credit him with having been the first to show that only a hemispheric treatment could enable us to understand the relationship between slavery and race relations and the social and political dynamics of the transition from slavery to freedom."

In his overall interpretation of Latin America, Tannenbaum always gave considerable attention to the foreign policy of the United States there and to what he called the American tradition in foreign policy. He was inclined to believe that this tradition was democratic, reflecting the ingrained values of equal opportunity and the upward movement of individuals in American society; benevolent and constructive in effect, reflecting the goodness and innocence of the American people; and pluralistic, reflecting the American experience that each state was accepted and dealt with on a par with every other state. In his book on the subject, *The American Tradition in Foreign Policy* (1955), he wrote that "the American commitment to the ideal of the juridical equality and moral integrity of states explains our participation in two world wars." He went on to the specifics of his argument:

> *There is a peculiar consistency in this belief of ours that the little nation has the same rights as the big one. Our quarrel with Russia is upon this ground. . . . We really believe that Ecuador and Haiti are coordinate with the United States, just as we believe that Poland and Bulgaria are coordinate with Russia.*
>
> *To some these American notions seem impractical and foolish. Influential scholars and counselors would have us abandon them. They suggest that we cease being childish and idealistic and recognize that the national interest requires us to become disciples of Machiavelli, take our lessons from Richelieu, Bismarck, or Clemenceau.*

With regard to the relationship of the United States to Latin America, Tannenbaum felt that "the growth of the Organization of American States extends to the Western Hemisphere the ideal of a federation of indestructible states upon which the United States itself is founded."

In *The Balance of Power in Society* (1969), Tannenbaum describes the coordinate state in terms of the equal dignity and "historic personality" that each sovereign state brings to a federal relationship with other states regardless of wealth, power, size, population, and culture. He saw this principle in America's domestic history deriving from the conditions for admission to the Union contained in the Northwest Ordinance (1787). And, Tannenbaum strongly felt, the relations of the United States with other nations had perforce to be shaped by this principle and our long experience with it. For him there could be no getting away from it. He recognized a long string of violations of the basic principle as he defined it, including, of course, the many instances in Latin America; but he still maintained that they were "side currents at the edge of the broad stream of our foreign policy. The major drift of our relations with the rest of the world has with more or less consistency responded to the basic tradition of the coordinate state."

Tannenbaum willingly pitted these underlying American ideals against the doctrine of balance of power. In the end, he thought that they would win out and that they represented the real and incontestable strength of the United States. Tannenbaum believed in the goodness and decency of the American people, their government, and their relations with other states and peoples. He saw the aberrations but he did not believe that the many exceptions disproved the rule. He may have been right—one hopes so. Certainly, Tannenbaum's fervent rejection of the balance of power doctrine as un-American can be criticized as being naive and as excessively approving of U.S. policy. His scholarly error lies in his having allowed himself to become a partisan advocate.

The error was perhaps unavoidable: by seeing and stressing the inherent benevolence of America's intentions because of the persistence of its ideals, Tannenbaum revealed at the same time the effects of his Americanization and his discovery of the best in the American experience. That Tannenbaum could identify himself so fully as an American, being a Jewish immigrant from Eastern Europe, and feel so ardently and honestly that the best values of American society were ultimately operative was the essence of the American Dream. And it was, at the same time, the weakest link in his argument against an American application of the balance of power theory.

A curious element in Tannenbaum's outlook was his attitude towards Europe. He never exhibited any desire to travel overseas, and the only time he did so was in the early 1960s to attend a conference sponsored by the Ford Foundation and held in Bellagio, Italy. He went straight to the conference—with no side trips and no delays; he was away from New York for only five days. He had no wish to see Spain, or Portugal either. In fact, the only place he enjoyed traveling in was Latin America; otherwise it is probably accurate to describe Tannenbaum as a homebody. This rather limiting attitude may be explained by the thoroughness of his Americanization; by his acceptance of the Jeffersonian notion that somehow the New World was purer than the Old World; and by the high degree of seriousness he felt that one should bring to the calling of a professor. He no doubt believed that a trip to Europe would be a frivolous venture unrelated to his studies in the United States and Latin America.

The seminar technique was a way favored by Tannenbaum in looking at a problem. As he defined the seminar, it had to be a multidisciplinary and Socratic analysis. One found one's ignorance by putting oneself and one's colleagues "on the rack." One arrived at an understanding of a problem, not its solution, by seeing it from different angles. The sequences of conversation were the steps towards such understanding. But still there was the human element, the interplay of minds and personalities, and Tannenbaum believed that seeing the problem, being exposed to it personally, would add to intellectual comprehension. Thus, it was natural for him to have three different seminars on Latin America, all going on at the same time. One, naturally, was conducted each year at Columbia, and it was this seminar that became the predecessor of the other two and the basis of the Institute of Latin American Studies. The second was with businessmen who had dealings on a day-to-day basis with Latin America. And the third, the so-called Canopus Hollow Parochialists, held at the Tannenbaums' farm in Peekskill, New York, was with future army professionals from West Point. The technique in each of the seminars was to pose a problem— for example, political stability, economic advancement, the impact of United States diplomacy, or the role of the soldier— and to discuss it with students and nonstudents of different backgrounds.

The Latin American Seminar at Columbia, which lasted from 1944 to 1970 and was itself a peculiar institution, existed, as Tannenbaum used to say, *"a la buena de Dios."* It was always held in Tannenbaum's office on Thursday afternoon from four to six; before it began, *mate,* brewed in a steaming Russian samovar, and cookies were served. Anywhere from six to twelve graduate students, three to six professors, a fluctuating number of occasional or regular visitors, and many Latin Americans were there. The group was usually about twenty or twenty-five, and each seminar lasted approximately two hours. The speaker of the day was briefly introduced and then spoke for one hour on a subject about which he had special knowledge or interest; afterwards followed a question-and-answer period. Tannenbaum would always state in a jesting but firm way that during the discussion, *"Aquí no se permiten discursos"*—that no one would be allowed to harangue or pontificate before the group. The whole seminar was always conducted in Spanish or Portuguese, and Tannenbaum always presided.

Over its twenty-five-year life, the Latin American Seminar welcomed many important Latin Americans as guests, partici- pants, and speakers. Professors, ex-presidents, journalists, poets, artists, economists, students, labor leaders, and diplomats were among those who came to the seminar. They came because it was well known by Latin Americans as their forum in the United States. Germán Arciniegas was for many years a regular participant. Daniel Cosío Villegas, Mariano Picón-Salas, Arturo Uslar Pietri, José Luis Romero, Eduardo Santos, Gilberto Freyre, Luis Alberto Sánchez, Luis Válcarcel, and Vianna Moog all attended the seminar for one semester or longer. Colleagues from different departments, but all with an interest in Latin American problems, included Federico de Onís, Ángel del Río, Andrés Iduarte, Albert O. Hirschman, and Charles Wagley. Stanley R. Ross, Robert J. Alexander, and Richard M. Morse, at one time graduate students attending the seminar, are leading Latin Americanists today. Herbert Matthews and Mildred Adams came regularly for ten years. And when Fidel Castro visited the United States in 1959, it was only natural for him to come to the seminar.

At Columbia, there is now a University Seminar on Latin America. And the businessmen with whom Tannenbaum met once a week in his "downtown" seminar have continued to meet once a month at the Center for Inter-American Relations in New York City, calling their group The Frank Tannenbaum Roundtable on Latin America.

Frank Tannenbaum's marriage in 1940 to Jane Belo was a happy turning point. His first marriage in the 1920s had ended in divorce by the end of that decade. But with Jane Belo there were bonds of deep affection and common intellectual interests. She had spent eight years on the island of Bali studying ceremonial life, trance and other aspects of religious behavior, and children's art. From 1947 to 1950 she worked with Ruth Benedict, Rhoda Métraux, and Margaret Mead as a member of the Columbia University Research Program in Contemporary Cultures and made major contributions to the comparative study of French and Chinese cultures. Jane Belo came from a well-established, well-to-do, Episcopalian Dallas family; although herself a scholar and anthropologist, she observed the social amenities and enjoyed the company of bohemians in the aristocrat's way. She was a sensitive artist who expressed herself in paintings, drawings, and photographs. She literally filled the houses they lived in with art that she had produced herself or bought. What Jane Belo brought to Frank Tannenbaum's life was a rediscovery of the enduring qualities of family life (even though they had no children), an appreciation of various forms of beauty, and a greater sense of belonging and security. When she died in April 1968, she left what seemed to their close friends an irreparable void in Frank's life. Her death exhausted his youthful reserves of physical vitality.

Almost until the end, Frank Tannenbaum was strong of body and vigorous of mind. However, early on Sunday morning, June 1, 1969, the crippling disease of cancer took its toll. He was an outdoorsman—not in a sporting sense, but as one who enjoyed the sensations of being exposed to nature— who always loved his long summers at Pine Lodge Camp in Saranac, New York, where he could fish each afternoon or go canoeing. He could handle a heavy Adirondack guide boat with muscular ease, and once he spent a summer paddling down the Susquehanna River, camping out along the way. Or he would often putter around his farm in Canopus Hollow, repairing fences, milking cows, driving the tractor, and occasionally riding horseback. When not outdoors, he could be found in his large log-cabin study reading and writing; or conversing animatedly at the dining table or between meals with his wife and friends. At home he would usually dress casually and almost always eat carelessly. He tended to concentrate on the ideas at hand and not the food. The Tannenbaums' two dogs, a dachshund, Lanny, and a Saint Bernard, Samson, now and then received scraps or bones from him. The big dog was almost always with him and when Samson and Tannenbaum played, a big boyish grin would come on Frank's face. In accordance with John Dewey's precept of learning by doing, Samson was never properly trained, not even to sit down when gently instructed to do so by his indulgent master—much to the occasional distress of some houseguests.

At a memorial service held on January 8, 1970, at Columbia University's Low Library Rotunda, Margaret Mead, a long-time personal friend of Jane Belo and then of Frank Tannenbaum, spoke of the affection that had brought and held them together:

> *Jane thought it frightfully romantic to be married to a Columbia University professor. She had lived in Europe and in many parts of the world in the company of painters and musicians, but she saw being a professor through a veil of romance—which, of course, Frank shared. . . . He loved Columbia with a kind of feeling that he also had, I think, for the United States. I mean the feeling of someone who came from a long way off, and discovered essences that were not always there in everyday practice.*

Other eulogies were given by Germán Arciniegas and Richard Morse. Messages of condolence were cabled by Lázaro Cárdenas, Eduardo Frei, Eduardo Santos, and Fernando Belaúnde Terry, among others.

The memorial service paid tribute to a man of diverse intellect. It was impossible to categorize Frank Tannenbaum as a Latin American historian, for he was many things more than that. Perhaps the best label for him would be that of social philosopher, although he called himself a "generalist." He investigated human experience as a philosopher would, drawing from his own experience and observations. He had acquired much formal knowledge throughout his lifetime, but he knew that the complexities of social organization and human motivation could not be understood from afar. His focus essentially was upon institutions singly and in competition with each other and he understood that all human experience must occur within institutions of one kind or another. As Tannenbaum wrote in *The Balance of Power in Society:*

> *The road to social peace is the balance of the social institutions, and a wise statesman would strengthen those institutions that seemed to be losing ground, even if he were*

not addicted to them; for the only way to peace in this world of fallible human nature is to keep all human institutions strong, but none too strong; relatively weak, but none so weak as to despair of their survival. It is only thus that peaceful irritation and strife, so essential to social and individual society, can be maintained.

Joseph Maier
Richard W. Weatherhead

The Future of Democracy in Latin America (I)

There is no reason for believing that political stability in Latin America is greater in the nineteen fifties than it was a hundred years ago. Revolutions in the last thirty years have been as frequent, and dictatorships as numerous, durable, and oppressive, as they were a century ago. It may, of course, be argued that the reasons for instability have changed, and the contention may or may not be true. But the fact of revolution versus dictatorship has remained constant. It cannot even be said that the contemporary revolutions are less bloody or that the tyrannies are more humane. What happened in Colombia between 1946 and 1954 is sufficient to disprove that thesis. Democratic government has remained an unfulfilled hope in spite of the many interesting constitutions that have been written during the last century. The aspiration to achieve the ideal of legality has failed. I shall seek here to suggest some reasons for the failure and to argue for a way out of the dilemma posed by the dream of representative democracy and the fact of revolution or dictatorship.

Contemporary Latin American political difficulties cannot be divorced from their historical past. The Spanish tradition is authoritarian, bureaucratic, and centralized. The tradition is to leave political responsibility to the government and expect it to do everything. The extreme individualism of the Spanish character and the authoritarian tradition of the Spanish government seem to go hand in hand. The bureaucratic colonial administration controlled every agency of political administration—with the exception of the *cabildo* (township), and the township government was immersed in petty localisms. It was aristocratic in character and incompetent to become the base of a national government. The descendants of the Spaniards, the *criollos*, who led the independence movements, were inexperienced in politics and possessed no clear concepts of nationality. The nation was in the future, something to be forged, molded, and solidified. This was true territorially as well as ideologically. Either there was no American tradition to appeal to, or it was nebulous and fanciful—such as the attempt to resurrect the Incaic past. There was certainly a sense of identity of the American as against the Spaniard or the European, but the form and substance of this something-new upon which the future political life of the people was to be reared had not been molded and the process of integration remains incomplete.

The character of the Latin American people is still being formed, and a sense of inner identity and unity such as characterizes the Italian, the French, or the English people is something that lies in the future. The king and crown of the Spanish past were unacceptable, and the local milieu, as Bolívar so clearly saw, would not tolerate an American monarchical system. But the milieu proved recalcitrant to all other forms of government. If it visibly rejected the rule of the absolute king, it also resisted and found unpalatable the ideas that derived from the French *philosophes* and United States constitutionalism.

The bitter and disorganized wars of independence, which had no official date of termination and ended in no peace treaty, had shattered a great empire and stable government and led to a political vacuum and social disorganization. The end of the wars found Latin America divided into many separate countries, each in turn fractured into regional provinces governed by municipal oligarchies and ruled by local military *caudillos*. The king as the symbol of government had disappeared without leaving as substitute any other universally accepted idea around which a common loyalty could be evoked and in the name of which government could be carried on. The magic words of "liberty," "equality," and "fraternity" had a hollow sound, for the society remained stratified, and divided into *castas*. Neither the sacrifice nor the heroism of the wars of independence made the ideals of the French *philosophes* and American constitutionalism operative. Of the two great public institutions—the crown and the church—the first had been destroyed and the second had been seriously weakened. The traditional sources of recognized authority were no longer sufficient. They were replaced by the informal and legally nonrecognized rule of the plantation family associated with the local military. The *hacienda*, with its control of acreages sometimes greater than a European principality, became the effective source of local political power. The fact that the power it exercised had no basis in law was irrelevant to the rule of its own domain. With the *hacienda* went the control of hundreds and sometimes thousands of people. These retainers and *peones* provided a personal militia useful for defense and, if need be, for attack. By intermarriage, by the institution of *compadrazgo* (godfatherhood), by alliances forged of mutual dependence and neighborliness, the plantation system ruled the region, and the leading landowner was "king of all he surveyed." The independence movement had substituted this locally effective but legally nonexistent means of rule and governance for the authority of the king it had destroyed.

The national governments in the early days were so busy trying to stay in power that they had little time to "govern." When there is a new rebellion to suppress every month, and when for many years there is annually a new "national" administration brought in by a new revolution, it is idle to talk about the details of governing—that task fell naturally to those that had both stability and power locally. Someone had to protect the locality, its families and its animals, and they who could do that were in fact the governors even if not graced by the name or sanctioned by the requisite legal formula. A detailed description of the life of the older plantation would show it to be both a society and a government; so it had to be, and so it remained during the nineteenth century, and to some extent so it is—or was until 1910, if not until 1930. There have been some changes—by revolution in Mexico, by the effect of new means of communication, industrialization, social theories, movements, and agitation. But the plantation was until the day before yesterday, or the year before last, an economic, a social, and a political system with powers of local rule and governance and with a powerful role in controlling the provincial and the national political systems. Only in Chile was this substantial fact recognized for what it was—a political force—and a government frankly designed to rest on the plantation family gave to that country peace and quiet through the years when the rest of Latin America was trying to build governments upon an individualism that did not exist and upon ideas that had no local relevance.

The splintering of political authority and the rule of the local *caudillo* were fortified by a social stratification that has persisted in spite of the racial tolerance characteristic of Latin America. Certainly since the Independence, if not before, it has been possible at least in some countries for the pure-blooded Indian, like Juárez, to reach the highest office. There has been room for the exceptional individual who, by some magic, had shed his Indian ways and taken on the outlook and interests of the *criollo*. It was possible for him to become a respected member of the non-Indian community. Very much the same thing may be said of the Negro. An age-old law defined him as a legal person and the rule of the Catholic Church identified him as a moral person. Hence, manumission was relatively easy, and the social system was sufficiently flexible to permit the abolition of slavery without violence and to allow for the acceptance of the ex-slave as a freeman rather than a freedman. This tolerance opened the doors to cultural participation and made possible important contributions by the Negro and the mulatto to art, architecture, music, and literature. Latin American society has certainly been friendly to the non-European, and the Negro, at least, has long felt himself identified with the people in Latin America. This is in sharp contrast to the fear and isolation that for so long have beset the Negro in many parts of the United

States. Nevertheless, it has to be added that Latin Ameri
society has remained stratified, immobile, and, if a colon
expression may be used, divided into *castas,* and when compare
to the United States, there is noticeably less vertical mobility
The countries vary among themselves. There is more mobility
in Argentina, Southern Brazil, and Cuba than there is in
Ecuador or Colombia, and a great deal more than in Peru. But
the role of the important family, the barrier made by wealth,
race, and occupation, is markedly obvious in its effect upon
social mobility.

More important perhaps than the above sources of social
stratification is division between country and city, between
urban and rural. The city belongs to one world and the country
to another. The capital of the country, like Mexico, Guatemala,
or Lima, will have all the modern conveniences, newspapers and
universities, electric lights and refrigeration. But the little village
in the country will in all likelihood have neither literacy nor
shoes nor electric lights—it may not even have the Spanish
language. More than that, the rural communities may have value
systems of their own; their own inner hierarchy, their own
sense of propriety, make them a world apart from the city,
nation, state, or government. A village of Trique Indians in
Oaxaca, a Cakchiquel village in Guatemala, a Quechua Indian
village high in the mountains of the Peruvian department
Ayacucho have little in common with the world to which they
officially belong, and the political life of the "nation" remains an
unrevealed mystery. They do not know the meaning of the
activity called politics.

For these and many other reasons political leadership has
been regional and personal. The local *caudillo* was secure from
outside interventions and beyond the need of support from
"political party" because his power rested on the loyalty of
extended family, rich in lands and sure of the cooperation
neighboring towns entwined economically and socially with t
dominant *hacienda* ownership. This leader was the "politi
party" in his region. The people were his. The phrase wen

ople of Don Pancho," or "of Don Pedro," or "of General
ontreras"; there were no other people in the region—and the
gion might be larger than a good-sized state in the United
tates. In that area there was only one politician, one party, one
loyalty. Everyone belonged to him, and all affairs, even the most
personal, the most trivial, were brought to him for settlement
and adjudication. He knew and tolerated no opposition, and no
stranger could travel in the country without his explicit or
implicit consent; for he controlled all the agencies of government, insofar as there were such agencies, including the tax
gatherer, the judge, the sheriff, the schoolteacher, and the local
militia. He was the *patrón*, the father, the judge, the protector of
all "his people," and they were loyal to him. If he wanted to run
for office, he could always be elected unanimously—for it would
occur to no one to oppose him—and his politics did not matter.
If he did not wish to run for office, his blessing was sufficient to
elect anyone it was bestowed upon. In fact, his mere consent
was equivalent to an election—with or without a counting of the
votes. The *caudillo* could die but he could not be removed. He
could be murdered, or driven from power either by armed force
coming from another part of the country under another *caudillo*
or by the national army controlled at the time by his enemies.
But short of these exceptional circumstances, he enjoyed lifelong
tenure and his place was secure and his rule absolute.

Under these and similar circumstances, the government
could rest only upon the army, and the political party could be
only personal. Admittedly, this is a somewhat overdrawn
description if taken as applying universally to all parts of Latin
America—but not so overdrawn as to be misleading. Admittedly, too, this is a picture of rural rather than of urban social,
economic, and political structure. Latin America is rural, and the
urban has been deeply influenced by this leadership design of
the countryside. In the smaller *mestizo* towns and cities this
influence is immediate and visible—because the "family" and its
many ramifying alliances fill the important places and are
conspicuous in the economic and social life of the community.

To an extent hard for New Yorkers to understand, but not so difficult for people in Charleston, South Carolina, or Richmond, Virginia, the important families rule the state, and not only socially. Lima and Quito are good examples of what I am trying to say. But Popayán, Mendoza, and Bahia would be even better examples of a rule over the town by families whose roots are in the country. National politics were shaped by the antagonisms and alliances among the regional *caudillos* and their extended families.

Since 1910 a number of influences have tended to change this picture. Better communication, increased literacy, a growing industry, a larger middle class, a trade union movement, the impact of such exotic ideologies as fascism and communism, the great role of a strident nationalism, the criticisms of and legislative attacks upon the *latifundia*, the very rapid expansion of the large cities with their tendency to dissolve the older family loyalties and dependencies, the wealth produced in some places by oil, minerals, and large investments in agricultural enterprises—these have, taken together, weakened the role of the regional *caudillo* and the dominion of his imperious family. Another reason for his lessening power and prestige has been the acquisition of more efficient arms by the government in power. This has tended to weaken the "democratic" impact of regions against the national *caudillo*, who has the machine guns, the tanks, and the airplanes so generously provided him by the United States on the assumption that it was in the interest of the defense of continental democracy—but for the time being helping to perpetuate the self-elected ruler in the control of the government. Under the circumstances, political parties continue to be personal.

The trade unions have made some differences, but they, too, are largely dominated or controlled by the government in power. Presumably, the middle class has interests of its own and would—or should—have independent political aspirations that manifest themselves in political activity. But the middle class, like the trade unions, is so much under the thumb of the administration and so beholden to the government for favors received that it has in fact no effective means of opposing the administration. The mass of the people in most places are beyond the political horizon: they do not vote, are indifferent to the elections, and in many instances, especially in the Andean countries, are unaware of the nature and meaning of the political process. It must by now be clear that the government rests upon the army and why it can in fact rest upon nothing else. In the Andean countries at least, the local leadership, which was the natural foundation of political power in the past, has not been adequately substituted for. From some points of view, the political foundations in Latin America are weaker and less stable than they ever were, because nothing so clearly representative of a region or a class or an interest has replaced the local leadership.

Under these conditions, the president of the country must be the author of his own political party and must unite about himself the group with which he governs. Once in office, he can brook no opposition because disagreement is a challenge to the power of the president and not to his policies. All dissent leads in the direction of revolution, and criticism is taken as a prelude to political violence. The president must make all the decisions, even the most trivial. He must rule the army, the civil service, the judiciary, the legislature, the universities, and the economy. And, with the current penchant for increasing governmental participation in the economic affairs of the nation, the president is ever more competent to favor his supporters and to punish his opponents. He must and does control the national and the local elections. No governor of a state can come to office against his will or remain in office against his wishes. The frequent use of the constitutional provision for "intervention" in Argentina and Brazil, and the equally effective powers exercised through the permanent committee of the Congress in Mexico, make that clear enough. What holds true for a governor also applies to the election of members of Congress and of the Senate. The power of the president is pervasive and nothing escapes it completely, not even the judiciary.

In addition, the president must decide who is going to

succeed him, and he must be able to enforce that decision or face a revolution. This is true whether there is an official governmental party, as in the case of Mexico, or not. The president will either choose his successor and place him in power, even if he decides to succeed himself, or someone else will make that choice and overthrow the regime to ensure the election. This is the most important political decision of the president and will affect his ability to pass on the executive powers peacefully to his successor. The more peaceful the election, the larger the officially announced vote, the quieter and the more democratic the electoral process seems, the more effectively has the original decision been carried out. Doubtful governors will have been removed, the police heads changed, the army's loyalty made sure of, the control of the voting machinery securely placed in the proper hands, and the final result known long before the formal decision-making process has been set in motion. That is why opposition parties frequently refuse to participate in the voting. They, like everyone else, know the outcome in advance and have no desire to lend moral sanction to an executive decision by taking part in the election. If, however, they do participate, it is in the hope that some accident—a rebellion or division of the army—will upset the official plan and a revolution will pave the way for their own candidate. One could point to Costa Rica, Uruguay, Chile, and possibly Brazil as exceptions, but both Chile and Brazil have relatively recent histories that would neatly fit into the electoral process just described. The recent history of Bolivia is in some ways an exception. The government in power failed because of ineffective executive leadership to produce an electoral majority, the army took over the government, and a revolution based upon the miners and the urban workers ousted the army. But the entire electoral apparatus as revealed in the election of 1951 involved for all parties only 50,000 voters out of a population of more than 3,500,000. The parties do not represent the people— they represent the leaders.

In fact, party organization does not attempt to embrace the mass of the people and there is no experience that would lead a political party to the idea that it needs to be based upon the local communities, representing local interests meeting together to hammer out national policy. It might be questioned whether there are, in fact, any political parties in Latin America that fit a meaningful definition. The APRA is a movement rather than a party. The fascist and the communist "organizations" are exotic groupings that may have significant political consequences but are not describable as political parties; they are organized from the top down, have centralized control and discipline, and lack the local spontaneity so essential to representative political activity. The intellectuals in Latin America are an important political influence, but they are not organized, have no power, and serve a purely critical and negative function.

This bleak political panorama leaves little room for an optimistic formula on how to establish democratic and representative government in Latin America. What then is to be done—if anything effective can be done—in the face of a personal leadership tradition and a tenaciously stratified social system? The first need is to draw the people into political activity, and these are mainly rural rather than urban folk. In most of the countries, 50 to 80 percent of the people live in country villages, and many of the seemingly urban communities are essentially rural in their outlook, interests, and activities. More important, the rural folk are, in the Andean area, in Central America, and in Mexico, *communal* rather than individualistic. The concept of the individual as the base of the political party system, so characteristic of the United States, is not really applicable to vast areas in Latin America. If we are going to talk of effective participation in politics by the mass of the people in most of Latin America, we must recognize that we are talking about isolated and often highly integrated rural communities possessed of an internally tenacious value system. These communities must become part of the political party system if the parties are to represent the mass of the people or become instruments of effective democratic governments. But it will be hard to come by these aims.

In the Andean countries, with the possible exception of

Venezuela, in Central America, and in Mexico, the special character of Latin American rural organization, so largely neglected by intellectuals and politicians, hampers the easy development of effective political parties. The individual peasant-*ranchero* is a relatively rare specimen; perhaps not more than 5 percent of the total rural population and certainly not as high as 10 percent live on individual small farms that they own. One needs to make an exception here of Costa Rica and the highlands of Venezuela and parts of Colombia, but in countries like Mexico, Guatemala, Ecuador, Peru, Bolivia, Chile, and to a lesser degree in other places, the people live either in *hacienda* communities or in free villages. And these villages, as suggested above, are isolated from the nation politically, socially, and, to a very considerable extent, culturally. In vast areas they are Indian rather than European, and even the *mestizo* villages are often immersed in an Indian rather than European cultural milieu. These rural communities live on the fringe of the monetary economy. They build their own houses, weave their own clothes, raise their own food, make their own utensils, and what they secure from the outside comes through a parochial market from other villages and frequently by barter. Many have little or no knowledge of the Spanish language; they are illiterate, and those who can read have neither newspapers nor books. They are in fact nonparticipants in the affairs of the nation.

These communities are the actual base of the nation, whatever city folk may think of the matter, and the future of the Latin American countries will be largely shaped by the changes that occur in these little human groupings. Mexico alone has over 100,000 rural villages. In countries where the *hacienda* system remains in full vigor, the problem is complicated by the fact that a majority of these villages may be located within the confines of the plantation and have no possibilities for independent political life and no room for initiative in their own community affairs. They cannot build a school, hire a teacher, or freely shape their own agricultural activities. We have no statistics for the distribution of the rural communities between the free village and the plantation, but it would require great boldness to suggest that less than 50 percent of the inhabited places in Ecuador, Peru, Bolivia, and Guatemala, not to mention other countries, are located within *hacienda* boundaries. The point is worth stressing because it complicates the attempt to integrate the rural folk into the political life of the nation. To bring these communities to participate in the active political parties is difficult enough and the plantations make it more so—perhaps make it impossible. The preliminary to the growth of peaceful and representative government in Latin America is the disintegration of the present *hacienda* system. This may for many reasons prove neither possible nor practical. If so, then hopes for democratic government in Latin America are dim indeed.

The plantation system is not the only thing that stands in the way. The cultural isolation of the rural community is equally formidable as an obstacle to the growth of national representative government. This isolation makes the community apathetic and indifferent, almost unaware of the nation. The major single issue in the political destiny of Latin America is to bridge this gap between the rural Indian and *mestizo* community and the nation. This can be done only with an adequate system of rural education. At best, it will take—even with heroic effort—generations of unremitting devotion to the task.

The successful pursuit of this task requires a new vision of the nation itself: a nation of thousands of free, economically competent, and culturally developed rural communities. The stability and well-being of the nation must be seen as depending upon the initiative and leadership shown by these villages. Latin American nations—at least the nations facing the Pacific—are multicellular, and each cell is frequently a community with its own value system. These communities have to be developed as such. The emphasis has to be on the group and not on the individual in the group. The needs of the community determine the school curriculum. The available resources are the raw materials which the school must use in its program, for in the long run it has no others. It needs to be remembered that a rural community has a fixed habitat; the mountains, the woods, the earth, the spring, brook, river, or lake are given, and little can be done to change them. If the community is to achieve the good life, it must do so in *that* place—for there is no magic to move the mountain or change the course of the river. The climate, too, is given. The heat, moisture, and rain are what they are, and man must find the skills and the wisdom to abide in comfort within the limitations nature has provided. Literacy may be useful, but habits, techniques, practical wisdom that derive from experience, and the special knowledge modern science can offer, are more immediately effective.

The question to be resolved is how to fit what modern science has to offer into this specific and limited environment. How to use and conserve the resources, how to keep the soil from eroding, how to purify the water, how to drain the swamp, or how to irrigate the land with the available waters and with the little means at the disposal of the community, how to make two blades of wheat grow where only one was grown before, how to increase the yield from the stalk of corn, how to select the new fruits that could thrive in the specific place, how to prune the tree, how to protect it from disease, how to conserve and use the fruit, how to build a good house out of the available stone, clay, or bamboo, how to improve the diet by growing vegetables that will not wither or die, how to tap the underground for water in a desert area, how to make new uses of the local fibers, how to improve the weaving, how to design and cut a dress, how to improve the cooking, how to breed good pigs, how to smoke, salt, or otherwise conserve the meat, how to improve the cattle of the village, and how to adapt the hundred different possible uses of milk—all of these activities and a thousand more are the legitimate curricula of the rural school, not to mention the town band, the arts and crafts, and, if one lets his imagination go, the reading of good fiction and poetry.

The program of the school is how to discover the ways to

the good life within the place where the community is located and with the available resources—for there are no others, and even the best of governments can do little to substitute for what nature has provided. The emphasis must be on creativity rather than on book learning. The school becomes the "House of the People," which is open from sunrise to the middle of the night; for the life of the community itself is mirrored in the school's activities. The children are there, but so are the womenfolk who use the school sewing machine or school medicine chest or consult the teacher who is a practical nurse; and the men are there when not at work to learn how to read or to use the tools from the school carpenter shop, or to discuss one of the many questions that arise every day of the year. The emphasis is upon the development of local leadership and the tapping of the tradition of cooperation embedded in the rural community. Everything is done cooperatively. The school is built by the community with its own labor, all taking part, including the women and children. And every activity has to have its committee, its mutual responsibility, its special leadership, its special discussion. The school has to be built and largely maintained by the community, for the simple fact is that the governments do not have the financial resources with which to build the schools, equip them, and pay the teachers as well. *If it cannot be done by the communities it will remain undone.* Even in Mexico, where such heroic efforts have been made to develop a rural school system, at least half the children of school age are not going to school, and this is probably an understatement. In fact, the villages must learn to build and maintain their rural schools as they once built and maintained their rural churches; otherwise, the dream of a matured and self-confident rural community will remain a dream and representative democracy an unfulfilled hope.

It is easy enough to pose the issue in these, shall I say, romantic terms. It is difficult to visualize a realistic effort to meet the challenge the rural community represents. For one thing, this kind of program requires an almost religious devotion to the idea of an independent and mature rural community. Such a devotion to a rural ideal is hard to find and difficult to generate. Latin American intellectuals are urban and not rural minded. They are filled with the ideal of literary rather than practical education, and they simply do not know their own rural community and are, on the whole, indifferent to it. They do not see that the strength of the society and its stability require a healthy and vigorous rural basis, which in the Andean areas means thousands of self-sufficient rural villages.

What is true of the intellectuals is, in most cases, even truer of the governments. The government bureaucracy is urban minded and preoccupied with the large city. The capital of the country crowds all other communities to the very thin edge of the bureaucratic conscience. And equally serious is the fact that such a program cannot be developed in a country where the large plantation is the dominant rural institution. Unless the government has an effective agrarian policy, it cannot have an effective program of rural education—and the first may, for political reasons, be impossible and the second appear undesirable.

Even where the intellectuals—or some of them and the government as well—have a commitment to building a healthy multicellular nation based upon rural communities, the difficulties are so great as to seem almost insurmountable. The program of bringing these communities and their leadership into the nation will require many years of continuing effort in the *same* direction. There is, to begin with, the lack of funds—a chronic state of affairs and, except for a windfall as in the case of Venezuela, not visibly remediable. Even with funds, where are the teachers to come from? The ordinary teachers' training courses do not prepare them to meet the thousand needs and skills essential for living and working in the rural community. And worse, perhaps, teachers raised in an urban environment, unless moved by missionary zeal, find the rural community— where no Spanish is spoken, where there are no electric lights, no moving-picture houses, and no newspapers—a place of exile.

To be a schoolteacher in these surroundings calls for a high degree of self-sacrifice and devotion to an ideal. The Mexicans have tried to meet this difficulty by instituting the "Cultural Mission," which, by periodically bringing the poorly trained rural schoolteachers together, gives them a renewed stimulus, additional training, and a feeling of working on a task of national importance. A fully staffed and wisely administered rural normal school to train teachers for a rural environment would meet part of the difficulty only if it succeeded in imparting many skills without so changing the habits and attitudes of its students as to make them wish for an escape to the city. And that, unfortunately, is all too often the case.

All of these obstacles are perhaps secondary to what is, after all, the major difficulty—making the educational efforts constructive rather than disruptive of the life of the rural community, where prejudices are tenacious, values noncommercial and noncompetitive, and where the local mores are something apart from the urban and sophisticated world whence the educational impulse must come in the first instance. To be useful, the teacher, the administrator, must learn respect for the idiosyncratic cultural traits of the rural folk as a preliminary to the acceptance and trust without which nothing useful can be done. The emphasis must be upon building new habits, attitudes, and institutions inside the rim of an older culture complex and not against it. It should always be kept in mind that the new habit or institution must make its way and be absorbed by the community, that changes must come from the inside, from accommodation, and not be forced. If this can be accomplished, there will be vast resources of possible cooperation, initiative, and leadership to be tapped. But confidence and good will must first be won, and they can be had only if the administrators and the teachers can accept the communities as moral entities with their own integrated value systems.

We have had some useful experience in this matter, most of it in Mexico, where the rural education endeavor dates back to at least 1923. Here, however, the original impulse derived from a social upheaval that emphasized the needs of the rural community and the worthiness of the rural population. But even here some of the original impulse has been lost: impatience and too much sophistication have, as they always do, borne their usual fruit—skepticism and indifference. The experience did show that, when given the opportunity, thousands of rural communities not only built their own schools but took on, with an almost childlike faith, the many new responsibilities that the school brought.

It still remains a question whether or not such a program is sufficient for the purpose of bringing the communities into the political life of the nation. In some way the leadership developed in the rural communities must become related to or identified with the leadership of the larger world; the schoolteachers and the inevitably bureaucratic personnel of a department of education are not the real leaders of either the community or the nation as a whole. Lázaro Cárdenas supported a voluntary and nongovernmental effort by people around Uruapan, in the state of Michoacan, each adopting a rural community as his special interest and responsibility. The individual in a sense was elected as the *padrino*-godfather of the village and took on this role, establishing contact for the community with the larger world. He was the adviser and consultant, the guide and the counselor of his village, and tried to help it work out its own problems. This group contained doctors, lawyers, engineers, chemists, agronomists, foresters, specialists in cattle, in fruit culture, and so on. The scientific and cultural resources of the group were impressive. And at the meeting that I attended it was interesting to see that these men would call on each other for help. One man said to another, "I have a water problem that my village does not know how to deal with. You know about these things. Could you come and spend a day with me?" It was evident that here were substantial resources that could be tapped in behalf of any one community. Equally important, here were possible contacts with the active leaders of the larger world.

Any such program, difficult in itself, would have to hurdle

two stubborn "states of mind" so deeply embedded that they are likely to survive whatever political changes the winds may blow across Latin America. It would require the toleration of increased local independence and a modification of the tax system so as to give the localities an increasing measure of income. As things stand at present, and have stood from time immemorial, the central government absorbs most of the available income and leaves a pittance to the states and the municipalities. Everyone expects it to be that way and local officials beg hat in hand as a favor what they could have had on their own if the tax monies were differently distributed. I would like to believe myself wrong in this characterization—for it will largely determine the prospect of political stability in Latin America—but the one revolution that has no advocates, no parties, and no prospects is the one that would strengthen the parish, the township, the county, and the state at the expense of the central government. And yet without such a change, neither the rural education we have been suggesting nor the political party to which it is antecedent can fully make its way.

The other "state of mind" is the well-nigh universal expectancy of centralized control and guidance of the economic and social life of the nation. The tradition of governmental regulation and "planning" antedates the Independence and is so much part of the milieu that all political credos take it for granted. The idea of planning, seemingly so new and so revolutionary, is congenial even to the most conservative Latin Americans, for to them the notion is old and inevitable. The government must do everything, for no one else will. That is the conviction and the expectancy. The friends of Latin American democracy who look to the planning of the economy as a means to political stability and representative democracy will, to their disillusionment, discover that they have strengthened the central political machine at the expense of the localities and increased the barriers to representative government and political stability. The route out of the dilemma lies in the growth of local and national institutions with resilience enough to survive the all-absorbing tendency of the central government. But that growth will be slow and painful.

[1955]

The Future of Democracy in Latin America (II)

In Latin America there is a prevailing expectancy of arbitrariness on the part of the chief executive and his agents. What most of the countries have known as an integral part of their political experience is that where the administration's prestige or interest is involved, the will of the president is the law of the land. And this expectancy should be generalized to include his political family. The laws, the courts, the constitution become irrelevant, and cease to be. When the executive goes beyond the constitution or the law, there is no adequate legal resource available to oppose or stop him.

When Perón expropriated *La Prensa* in Buenos Aires, and when Rojas Pinilla silenced *El Tiempo* in Bogotá, the owners of the papers could not go to the courts. The judges from the humblest magistrate to the members of the supreme court were helpless to prevent the peremptory and illegal seizure in the first case and the forced suspension in the latter. They were not only helpless but intimidated because they knew that the president could replace judges or could close the courts at will. This arbitrary way of the executive with the courts is an old tradition and has survived in nearly all countries. Some might think that it could not happen in Chile. Could one be sure? In the thirties, Alessandri found it easy to establish a dictatorship which gave him dominion over all government agencies including the courts. It was, after all, a matter of tradition. The age-old expectancy that *él que manda, manda* reasserts itself in any serious crisis. The dominance of the executive over the courts tends to apply as well to the legislative branches of the government. In most cases, and at times for trivial reasons, the president is empowered to declare a state of siege or martial law. I discovered this on my first visit to Honduras where the president kept the nation under a state of siege. When I inquired why, I was told that it enabled him to collect certain taxes which would not otherwise be available. Trujillo's thirty-year regime in Santo Domingo is a classic example of the arbitrariness of the executive. Haiti under Duvalier was a recent demonstration of an ancient practice. So, too, is the case of Castro in Cuba. Castro is a Latin American *caudillo* first and a self-declared communist second.

A personal experience may further illustrate the point under discussion. It occurred in Mexico and could certainly have been repeated in some form in other areas and in many countries. While visiting a large sugar cane area under the control of the government, I became aware of considerable discontent among the *ejidatarios*. I learned that the manager of this very large sugar enterprise was not only unpopular but hated. The *ejidatarios* were obliged to grow sugar when many of them wanted to grow rice instead. Rice, they said, would have given them a larger net return. They complained of being cheated. The administrator, they said, had tampered with the scales and short-weighted their loads of sugar cane. He had surrounded himself with armed gangsters for fear of his life. When an American woman had occasion to call on him in his office, his guards searched her pocketbook for a hidden pistol. Within a few years he had grown richer than he could have dreamed. Finally, he was *fuereño,* an outsider, from a distant state imposed upon the area by the secretary of agriculture on his own authority or, more likely, on the recommendations of the president himself. This happened at the time that Ruiz Cortines was in office. The situation contained prospects of violence and rural rebellion.

When I returned to Mexico City, I took occasion to mention this to Lázaro Cárdenas, then long in retirement. It was clear from his attitude that he was aware of the difficulty. I explained to him that in the United States we had and will most

Economic Efficiency and Social Justice: Toynbee on Revolution in Latin America

Arnold Toynbee's lectures on Latin America* are refreshingly simple. As in so many other instances, his genius for broad and all-inclusive generalizations seems to reduce a long historical process to manageable terms; the complexities seem to fall away to make a baffling world intelligible. In these lectures, as appears so natural to Toynbee, petty details of human life are given their proper place in the broad stream of history and man's daily projects are related to human destiny. To Latin Americans, these lectures may seem like a revelation. To say, as Toynbee does, that the great issue in the world lies between economic efficiency and social justice; that social justice always wins in the end; that, unless the United States takes its stand on the side of social justice, it will be swept away like empires of the past—like the Persians and the Romans—will make all things seem easy and provide an answer to every difficulty. Unfortunately, it makes the issues too simple—so simple, in fact, as to make them meaningless. It also tends to lend support to a devil theory of history.

The dichotomy between economic efficiency and social justice is false, as Toynbee himself recognizes in the end. It is false because, in the historical process, it would be difficult to identify economic efficiency and equally difficult to define social justice. They could only be identified in a given place and for a given purpose and only if the ends in view were agreed upon by all concerned—that is, if the historical process were a rational

* *America and the World Revolution and Other Lectures.* N.Y.: Oxford University Press, 1962.

one. When one thinks of the suicidal wars of the Greek city-states, of the tyrannies that shaped the demise of the Roman Empire, of the two last world wars, and the present nuclear arms race, it is difficult to phrase human issues anywhere, not only in Latin America, as the dichotomy of economic efficiency and social justice.

This simple rational set of alternatives reflects Toynbee's English political experience. In England, one can get what looks like a consensus of public opinion on many issues. And on most questions, no matter how difficult, it is possible to secure a political decision without violence. English historical experience is such that political judgment can be informed, registered, made into law, and enforced without splitting the society apart and without convulsion. It has not always been that way. The Reformation, the beheading of Charles I, the Cromwellian interregnum were matters that it would have been difficult to set in the frame proposed by Toynbee. And if England worked its way through to political forms where economic efficiency and social justice have come closer and closer together, to use Toynbee's formula, it has been mainly because a thousand-year-old system of local government has trained, disciplined, informed the mass of the English people to take their turn governing and being governed by their neighbors. Without the long participation by the populace in disciplining each other, it is doubtful that English politics would have achieved the degree of reasonableness that makes so simple a formula a rational proposition.

To take this formula to Latin America and use it as a key to an explanation of its difficulties, and as a guideline to its future, is a most dubious intellectual venture. It can, if taken seriously, probably do more harm than good. For Latin America has nothing of the sweet reasonableness of English political tradition. It does not even know the meaning of the raucous hurly-burly of popular exuberance of American politics, which arrives at political decisions by the devious routes of continuous self-contradiction and name-calling. It is doubtful whether a formula derived from either English or American experience can be used for satisfactory analysis of, not to speak of policy making in, Latin America.

One must begin by recognizing that, in spite of appearance, Latin America is not like Europe and in many ways unlike the United States. It is a Western society that has missed some of the key influences that shaped Western culture. Latin America was by-passed by the Reformation, the Enlightenment, the French Revolution, the Industrial Revolution, and the "Great Transformation" that incorporated the masses into the political process on the national level. Certainly, some individuals and small sections of the population have shared in the culture and partake of the attitude that these broad historical movements precipitated. But not so with most of the populace. More than that, a considerable part of the people are of Indian or African extraction, neither of which has fully absorbed even that limited repository of European culture which is also Latin American.

Where the Indian has survived, he lies psychologically and morally beyond the reach of his present masters. In Bolivia, where he has become a citizen, he continues on the rim of European civilization as it is known in that unhappy country. The present situation will certainly change. But in exactly what direction? What is the future of the white and *mestizo* element, that is, the city folk in Bolivia? Who is there that can assure their survival in the nation? Is there anyone who can speak of this with certainty? Surely no one in Bolivia, in the innermost recess of his private feelings, can be certain. To speak of economic efficiency and social justice as an explanation or as a formula is as meaningless here as it is in the religious conflicts between Hindu and Moslem in India. This is, of course, also true of Peru, Ecuador, Guatemala, and, to lesser degrees, other places. In countries with large Negro populations like Brazil, Colombia, the West Indies, Venezuela, it is difficult to apply this formula because politics, here for reasons different than in Indian countries, is also given to little rationality or discipline.

One need but examine the history of Haiti to see how difficult it is to apply any rule whatsoever.

The dominant group in most countries is *mestizo,* and the *mestizo* is a child of yesterday only. His historical outlook and experience are not European and his political training is not conducive to sweet reasonableness. A look at the history of Venezuela or Honduras or Mexico will make that perfectly clear. The exuberant passions that ride their political activity are *native,* have little to do with the United States, and the United States can do little about them.

When one talks about economic efficiency and social justice, one assumes the existence of a national government, a national policy, a disciplined bureaucracy, and political activity meaningfully identified with national interest and national purpose. But in Latin America, who speaks for the nation—who exactly is going to apply the formula in Guatemala? The Indians, who are half the nation but are mute on national issues in a dozen mutually unintelligible languages? The *ladino* (as the *mestizo* is called in Guatemala) in the little village and the small town who dislikes the Indian, looks upon him with contempt, and lives by exploiting him? The upper-class *ladinos* who run the government but who have no base other than the army for political power? Is the army destined to simplify all things and apply this formula? Or is it the United Fruit Company? Surely, this company has been abused for powers it does not possess. It could not change the racial, social, political, and economic structure of the country even if that were its reason for existence and even if it possessed inexhaustible funds. The power of a foreign private agency to modify the social design of any nation is small indeed—even if it knew the direction in which the society ought to move.

Social institutions do not change easily; human habits and customs have a resistant way of perpetuating themselves, and it is easier to grind diamonds than to change human beliefs and prejudices. When we talk about the sweet reasonableness of "economic efficiency versus social justice," we are almost talking about a moral vacuum where people have no passions and no interests. One is led to suspect that economic efficiency and social justice are by-products rather than matters of intent. Whatever they may be, they cannot be planned for long in advance. They derive from other preoccupations just as popular suffrage was a by-product of the individualism that followed the Industrial Revolution and the growth of "free," or rather unattached, labor.

Any attempt to apply Toynbee's formula, even if one knew what policy formulation it called for, presumes a universally accepted government, a government based upon a general consensus. It presumes a political system where choices can be made rationally, where the law has universal application, where there are representative political parties, where the executive governs with the consent of the people, where the purely political problem of staying in power has been settled long ago, and where the transfer of the presidency is expected to occur peacefully and in accord with long-established law and tradition.

Unfortunately, these are not the usual attributes that govern political life in Latin America. One need but look at the recent history of Cuba, Haiti, Santo Domingo, Venezuela, Ecuador, Brazil, Argentina, Guatemala, Honduras, San Salvador, and Nicaragua to recognize that politics in Latin America is not wholly rational. Anyone who can give a "rational" explanation to the role of Santa Anna in Mexico in the last century, or to that of Velasco Ibarra in Ecuador at present, is endowed with more than "human" insight.

Toynbee's lectures are eloquent, interesting, appealing, morally and politically right when addressed to a European or an American audience, but of little consequence, if not irrelevant, when addressed to Latin Americans. And, strangely enough, the intellectuals in Latin America will lap these lectures up as if they had been written in honey instead of ink. The intellectuals are closer to Toynbee than to their own people. They have read Toynbee, of course. They have also read Freud, Sartre, Marx, and Lenin. They may even have read Walt

Whitman and William James. The trouble is that half of their compatriots cannot read at all, and two thirds of those who can are functionally illiterate because they have had less than three years of primary grade schooling. The masses, especially in the rural districts, belong to a different world from the one the lectures are addressed to and the folk are indifferent to the issues posed by them. If they have any political ambitions at all, it is to follow their local *cacique* to glory and victory over the visible enemy of their own leader, usually a regional leader without any concern over the broader national questions posed in Toynbee's lectures.

It is at this point that Toynbee's discussions of the revolutions in Mexico, Bolivia, Guatemala, and Cuba seem so beside the point, so basically uninformed. They are written as if revolutions were made in a rational universe where everyone knows what he wants, as if the public good were clear to each person and where only the evil ones, the oligarchs, the imperialists, are opposed to what is so obviously just. They are written as if the issues of economic efficiency and social justice were there for everyone to see and choose. But that is not the case.

If one takes the revolutions of Mexico, Bolivia, and Guatemala, the fundamental issue was how to make a nation. During the bitterest days of the Mexican Revolution Manuel Gamio wrote a series of articles, later collected in a book under the title *Forjando Patria* (1922), and Manuel Gómez Morín published a pamphlet entitled *1915*. Gamio's book concerns itself with the question of amalgamating the many culturally and linguistically different regions into a unified Mexican culture, a Mexican nation. He was preoccupied not merely with how to induce the government of Mexico to identify itself with the people, but with how to persuade the people to identify with the nation.

To Gómez Morín, on the other hand, the year 1915 was the time when the students and the intellectuals awoke to the idea of a nation. They discovered that Mexico was something different from what it was supposed to be, something ruled by men who had their real psychological base and moral allegiance in Europe and who looked upon the Mexicans as an inferior people. And Gómez Morín was describing the traditional Mexican families, not Europeans or Americans. He was discussing the Mexican families that did not feel Mexican, that were ashamed of being Mexican.

Mexico has now measurably succeeded in "making a nation," but it took twenty years of bloody strife and cost over a million lives. The success, however, is not complete. There are still some 13 percent of the people who do not speak Spanish and are not in real communication with the nation and do not know what it is all about. The forging of a nation was an aspiration of a few intellectuals. If it succeeded, it was by accident. Pancho Villa, Saturnino Cedillo, and a thousand local chieftains who fought and died in the Revolution did so for reasons other than nationhood—or for no logical reasons at all. They were driven by a passion and a restlessness that had no preoccupation with either economic efficiency or social justice. They were like the people in *Los de Abajo*, by Mariano Azuela. If they helped create a nation, it was by accident. It is probable that the hostility of the United States to what was going on below its border and the fear of the effect the upheaval might have on the United States were more important in creating a nation in Mexico than anything that the Mexicans themselves did or planned.

The jubilant pride of the Mexicans in themselves, in their culture, in their aspiration to reveal what is really Mexican in the Mexican no one planned or dreamt of, yet it is the most important thing the Revolution produced. It would not have emerged and flowered if there had not been the United States against which to test one's inner self, against which to cast one's reckless *Yo*, even if it meant death.

The wage dispute at the time of the oil expropriation in Mexico in 1938 had little to do with the dichotomy posed by Toynbee and much with fatalism and national dignity. The expropriation acted as a psychological catalyst and freed the Mexicans. When nothing happened, the overwhelming fear of the United States, which had hung over Mexico for more than a hundred years, passed away. They were now free and unafraid. But this, too, was an accident brought on by the oil companies that insulted the president of the country by saying that they doubted his word and by publishing a full-page advertisement in the local press announcing that they would not obey the decision of the Mexican supreme court. The Revolution, as it developed in Mexico, was something other than a mere conflict between economic efficiency and social justice.

Similarly, the case of Guatemala. Whatever it was that Jacobo Arbenz tried to do, he was in no position to harmonize the four-hundred-year conflict between the Indian and the *mestizo,* nor that between the army and either group. It is always worth remembering when discussing this episode that Arbenz deserted his post when Guatemala was invaded by Colonel Castillo Armas with 181 men, and that neither the army nor anyone else rose in his defense. The United Fruit Company, whatever other role it has played in Guatemala, in this case served as the image of the devil to be beaten in public with a stick. The objectives of the Arbenz regime were pointed towards embarrassing the United States and offering up Guatemala as a sacrificial lamb in the Cold War. The Guatemalan Revolution could not serve the purpose of national unification— because there is no one who can speak for Guatemala as a nation.

Anyone who governs in Guatemala does so not for ideological reasons but because he can. The president of Guatemala has never been elected in any real sense. He has been chosen by those who have the will to play the political game to the point of revolution and civil war. There is no solution to the Guatemalan difficulties in the immediate future. The problem is not primarily economic or political, nor primarily the United Fruit Company, imperialism, or colonialism. The difficulties stem from the stresses and strains of unlike cultures and languages, habits, beliefs, and attitudes. The two halves of the population are incompatible and the differences that divide them are not soluble, even by a revolution. For a revolution might well become a civil war between the Indian and *ladino*, especially if the Indians could get arms. To talk of the Guatemalan Revolution of Arbenz as if it were anything more than an attempt from the outside to make trouble for the United States is to give weight and importance to people whose real concern was with international politics rather than internal change. Guatemala's first order of business is to become a nation, for, up to now, it has only been a legally recognized state. Not until all the people in Guatemala have equal access to the law and equal share in the shaping of the politics of the state will it be a nation. No one can now tell how long that will be.

Something similar may be said of Bolivia, which, in spite of its revolution of 1952, is not yet culturally a nation. More than half of the people are isolated in Quechua or Aymará, and do not understand Spanish. The country is continually on the brink of violence between the Indians (now called *campesinos*) and the *mestizos* in the towns and cities. No one really knows, or can know, where economic efficiency ends and social justice begins. The survival of the government is in almost daily jeopardy. Since 1952, there have been many violent efforts to subvert it. The threat of a general strike by labor led Hernán Siles Zuazo, then president of the country, to go on a hunger strike. The administration was thus saved by a show of moral courage.

To save the government from bankruptcy, American financial aid has been used to meet internal budgetary obligations. One of the reasons for this difficulty is that the miners' union, which helped make the revolution, has become accustomed to living on subsidized foods in addition to wages higher than any in the country. The miners added to their income by selling the food they bought in the subsidized commissary at a profit. The subsidy to the miners was the greatest burden on the national budget and incompatible with the political survival of the government. And the subsidy could only be continued with the help of American loans.

To say that the American government favored economic

efficiency as against social justice in Bolivia is simply meaningless. The situation is so complex that all one can say is that American aid kept this government in office on the grounds that, if it collapsed, there would be complete chaos, which might well have endangered the urban population. This, in turn, would possibly have led to other equally serious consequences, such as military intervention by Bolivia's neighbors.

The primary problem in Mexico, Guatemala, and Bolivia was and remains, especially in the latter two, the making of a nation. Almost equally pertinent is the question of how to establish internal peace and security. People living in a society where life is relatively secure have no idea of how little value life has in unstable societies. They have no notion of a world in which, when one asks for a friend, he may be told *ya lo mataron* (he has already been killed); in which it is possible to sit at breakfast and hear a genteel woman tell the president of a country: "This is the way things go on here, so-and-so killed so-and-so, and then his friends killed so-and-so; by now sixteen people are dead and no one does anything about it."

An unstable society, where violence is traditional and endemic, continues to be violent even after the so-called revolution is over. Such a society cannot be talked of as liberal, conservative, or socialist. It has first to find some basis of internal peace and security. How difficult this is one can learn by looking closely at the record of the Mexican Revolution. In that revolution, a degree of internal peace was ultimately achieved by leaders who could not only gather a following, but also severely discipline it—as President Calles and his secretary of war, General Joaquín Amaro, did by shooting all the officers of any rebellion. How to establish peace, respect for the law, public confidence, the freedom of movement without fear is a primary matter. For years in Mexico highways were patrolled by the army, and railroad trains escorted by soldiers. An instance of highway robbery was punished by summary execution on the spot. How to establish order is a foremost concern and without it nothing else can be done.

When the Bolivian government raised the price of gasoline because the national petroleum industry was close to insolvency, the action was followed by a riot that cost fifty lives before order could be reestablished. How to provide for freedom of the press when a newspaper might call for armed revolution, for freedom of assembly and yet prevent riot and subversion at every turn for any reason, or no reason, is an unanswered question both in Bolivia and Guatemala.

In an unstable society these are primordial issues and cannot be reduced to nice formulas. A government that has fifty rebellions against it in one year has little time for anything except to keep itself in power—and it is ultimately overthrown or is converted to a tyranny. In Latin America, with or without a revolutionary situation, the problem always remains, who is the real leader? Where does power lodge? In whom and in what particular person? For it does not lodge in an institution. It belongs to an individual. The case of Trujillo in Santo Domingo was one example. Fidel Castro in Cuba is another. If these seem extreme cases, they only differ in degree. The president, whoever he is, has overriding power. He is usually stronger than the legislature, the judiciary, and the political parties combined. And as long as he has the support of the army, he can continue in office; otherwise he becomes a puppet of those who control the military.

The social justice that Toynbee sees as the alternative to economic efficiency in the Cuban, Mexican, or Bolivian revolutions was not the result of a rational choice by a political party. The choices were made by the individual leaders who happened to be in power. If someone other than Cárdenas had been nominated for the presidency in Mexico, the agrarian reform program would have developed differently. If Castro had been killed a few weeks after he came to office, the Cuban Revolution would have taken a different turn. There is no basis for suggesting that what happened in Cuba, or even in Mexico, was the logical, necessary, and inevitable outcome, or that reasonable men devoted to social justice would have made these particular choices. It would be more accurate to say that the leaders are driven by anger, ambition, passion, illusive ideas of grandeur, and notions of hostility against outsiders, capitalists, and whatever. They may have also been captivated by the idea of revolution, without having any clear notion of what they were trying to do. The direction a popular revolution takes is often determined by the temporary *caudillo*. And the *caudillo* is a self-appointed and self-centered individual, relatively indifferent to ideals of social justice. The Mexican movement was driven by neither a political theory nor notions of a planned society.

In Latin America, anyway, the social revolutions occurred in a milieu where ideas of economic efficiency and social justice were ephemeral. The first issue a successful leader has before him is to establish a government, one that will not fall to pieces or be overthrown, but can survive internal corruption and leave something over to pay the police and the army. In Cuba, it was said that the bureaucracy used to pilfer about two hundred million dollars a year. When robbery becomes endemic, it almost becomes honorable. It has even been defended as a device for capital accumulation in a non-industrial economy. The question of having a viable government is not something that can be settled in a day or a year.

Toynbee's treatment of the Mexican Revolution, as if choices were made by scholarly men over a cup of good tea, must be considered in the light of the available human and material resources. For many years, the land was filled with hatred and violence and no program could be effectively carried out, even if a program could have been agreed upon. The amount of human recalcitrance, dogmatism, and sheer cussedness and greed, and the favoritism natural among friends, were sufficient to sidetrack, or cripple, nearly every project. This is not an accusation; it is an attempt to face the hard realities of a violent society riven by irreconcilable values, attitudes, and beliefs, not to speak of persistent differences in culture and language. To say, as Toynbee says, that the present situation in

Mexico is like what it was at the end of the Díaz regime is to deny the history of the last fifty years.

In 1910, Mexico was a primitive rural society with the mass of the people tied to the soil as *peones*, who, if they were not slaves, were not greatly removed from slavery. The *peón* could be sold with the land and was not free to leave the *hacienda*. It was a stratified social system with a minimum of vertical or spatial mobility. It was a world governed by a small landed aristocracy where each *hacendado* was the ruler of all he surveyed. The land was held by something like 1 percent of the population and a little over a hundred families owned one quarter of the country. Entire states were divided into a few *haciendas*. There was no freedom of assembly, speech, or press, and the government, both national and local, was in the hands of old men perpetuated in office by a dictator. The country had no roads, no rural schools, no trade unions, no labor legislation, no social security system, no middle class. It was an arbitrary, cor-rupt, and static society. And this is not contemporary Mexico.

In the Mexico of Díaz, the large mass of the people had no aspirations. At present, it is quite the opposite. The people may be poor but the middle class is increasing. The large number of urban workers and a considerable part of the *ejidatarios* who have land in effect belong to the middle class because they have a sense of mobility and growth. Their children can, if they have it in them, join the "upper" class, all of whom were, in their day, barefoot children. To date, over 45 million hectares have been distributed to more than two million families, which means that more than 11,000,000 people in Mexico are living on lands given to them in *ejidos*. This is about one half of the rural population and one third of all the Mexican people. It is true, of course, that there are now perhaps half a million families who are entitled to *ejidos* but have received no land. It is also true that the population of Mexico has about tripled since 1910; that in Central Mexico, where most of the people live, there is no more land to be distributed; and that it is difficult to move people from the highlands to the warm lowlands.

In the future, except for minor changes and for possible increases in lands under irrigation, higher agricultural production rather than land distribution will have to serve as the means of raising the standard of living of the rural population. This is so because 52.2 percent of Mexico is arid and 31.9 percent is semi-arid. The growing population has made irrigation indispensable. Up to 1959, 2.2 million hectares had been put under irrigation. This has allowed for an increase in the production of wheat and corn and has permitted cotton to become a major export item. To assume that land is available for all those who want it and that a "bad" government is withholding it is simply to misread the situation.

Toynbee's discussion of Mexican education is as unsatisfactory as his treatment of agrarian reform. Admittedly, approximately half of the children are not in school. But it is also true that the other half are, and this represents an enormous increase since 1910, when there were few schools in the cities and practically none in the country. If there are so many children out of school, it is not because the governments of Mexico since 1922 were indifferent to the problem. They have certainly struggled with it. The country was in a state of internal strife until about 1930 and not completely at peace until 1940. And there was so much to do and so little to do it with. There were demands for roads, irrigation, public sanitation, and the villages needed water; there were needs for rural credit; the land distribution program was initiated and had to be carried forward; the army had to be maintained and ultimately disciplined so that it belonged to the government rather than to individual generals; the oil industry was expropriated and had to be administered; the railroads were nationalized and needed management.

Among the undertakings was a heroic effort at an educational program in the rural districts. The expenditures for education have gone up to what is now about a fifth of the national budget. All of this, including an industrialization program, was carried forward with a bureaucracy that practiced the traditional habits of peculation and favoritism. A culture which expects peculation in public office is not seriously affected by good laws or pious declarations. And that raises problems that cannot be contained in a formula of social justice versus economic efficiency.

The problems here considered have something to do with the nature of centralized government. The educational program in Mexico is essentially national, especially in the rural districts. The central government receives most of the income from taxation and leaves only a pittance to the states. The villages have almost no income from taxation. Everything flows from the center. Somehow, the impulse from the Department of Education in Mexico City must reach every little corner in the Republic where there are children. It must provide teachers, schools, books, papers, pencils, blackboards, chalk, school benches and desks, and the thousand other things that go with a school program. There are now something like a hundred and fifty thousand places where people congregate in little communities, most of them under three hundred inhabitants, including women and children. There are no roads to many of them, and in many no Spanish is spoken. It would be materially impossible for the Mexican government to provide an eighth-grade school, equipped as a modern school ought to be equipped, with personnel and materials equal to those of Birmingham or Rochester.

We tend to forget that education in England and in the United States was initially a private venture. This is true not only of the universities but of the village and township schools. Families would combine to hire a teacher the way they hired a preacher. It was a long time before the county took cognizance of the school and longer still before the state did. Had we waited for the federal government to build every rural school, every college, every high school, the English and American school systems might have turned out no better than the Mexican, if as good. The question that lies at the bottom of this issue is whether education is something separate and apart from the total social system. One would suppose that a school system is a function of a given state of economic, political, social, industrial development, and that no school system can be expected to be anything more than the culture requires. It is a question that is only decided by the inner necessities of the culture and its functional readiness and has little to do with any abstract formula.

The treatment of Mexican education as if it were a failure rather than a great achievement of the Revolution is like Toynbee's statement that Mexico's failures to achieve social justice are comparable to England's at the beginning of the Industrial Revolution. For if one thing can be said about Mexico's industrialization, it is that it did not reproduce the experience of the English Industrial Revolution. England had no social legislation at the beginning of the Industrial Revolution, and, for a period, the life of the laborer in the cities worsened. The story of child labor in the cotton mills is notorious. It was not until the end of the first and the beginning of the second quarter of the nineteenth century that the first child labor bills were enacted by Parliament. Not until the first and second parliamentary Reform Bills were passed could any adequate social legislation get under way. The trade unions were hampered and persecuted until the third quarter of the nine-teenth century. An effective trade union movement did not really come into being until the seventies and eighties.

Quite different is the story in Mexico. There, social legislation was written into the Constitution of 1917 long before there was any significant industrial development. A trade union movement was encouraged and brought into being by the state and, in a sense, entrusted to the labor leader before he had time to organize the workers. Article 123 of the Mexican constitution reproduces the most advanced social and labor legislation on the statute books of the industrialized nations, including England, the United States, Germany, as well as Australia and New Zealand.

Mexican industrial development began with an eight-hour

day, a minimum wage, prohibition of child labor, the right to strike, compulsory recognition of the unions, payment for injuries during sickness, displacement, and retirement. In effect, if anything may be said in criticism, it is that the industrial worker was favored over the rural laborer and that industrialization has weighed more heavily on the rural population. It is true that in recent years government policy has sought to stimulate industrial growth by keeping wages steady and giving inducements to capital savings and investment. It is probably true that real income measured in wages has declined due to inflation. At the same time, services in terms of medical care, social security, health, housing, and schooling have improved for large sections of the urban population. As of 1960 as many as 54 percent of factory laborers were covered by social security. The number of obviously poor that one used to see in Mexico City has greatly decreased.

On the issue of foreign investment, Toynbee's treatment of present-day American investment in Mexico is incomplete. It may be true that the United States, at the moment, is the largest foreign investor in Mexico. But all foreign investments in recent years amount to less than 10 percent of the local private and government funds in industrial development. And when Toynbee says that the largest companies in Mexico are branches of the United States' corporations, he should add that these corporations are required to accept 51 percent of local capital. This, I think, changes the relationship of the foreign investor to the government.

The Mexican government has consistently pursued a policy intended to eliminate foreign capital in the basic industries—oil, mining, transport, and power. To what extent this is good for Mexico, with its growing population and limited resources, is another matter. It would be hard to say whether this policy is on the side of economic efficiency or social justice. Mexico needs to double its gross national product every twenty-five years to remain even as poor as it is now because its population is doubling every quarter of a century. Just who can tell which of these policies will, in the next fifty years, so increase Mexico's income that it will be able to feed better the nearly 100 million mouths that it will then have?

This discussion of the Mexican Revolution leads into Toynbee's treatment of the Cuban Revolution. For him, Cuba is the model in agrarian reform and social accomplishment that the other nations in Latin America ought to follow. He even speaks of the day when Mexico and the rest of Latin America will accomplish what Cuba has accomplished. Surely, this is strange language. In his treatment of the social changes to be wrought by revolution, Toynbee equates the movements in Cuba, Bolivia, Mexico, and Guatemala. The only commonality among them is the word "revolution." The conditions, political and social, under which the effort to remodel these different societies was made were so various that it is misleading to classify the upheavals referred to by a common denominator.

Mistakenly, Toynbee identifies Castro's enterprise with what occurred in Mexico, Bolivia, and Guatemala. Mexico, Bolivia, and Guatemala are Indian countries. Each has numerous villages with long memories of the lands taken from them by others. They are countries where the rural population has age-old traditions of farming and where there is an ancient love for the land by the people who have tilled it from time immemorial. In these countries, the great mass have continued to live on the land and, for the most part, in a nonmonetary economy. They are subsistence economies. In the end, an agrarian reform program would give some hope of raising the standard of living of the rural population.

Cuba was a very different case, indeed. Over 60 percent of the population is urban. Havana alone has more than 20 percent of all the people in Cuba. In a country where the majority of the people are urban, where the economy rests on the export of sugar (80 percent of the export value of Cuba), over the price of which the country has no control, there is no agrarian problem. Nothing that can be done with the land by breaking it up, by collectivizing it, by placing it in the hands of cooperatives, by turning it over to the government will increase the market abroad, or raise the price upon which the economy depends. This is true of the other Cuban export crops, tobacco and coffee. If the income of the people were to be increased, it would have to come from lower costs of operation or greater efficiency. There is no ground in experience for such an expectancy and the evidence, at the moment, shows deficiencies not only in the sugar industry, but a decline in the production of those items in common use by the poor people. Not only has there been a decline in imported goods—and that began before the suspension of the sugar quota by the United States—but in the production of native agricultural products and manufactured goods as well.

To speak of these changes as evidence of economic efficiency is not really conducive towards an understanding of the nature of revolution in Latin America in general and Cuba in particular. There is the fact that much land held by private companies and by the government was not under cultivation. Castro explained this as an imperialist conspiracy. But most of the land was in Cuban hands. In the sugar industry, Cubans owned over 50 percent of the area. There must be other causes for the lack of utilization of land and the insufficient production of food.

Probably the policies of the Cuban government were part of the difficulty, but only part of it. The mass of the rural population are descendants of slaves freed in 1886. They have no tradition of land ownership; they have no love for the land; they are not farmers and lack the numerous skills and insights that, taken together, constitute the highly complex art that makes the "profession" of farming. If there had been a farming population in Cuba with their own villages and their memories of landownership, there would long ago have been a series of rebellions in demand of land. Somehow, the "farmers" would have reached out for the soil. But no such rebellion ever took place: there is no evidence of land hunger ever being an issue. The mass of the Cuban rural workers were cane cutters, common laborers with no knowledge of, or interest in, becoming farmers. In addition, there are, no doubt, difficulties embedded in the local culture, soil, and climate that would help to explain the failure to use the idle land for food-growing purposes. Whether the Cuban government can compel the rural population to become what it is not—farmers—and do so by force and propaganda, and do it quickly is something that remains to be seen.

It still needs to be proven that large-scale farming under government operation is economically advantageous or socially desirable. All the evidence is to the contrary. The Chinese and Russian evidence, now available, throws doubt upon the wisdom of such policies. The Cuban government is now rationing items of food locally grown and previously in abundance. It is perfectly clear that the government is trying to impose a plan upon the rural scene. For Castro has not only expropriated the sugar plantations, but he has also taken over the tobacco, pasture, and coffee lands. At the moment, over 30 percent of the land in cultivation is organized in *Granjas del Pueblo*, govern-ment-managed *haciendas* of one hundred thousand hectares (247,000 acres) or larger. The justification for this is that it is easier to get one good manager for a large farm than many for several small ones.

On an increasing scale, the government is converting the lands of Cuba into large farms managed by the *Instituto Nacional de Reforma Agraria (INRA)* on the basis of wage labor. This looks like a nice scheme to those who are innocent of agricultural life and so committed to statism as to be indifferent to the fortunes of the individual. In the sugar industry, where the "cooperatives" are being assimilated by the *Granjas del Pueblo*, the rural workers' status is now less favorable than it was before Castro came to power. The Cuban rural worker had an effective trade union, a wage based upon the price of sugar, and a body of legislation that protected his rights. He could appeal to the courts and call on the government itself to intervene for him against the plantations. He could go on strike as he had often done. Now, in the name of the revolution, the worker has lost his trade union and his own elected leaders; both have become tools of the government.

There are now no independent courts and no body of legislation protective of the worker. There is only the government that is also the owner, manager, purchaser, supplier, and employer. There is now no intermediary agency between the worker and the government. And the government is some unapproachable anonymous bureaucrat in a large office protected by a militia armed with machine guns. The employer and the policeman are now one and the same and there is no one to turn to. A major tragedy has overtaken the worker, rural and urban. The intermediary institutions that in a healthy society such as Great Britain stand between the individual and the government have disappeared. To identify what has happened in Cuba as a step towards social justice requires, indeed, a high degree of detachment from the tragedy that has befallen the Cuban people.

There are now more than one hundred thousand exiles in the United States and fifty thousand more in various parts of Latin America. Cubans are abandoning the land at the rate of about 2000 every month. If the early refugees were the well-to-do and the professionals, those presently escaping are poor people—workers, fishermen, little storekeepers. The Cuban upheaval has taken a turn that defies classification in either of the categories Toynbee employs for characterizing the drift of the changes being wrought in the contemporary world.

Is what occurred in Cuba comparable to the other Latin American revolutions considered by Toynbee? Is the Cuban Revolution like the ones in Mexico, Bolivia, and Guatemala? The answer, I think, is that they are not comparable. Cuba is not an agricultural subsistence society and therefore not capable of being reformed by an agrarian program. In fact, the Cuban experience puts in doubt the availability of revolution as an instrument of social change in an industrial or commercial society. The emphasis on revolution by Marxists, when opposing capitalism or when advocating socialism, has been so universal and cast in such general terms that it has been taken for granted by Marxists and their opponents that the path from the present to the future would be by revolution. Experience has shown, however, that cataclysmic revolutions have only occurred in subsistence countries, where the essentials of a stratified social structure may well exist. Such a society has ordinarily no built-in device for social change. The revolutions of our century have this in common. They have all occurred in a society that was neither urban, capitalistic, industrial, monetary, nor commercial.

The Cuban Revolution followed an agrarian model although there was basically no agrarian problem in Cuba. There were broad requirements for rural housing, health, and education. Most important, there was the need to bring a halt to corruption. But none of these changes required the overthrow of a total social system. Cuba did have the mechanism to bring the required changes into being without the convulsion precipitated by Castro. A monetary society has available taxation and income distribution devices that a subsistence economy does not possess. If Castro chose revolution, it was because he was raised in an intellectual milieu where Marxian doctrines seemed to require cataclysmic changes. But a monetary society neither needs nor benefits from convulsive revolution. What Castro's efforts have brought to Cuba is a decline in its standard of living and a totalitarian government. In addition, Castro can only enforce his programs by police methods that have destroyed the freedom of the people and their traditionally easy and friendly ways among themselves and their neighbors. To say that the Cuban Revolution is a model pointing the way for other Latin American countries is nothing short of the fantastic. It confirms our suspicion that Toynbee has not looked at this part of the world with the kind of attention he devoted to his earlier Greek studies.

[1962]

The Continuing Ferment
in Latin America

The political troubles in Latin America are neither recent
nor visibly terminable. Current difficulties have ancient roots
and present turbulence carries on a tradition in public affairs.
The manner of achieving public office is indifferent to the policy
to be pursued by the new administration, and almost independent of it. The looked-for means of coming to office is revolution.
There are, of course, other ways, such as political campaigns and
elections, but they are secondary, and usually follow the initial
uprising that deposed the president and laid the basis for a
popular vote that will "legitimize" the accession to power of the
leader who overthrew the government. It does not always
happen that way, but it occurs with sufficient regularity to make
a succession to the presidency by election and without violence
somewhat surprising and possibly misleading. All too often the
election is a staged affair, with the results known long before the
electoral campaigning begins, and the president, having risen to
office by revolution, has his occupancy legally sanctioned by a
casting of ballots as required by the constitution.

Despite the political turbulence, the ideal in Latin America
has been political stability and constitutional democracy. Philos-
ophers, statesmen, politicians, and soldiers have aimed at it.
Latin American countries have experimented with popular
constitutional forms to the point of extravagance. They have
written into their basic charters the classical separation of
executive, legislative, and judicial powers; incorporated broad
versions of the rights of man, and, since World War I, added
detailed enumerations of economic and social rights. Freedom of

speech, press, assembly, political activity, freedom of movement, security from arbitrary arrest, and the right to a fair public trial are specifically guaranteed. Constitutional mandates are broad enough to meet the most exacting definition of popular rights. But there is something amiss. It does not work that way. The governments usually come to office by violence, and are dislodged by revolution. Censorship of the press is widespread if not universal, freedom of association is restricted, jails are often crowded with political prisoners who have no prospect of an open trial, men are exiled by government fiat or flee the country to escape incarceration or even death. All of the civic guarantees so fully detailed in the constitution are a mere mockery. In fact, the constitution is not an instrument of government. Primarily it serves as an excuse for rebellion. The proponents of a forceful change of administration make the violation of constitutional guarantees their public justification for the upheaval, and ask for support on the ground that they, when in power, will maintain the liberties of the citizen, so often promised, so rarely fulfilled. This has happened with such frequency and over so long a time that it cannot be ascribed to the malice of this or that individual. Governments in most Latin American countries, whatever their motives, seem driven to be arbitrary. If the president allows his opponents the liberties they claim on constitutional grounds, they will use them to organize the opposition and will topple him from office—and soon. The choice seems to lie not between a good or a bad administration but between tyranny disguised by constitutional symbols and revolution in the name of constitutional symbols.

The easiest way to explain this political behavior is to blame it on the manner in which chief executives come to office. If the president achieves power by revolution, he must expect conspiracy and rebellion; for he who comes to power by violence usually can and probably will be removed by violence. The effort to stave off the impending upheaval requires continuing vigilance for the ubiquitous conspirator waiting his chance to replace the government by some sudden coup. In practice, such a contingency obscures the niceties of constitutional guarantees and the government has recourse to arbitrary rule, military government, the declaration of a state of siege in an emergency, or only a suspension of constitutional guarantees in an effort to avoid an emergency. These practices seem logical and necessary to those in power. In fact, it would not require too subtle a casuist to defend these arbitrary acts on moral grounds—as a way to ensure quietude and avoidance of bloodshed. But this still leaves the question of why the cycle of revolution, dictatorship, and revolution has come into being as a norm in the political life of Latin America.

Within a twenty-five-year period, from 1930 to 1955, there have been over fifty successful violent, mainly military, upsets of governments in Latin America, and many more attempts that ended in failure. The only place where revolution has not been resorted to since 1930 is the little country of Uruguay, whose admirers speak of it as the Switzerland of the Americas. In contrast, Paraguay and Bolivia have had successful and attempted revolutions that can be counted by the dozens, while Chile, Colombia, Argentina, and Brazil, with a certain claim on political stability, have seen their governments overturned by revolution or upset by military pressure on more than one occasion. Even Costa Rica, deservedly famed for its democratic and peaceful ways, was forced to improvise an armed force and battle against the subversion of its traditionally free institutions.

The many successful and unsuccessful rebellions and military coups are only part of the record. The rest is made up of what we call dictatorships and what might perhaps more accurately be described as tyrannies; for most of them exercise a power unrestrained by law or constitution and use legal formulas for decorative trappings, as a sort of symbolic acknowledgment that they have their being in the Western world and abide in a constitutional age. Not even a Juan Vicente Gómez of Venezuela or a Jorge Ubico of Guatemala could think of governing without a constitution. The constitution is like Milady's hat: it is the fashion.

The dictatorships we are going to discuss are not exactly of the same stripe, but they have this in common—they are all personal. They belong to the individual and they terminate only with the individual's departure from the scene either by death, revolution, or some other reason. They all have their beginnings in revolution or in the possession of preponderant military power and are then given respectability by an "election"—the result of which is always known in advance. It would be boring to detail a repetitious story for each country, and, in some ways, it would also be misleading. For in spite of the many things they have in common, there are marked differences in the role of these arbitrary regimes.

SANTO DOMINGO

The example of Santo Domingo belongs to the older tradition of Porfirio Díaz in Mexico and Juan Vicente Gómez in Venezuela. Trujillo converted the country into a family farm which he operated for the benefit of himself and his many relatives. The government was reduced to a personal instrument, the constitution converted to a flexible body of rules changeable at will to give specific sanction to immediate ends, and the rights, privileges, and immunities of the inhabitants of the country were as dependent upon the caprices and interests of Trujillo as were those of plantation laborers upon the owner of a private estate.

Santo Domingo has some claim to being considered a classic case of the use of totalitarian methods for personal and family ends. It would be difficult to find a better example of megalomania and nepotism disguised as government. There is, however, nothing new about this. It merely represents an extension of known ways on a fuller scale. Perhaps it could best be identified as a maturation of the methods of Juan Vicente Gómez.

GUATEMALA

In contrast to the personal dictatorship of Trujillo in Santo Domingo, the difficulties in Guatemala reveal an ancient rift in the body politic for which time alone can provide an answer. Guatemala is not a nation, a society, or a people. It is a government—a legal entity with administrative jurisdiction over a specified area. Its three million inhabitants are divided between Indians and *ladinos* (i.e., *mestizos*), of whom two thirds speak no Spanish, can neither read nor write, and belong, in fact, to a series of separate but related cultures that antedate the Spanish Conquest by centuries. Four and a half centuries of attrition have failed to mold a common society, and the Indians and *ladinos* take no comfort in each other.

This divided society has been tyrannized for seventy years after the Independence by four picturesque and cruel dictators, and in between afflicted by chaos and revolution. The country is poor, and the *ladinos*, who have little of the country's worldly goods, are isolated and parochial. Until World War II, the coffee plantations belonged to Germans, the banana plantations, the railroads, and the public utilities to Americans. In a country with a small and impecunious "superior" race, a wealthy foreign corporation favored by a hated dictator (Jorge Ubico in this case) may seem like an ogre incapable of grace or mercy. The fall of the dictator jeopardizes the fortunes of the foreign companies he protected in the interest of the national economy and the modern science they were bringing to the country. In a society lacking in cohesion and functional organization, party government does not exist, and power rests upon the only force that can sustain it—the army. So it was with Ubico. So it was (with some intermixture of the unstable forces let loose by the rebellion that overthrew Ubico) with Arévalo. Arévalo had to suppress twenty-seven rebellions to survive his six years of allotted time, and his successor, Arbenz, could only be "elected" after the deliberately staged assassination, in 1949, of Colonel Javier Araña, the most likely successor of Arévalo. Arévalo and, more so, Arbenz chose to sacrifice their program of social reform upon the altar of the Cold War and blame the United States for the age-old difficulties of this unhappy country, as if the people of the United States were responsible for the bitter fruits of more than four centuries of misgovernment and exploitation. One suspects that the communists, who dictated the public policy of the Arbenz government, were more interested in embarrassing the United States than in improving the lot of the Guatemalan Indians. In that they succeeded. It is, however, doubtful that the program of social and economic change suggested by Arévalo and Arbenz could have been carried through even if they had avoided the snares of the Cold War. To change effectively the political and social structure of the country would have involved the destruction of the army and the *ladino* elements upon which their power rested. The "new revolution" and the "new elections" were merely a repetition of an older theme. There was no basis for a democratic representative government. There has never been an honest election in Guatemala, and there will not be one for a long time to come. An effective election would reduce the *ladinos* to political impotence if not to a deprivation of their social and economic prerogatives.

BOLIVIA

If the Guatemalan difficulties left the country largely unchanged, the Bolivian Revolution that brought Paz Estenssoro to the presidency in 1952 precipitated innovations that gnaw at the very roots of a society reared upon the Spanish Conquest. Spanish colonial power rested upon the unparalleled wealth of the Bolivian silver mines, and the governments of Bolivia since Independence have drawn their major income from the export of minerals, which continue to supply between 95 and 98 percent of Bolivia's foreign exchange, of which tin has, in recent years, represented 75 percent. A fraction of the population working in the mines pays for the imports of the entire nation and for half of its food supply. Of the 8,000,000 people, only about 50,000 are miners and perhaps as many as 160,000 are engaged in manufacturing, building, transport, and communication.

Until the Chaco War of the early nineteen thirties, the native races (who constitute two thirds of the population) were a people apart from their rulers, and were treated as beings with no rights of their own. Like Guatemala, Bolivia was neither a people nor a nation. The Chaco War brought this fact home to the younger intellectuals raised upon modern notions of nationalism and social reform; and how to bridge the gap between the races and make a nation out of two peoples alien to each other has been a major preoccupation of the more sensitive and the more cultured younger political leaders. The effective power of the country was narrowly held. The tin mines that supplied three quarters of the exports belonged to three mining companies, Patiño, Hochschild, and Aramayo. The Patiño company alone had an income larger than that of the government—but the income remained abroad and did not go to increase or diversify the country's economy. Apart from the three mining companies, the country was ruled by a small body of great landowners from whose families came the intellectuals and political leaders.

The turbulent history of Bolivia reflected the narrow regional patriotism of a country divided by high mountains, and the competition of the leading families for power, pelf, and prestige. So fragile was the political base that an army officer followed by one or two loyal regiments could, if luck were on his side, overthrow the government and make himself president. But these were family quarrels within a narrow caste, all of whose members had a similar outlook and ambition. These many upsets of the government affected the personnel of the administration and left all other things as they had always been. The Indian on the land was forgotten. As late as 1947, it was possible to print an advertisement in *La Razón*, the leading newspaper in La Paz, which read as follows: "A farm for sale on the Altiplano a half-hour by automobile from the capital, on the road to Guaqui, with five hundred sheep, much water and twenty peons." Agriculture was routine, inefficient, and failed to supply the country with necessary food, while the government lived well or ill depending upon the price of tin on the international market. If one could speak of a stagnant social structure continually churned by political rebellion, one would be characterizing the scene during the last hundred and twenty years in Bolivia.

The government of Paz Estenssoro, which achieved power with the revolution in 1952, weakened the foundations upon which Bolivian society and politics had rested for four and a half centuries. In 1952, the tin mines were expropriated and in 1953 the landed aristocracy saw its properties given to the Indians. The turnover could not have been more drastic. The fact that the price of tin is often below production costs, and that the Indian has no adequate access to credit, education, or modern tools, merely increased the resulting difficulties. Even so, a society based upon private ownership of the mines, and upon a feudal hold of the land, has been transformed; and administratively the government is poorly equipped to deal with the complexities of a world turned over. What the structure of power will look like within the next twenty-five years, with the Quechua- and Aymará-speaking Indian armed, and in possession of his land, with the former rulers of the country impecunious exiles, and with the government administratively unable to prepare adequately trained personnel, is not predictable.

ARGENTINA

Different, indeed, is the story of Argentina. For Argentina was neither poor, nor illiterate, nor riven by racial and linguistic antagonisms. On the contrary, it was rich, European in culture and outlook, possessed of a magnificent territory and an ambitious people used to peaceful civil government and the rule of law. And yet within a few short years this progressive and self-confident nation saw its political institutions undermined, its liberties destroyed and its economy made poorer. All of this was accomplished by a military demagogue. Perón's promise of autarchy was an impossible objective in a country that lacked coal, iron, stone, and forest in adequate amounts, and whose present needs for fuel oil are only half-satisfied from local resources.

As late as 1870 the country had only two million people and its exports were mainly hides with some dried meat and increasing amounts of wool. In 1874 barbed wire was marketed in the United States, and subsequently it wrought a revolution in Argentina. The land hitherto of little worth could now be fenced to keep cattle out for sowing of grain, and to keep them in for breeding and fattening. Barbed wire and refrigeration made possible the first shipment of chilled beef to Britain in 1876, where a growing urban population offered what seemed like an ever-widening market. During the years 1895–1915, Argentina lived in an expanding universe, and optimists dreamed of boundless progress; the population would multiply, the market would expand, and worldly power would accrue to the people destined to be the leaders of Latin America in opposition to Anglo-Saxon materialism. But the dream came to a sudden end. Even before 1915, thoughtful Argentineans began to see that an agricultural export economy was limited by its market, and the market was reaching the saturation point. Exports after 1915 were high but not increasing, the flow of immigration was declining, the population, which had doubled between 1895 and 1915, was not increasing at the earlier speed, the birth rate was falling, and optimistic forecasters of a population of 16 million in 1930 and 30 million in 1960 were disappointed: in 1943 the country had fewer than 14 million and in 1950 about 17 million. All around, the world was expanding. The United States was growing by leaps and bounds and Brazil,

Argentina's neighbor, was rapidly increasing in population and resources. A feeling of frustration and anger took hold of the nationalistic-minded statesmen and their military coadjutors. Leading economists wrote of Argentina as a "blockaded nation" and statesmen and soldiers began looking for an escape—by expansion, by autarchy, or by both.

World War I dramatized Argentina's dependence upon the industrial world, and the depression of the thirties its helplessness in a universe where the price of its leading exports was beyond its control. World War II emphasized the previously learned lessons but also opened up a possible way of escape. If only Hitler could win the war—then expansion would be possible. The military leaders of Argentina felt themselves natural allies of a victorious Germany, and the tortuous policies of Argentina's governments, from Castillo to Edelmiro Farrell, have their explanation in this hope. When General Rawson said towards the end of the war, "We will not obtain anything by sheer force. We must not aspire to gain supremacy over other Latin American countries," he was arrested. The promise of saving Argentina from being a "blockaded nation" gave Perón support from the younger military, the extreme nationalists; and the offer of belated social legislation, naturally enough for an agricultural nation governed by a landed aristocracy, gave him the support of the relatively small union movement.

Perón's proclamation of Argentina's freedom from domination by foreign imperialism flattered an old dream and kept alive a hope that one way or another Argentina would cease to be a "blockaded nation." It explains the subversive efforts among other Latin American nations, the fostering of *peronista* trade unions in other countries, the personal alliances with military chieftains, the attempts to bring Uruguay, Paraguay, Chile, and Bolivia into some sort of Argentine bloc, as well as the misguided efforts at autarchy. It explains the policy of nationalization, the control of exports, the emphasis upon industrialization and the final ruin of the agricultural economy of the nation. Personal demagogy, showmanship, and bravado are integral likely continue to have instances of malfeasance of office, of corruption, and of abuse of power. Such wrongdoing could and did occur in city, state, and, with less frequency, federal government. However, where the United States differed from Mexico was that the matter we were talking about could, and probably would, be made into a scandal by the newspapers, that a committee of the legislature might be induced to conduct an investigation and hold public hearings, that the information supplied to the public prosecutor of the state might lead to the calling of a grand jury and an indictment, that some member of the House or the Senate would make a speech on the floor and give the matter national publicity. Finally, if none of these things occurred, a body of private citizens (for example, the League of Women Voters) could organize a committee and publish the facts, circulate them to the newspapers, or hold protest meetings, until the government responded to these pressures and tactics by taking some remedial action.

I remember vividly the puzzled look that crossed Cárdenas' face as I described the probable reaction to such a situation in the United States. In Mexico, neither the newspapers, the legislature, the public prosecutor, nor any private committee would undertake to scrutinize the actions of a public official. No one knew the many ramifications the scandal might have, how widely it might reach into the official family, or who would ultimately be dirtied by the inevitable mudslinging. Thus, nothing could, or would, be done publicly—the political implications were altogether too serious and perhaps all-encompassing to be discussed in public. If the administrator of the *ejidos* was to be removed at all, it would have to be done through personal influence with the secretary of agriculture, or perhaps the president of the country. This I understood. And such an event might or might not occur depending upon a thousand hidden human commitments amongst the men who are the governing element and their close associates beyond the official circle. A public airing of the matter would never happen, or only with the previous sanction from the highest source.

The bearing of this incident upon the democratic process is

evident: Mexicans and other Latin Americans have not learned to wash their dirty linen in public—*la ropa sucia siempre se lava en casa*. There is, however, an unwritten rule that the democratic process and public confidence can only survive when a people has the fortitude to examine its shortcomings and failings, its corruptions and its acts of injustice openly and for all the world to see.

Arbitrary government is an endemic habit in the political life of Latin America. How arbitrary is the Argentine government? Here is an administration governing without opposition or support from a political party, without a political philosophy, and without the constraints of parliamentary practice. It is a government of the police and the army, with the judiciary subservient to the will of a president who assumed office by a military coup. An irresponsible government is one under which the individual citizen has no protection against arbitrary action of the president and his agents.

On December 7, 1968, the *New York Times* reported that prisoners were being tortured, that the Argentine government removed judges and replaced them with officials willing to do the bidding of the executive. What occurred then had happened before under Perón and a century earlier under Rosas. What happened under General Onganía was not unique. It had a long history behind it. On February 27 and 28, 1969, the same newspaper reported from Brazil that the military regime of Arturo de Costa e Silva suspended federal elections and filled local offices without elections. Congress had been suspended for an indefinite period; the government removed three supreme court justices and also removed elected officials of the electrical and construction worker unions, closed down the morning newspaper *Correio da Manhã* for five days, and extended the prison term of its publisher. As in the case of Argentina, this is not a completely new catalogue of arbitrary actions by government. It has happened before and in all likelihood will happen again. Whether or not a culture can escape its own traditional habits remains a moot question.

In Latin America, when the government wants its way, the citizen is not effectively protected by any law, court, parliament, church, university, trade union, or political party. There is nothing that stands in the way of the will of the executive. Such capriciousness was evident in the administration of Rojas Pinilla in Colombia when he expropriated, destroyed, and punished without the rule of law. The fate of *El Tiempo*, the great newspaper published by Eduardo Santos in Bogotá, is another example of the process of executive arbitrariness we are examining. Rojas Pinilla required the paper to publish an apology to the president on its front page for 30 consecutive days. It had been prepared in Rojas' office and was meant to humiliate and to discredit *El Tiempo* in the eyes of its readers. The apology was to seem as if written by the editors and publishers of the paper. *El Tiempo* made a counter offer to publish the document as a statement by the president of the country, but was refused. The newspaper was given no alternative. It would either print the false and degrading statement or be closed down, and it was closed down.

Here was a country long known for its liberalism, its strong devotion to legality and a constitutional system, suddenly facing an official denial of law, justice, the rights to one's property, and the abrogation of a long-established freedom of the press, once considered as an inviolable constitutional mandate. For purely personal caprice and political purposes, a great newspaper, the most influential single voice in the nation, respected at home and abroad, was destroyed. It would be hard to find a better illustration of the precariousness of legal procedure, constitutional rights, and personal liberty in Latin America. For what happened to *El Tiempo* could happen today to any newspaper or to any other enterprise or to the rights and liberties of any individual in Argentina, Brazil, or Peru.

There is really no formal remedy for this state of affairs. It may in time pass away. Changes in political, social, and economic institutions may make arbitrary, personal, or vindictive action by the executive unacceptable and impossible. Such changes, however, would deny centuries of experience and can at best pass away only slowly. The Bolsheviks who destroyed the Czar for his arbitrariness and centralized state power ended by vastly extending the police powers of the state and, in the place of the Czar, made room for Stalin.

The point to be made is that in the tradition of Latin America the president can, as in Haiti, Cuba, Colombia, or Venezuela, act arbitrarily. Somehow, the cultural milieu condones it. It allows the government to resort to violence rather than law. No one could tell Melgarejo in Bolivia or Vicente Gómez in Venezuela that what he proposed was against the law. It was the will of the dictator. And one must ponder the matter by asking: how long does a tradition last, or when can one say that this particular way of behavior is no longer possible because the populace would not tolerate it? One might be a pessimist and argue that once a nation like Argentina has had a Rosas there is always the possibility of a reversion to the original model. One need only contemplate the recent political history of Spain or Russia to appreciate the force of cultural atavism.

Representative government requires the existence of political parties accommodating many contradictory interests under a common symbol. The Democratic party in the United States is a good example. Many points of view flourish under the same label. It is really a way of bringing the many party machines to some sort of agreement without absolutely surrendering to any one of them, and giving each some prospect of having its claims listened to and partially satisfied. The differences cannot be over absolutes. If a political party is going to function effectively, the differences among its constituents must be over particulars.

A national consensus is hard to come by in Latin America and, where it seems to exist, it is make-believe. In Peru, half of the population is politically outside the pale. The Indian has no idea of the nation, the party, the state, or the meaning of national policy. He is neither consulted nor considered. Whatever seeming consensus there is exists among the urban *mestizo,* the industrial groups, the labor movement, and the military. The little village is not part of the political community. It is governed, but has nothing to say about who is to be the governor or how it wants to be governed.

It has always been difficult to have political communication in Latin America. There are, of course, the physical obstacles. The high mountains, the rugged passes, the *altiplano,* the tropics with the heat, humidity, and heavy rains, the extensive rivers, the jungle and the forests, and the deserts have stood in the way of rapid and comfortable travel between one point of a country and another. Add to these the distribution of the population. Mexico, for instance, has 150,000 or more communities, but the majority of them are under 400 people—little groups of isolated villages, literally cut off from the rest of the nation. Things have changed somewhat, but millions of Mexicans still live in these isolated places with inadequate communication in spite of the vast road program of the last thirty years, and the expanding school system. An Indian village of less than 400 human beings hidden in the mountains or in the wet forests of Tabasco or Chiapas is not likely to have a school, or a doctor, or a dentist, or skilled craftsmen, or even a newspaper. The transistor radio may now penetrate into the most remote hamlets, but what it broadcasts has little meaning to nonparticipants in the language and culture transmitted on the transistor radio.

The problem of communication is compounded by the many languages and cultures that still exist—a hundred in Mexico, a dozen or more in Guatemala, Brazil, Peru, Colombia, Venezuela, Bolivia, and Ecuador. In Guatemala and Bolivia, it would not be surprising if an accurate count revealed that half of the population was really monolingual in a non-European language. I am reminded of what I saw some years ago in the little pueblo of Chamula, where the Chamulans had their church and gathered for the Christian festivals and where the local government had its seat. The scene in the one-room schoolhouse was typical of many things in Mexico and Latin America. There were perhaps twenty little children in attendance out of a population of many thousands. The teacher could not speak their language and the children did not understand Spanish. The teacher had written the word "papa" on the blackboard and found a translator in a seven-year-old boy who had lived with his mother in San Cristóbal, where she was working as a servant. The teacher would say the word "papa" and the little translator would repeat it and then turn to the other children and translate it into Chamula. This scene could be multiplied in thousands of places in Latin America. As the children, at best, only attend school for three years and in their vast majority drop out at the end of the first year, their knowledge of the official language of the nation is likely to remain minimal, unless they move to an urban center and acquire enough of a vocabulary to make themselves sufficiently intelligible to earn their daily bread.

Physical, cultural, and linguistic isolation is a poor foundation for the kind of political communication required in any system of democratic government. And the problem is a persistent one. The large cities may grow more rapidly than the countryside, but the total rural population may increase in numbers though declining in proportion. And even in the city it will take more than one generation for the *campesino* to steep himself in the urban culture to the point where the sophisticated and precarious workings of political democracy make sense to him and become a natural part of his way of life and being.

General Isaías Medina Angarita, former president of Venezuela, speaking in the Latin American Seminar at Columbia University, discussed the question of how to govern a Latin American nation, and told of two incidents from his own experience. As the commanding general, he was called in one day by López Contreras, who had succeeded Juan Vicente Gómez, and was told by the president, "General, I would like you to succeed me as president when my term is finished." "Thank you very much, Mr. President," Medina Angarita responded, "but how can I succeed you? I have no friends." "All I want is your consent," López Contreras said. "If you agree, I will arrange all the rest." This dialogue illustrates that the culture of representative government still has to be learned and that a congenial political climate is required for the lesson to be meaningful. The other incident Medina related was even more illuminating. After López Contreras assumed the presidency, he called a cabinet meeting and asked his ministers pointblank: "What is this thing about voting?—*¿Qué es esta cosa de votar?*— Have any of you ever voted?" None of them had.

Clearly, we are talking about a cultural pattern, a set of values that is best absorbed with the other things one learns at a mother's knee if they are to be a functional and truly integrated part of the political process itself. One sees the lack of such a cultural pattern in Russia, where it was legitimate for the government, under the aegis of the communist party, to declare that the majority of voters who elected the Czechoslovak government of Dubček were reactionary conspirators against the people's democracies. Obviously, the Russians never learned the virtues of majority rule under the czars and they have never been able to acquire them. The question really is, can a pattern of political behavior be transmitted from one culture to another? How effectively can it be done? How long does it take? This, after all, is the question that needs to be asked about Latin America, if we insist upon having democratic governments in the area. How many Latin Americans believe in majority rule, in a government under law? How many believe that the law ought to be impartial, equal for all men regardless of family, friends, or special cliques? The answer is that the majority do not, and this is true for states where there is a nominally democratic government; one cannot count heads in this matter, but many years of intimate contact leave this negative impression.

The physical and cultural obstacles to the communication necessary for stable democratic political patterns have tended to create two separate worlds, the one of the cities, the other of the villages. The two worlds may be close physically, but they are remote from one another culturally and politically. The Otomí Indians live close to Mexico City, but it is as improbable to think of them as participating in the national culture of Mexico as it is to think of the Quechua and Aymará Indians as participating in the national culture of Peru. Even where the sharp delineations of race, language, and special traits have lost their dominance, the difference between the rural and the urban remains and the rural is less responsive, less interested, less movable than the urban and has fewer means of understanding or experiencing the democratic process.

The villages and hamlets have long been a world where people lived on what they produced, ate the food they cultivated, lived under a roof they raised, and wore the clothes their women wove for them—a subsistence society without money, or with so little that it could not be counted as part of the money economy characteristic of the urban centers. The city was and is of another world. The rural community is still in the thirteenth century, and how to combine these different societies into a nation remains a puzzle for the future to unravel. It will not be easy. All one needs to do is to reflect, for comparative purposes, upon the unyielding cultural entities in the Middle East, or perhaps upon the differences that have kept the Hindu linguistic and caste societies in continuing dissidence and turmoil, to see how difficult it is to combine a variety of cultures into one nation. In spite of Gandhi, the Untouchables are still untouchable.

If democratic and representative government requires that people have equal rights before the law and share enough values to talk meaningfully to each other, then Guatemala is a long way from that point. So are Peru, Ecuador, Bolivia, and many others. And where there seems to be some basis for communication, the tradition of *personalismo* makes representative government a dream beyond immediate reach. If it is not a Somoza in Nicaragua, then it is a General Onganía in Argentina. How long this will last is impossible to say. Industrialism should change all of this, at least so those of us bred in the United States believe. However, Latin American labor leaders and industrialists are bred in the local traditions and behave like *caudillos*.

True enough, the theory, the constitution, and the law assume a society of equal citizens. But the realities are different; the theory, the constitution, and the law have little to do with practical government—and knowledgeable people avoid legal procedures and turn to friends, relatives, agents, men with the right connections and a reputation for manipulation. One survives by the skin of one's teeth and by the protection granted by a strong fellowship. The loyalty to friends, *gente de confianza compadres*, and to the family transcends the law, the rule, or the theory. Without friends one is no one and has no protection. With the right kind of friends, one is above the law.

The inability to trust others (*¿es fulano de tal gente de confianza?*), in business, in politics, or even in personal relations, is a persistent impediment to political decisions openly arrived at or even to the development of an industrial system that requires as a base that people assume the integrity of those they deal with. The anxiety of *confianza* that runs through society—and it becomes sharper as one goes from peasant and worker to intellectual, politician, and industrialist—is a matter of distrust of one's neighbors, the higher-ups, the politicians, the governmental officials, the police—everyone. In that kind of society, authority is built on sand. Education, wealth, professional standing are of little help, for everyone is bounded by a small circle of which the family is the center. And only this circle is trustworthy. All others are suspect, alien, to be treated with courtesy but not to be accepted, to be looked upon as potential enemies. If one cannot trust them, one cannot share power with them or take them into one's firm, club, or home. This insistence on *confianza* ties in with what outsiders like to call nepotism. But the favoring of your family, often an extended family, is inevitable in a society as fractured, distrustful, and self-centered as is generally the case in Latin America. The major concern is security for yourself and those attached to you. In the last analysis, it is only the *gente de confianza* who are the real friends and who offer the only defense and protection against outside enemies.

How to build a political party on such fragile ground is a continuing puzzle and a continuing failure. The party will last as long as the *caudillo* lasts, and when he goes all else goes with him. He has kept the party because his followers had confidence in him and have it in no one else. The prominent political parties have been built by outstanding individuals: Haya de la Torre, Rómulo Betancourt, Eduardo Frei, Pepe Figueres. They are all *caudillos* of varying kinds. When their grip loosens, the party splinters. It would require great optimism to believe that the APRA, the Acción Democrática, the Christian Democratic party, and the National Liberation party will survive their original architects and builders.

How to change this age-old tradition and replace it by the acceptance of a legal process politically free from interference is one of the crucial questions. It is true that new groups are coming to the fore—for example, labor unions and industrialists. But on examination they prove to be a new version of the older way of doing things. In the Cuba of Batista, if you did not find an inside track leading to those who had the local machinery in their hands and would bend its services in your direction, you could do no business. But this is true in Mexico, and was and probably is true in Venezuela today—as well as Argentina and Brazil, and I do not know that one could exclude any country in this matter. The law and the administration are pliable to influences of various kinds. And an impartial democracy is thus a long way from a reality.

The existence of the local *cacique* in the rural districts is a distinctive feature of Latin American political history. Traditionally, the capitals, where the law, the courts, the legislature, and the president resided, were *tras lomita*, over the mountains in another world that little knew or cared about what happened in the remote villages, the *barrancos,* the forests, and the swampy lands of the tropics. The best of intentions and the most energetic of administrations were defeated by distance, indifference, local pride, or local suspicion. Passive resistance proved stronger than the democratic ideal based upon the independent vote. The local *cacique* was unanimously elected even if no one voted for him. He was in fact the law because the law of the state only made itself felt sporadically. Everyone knew it would wear itself out. In fact, the government could only govern if it allowed the local *caciques* to govern for it, that is, if it accepted the local family and its doings as part of the law of the land. Justice, education, and tax collection were locally administered in a special way acceptable to the local chieftain or not enforced at all—unless the president of the country was prepared for a local rebellion. To what extent have these conditions changed or been so modified that they are no longer operative? How long does it take to abolish or reform a local political machine? And is it replaced by a new one? Is the enforcer sent by the central government? If he is effective, is he not likely to replace the older *cacique* rather than change the method of local administration? Are not local loyalties stronger than his promise or legal obligations? To think otherwise is a bit of piety believable only to a city reformer. Unless the new agent becomes a *compadre,* he would soon discover that he was not obeyed, that he did not govern, that he was a stranger if not an enemy and an unwanted presence whose life might well be at stake if he took his job and his duties too seriously.

In most countries, the governor, whether chosen by the people or by those with power to govern through other means, is distant from the mass either in city or country. In Latin America the governing bureaucracy is essentially an urban, if not intellectual, group. Even the army general has an education and contact with the world that place him a long way from the people he governs. The distance between the rulers and the ruled is much greater than in the United States, Canada, or Western Europe. The rural masses are outside the political orbit and even where there are peasant organizations, their leaders would mostly be intellectual and city folk. In Latin America the city is the political hub—Rio de Janeiro, Buenos Aires, Santiago, Bogotá, Caracas, Mexico City. The nation's capital is where the political game is played, lost, and won, where the politicians live, where the tax money is gathered and disbursed, where honors, jobs, ambassadorships, and governorships are given away. These political activities take place at times in a parliament, a congress, a senate. The newspapers and universities provide all the glamour, the sound and the fury of the game. But they do not reach much beyond the city's perimeter.

One of the issues facing a democratic society revolves about the division of power—the formula of executive, legislative, and judicial independence. This is always a delicate matter because there is always a tendency on the part of each to encroach on the powers and autonomy of the others. In Latin America, however, one begins with the omnipotence of the executive. That is the tradition. In fact, the constitution and the law tend to favor the executive. There is, for example, Mariano Melgarejo's famous remark, made at a banquet to celebrate the adoption of a new Bolivian constitution; he informed the select gathering that he would put the old constitution in his left pocket and the new one in his right pocket and that *"Él que manda acá soy yo"* ("I am the one that governs here"). It was a statement of the bare truth. It might have been in poor taste on such an occasion, but it was not beyond the recognizable limits of the real situation. If one thinks of some of the recent *caudillos*—Batista, Pérez Jiménez, Trujillo, Perón, Onganía, the Somozas, Rojas Pinilla, Vargas—then it is clear that Melgarejo's words were within the bounds of validity and applied far beyond Bolivia. What judge or legislator would have asserted the constitutional prerogative against Trujillo, Rojas Pinilla, Vargas, Onganía, or Castro?

The prerogative of the executive is deeply impressed upon the Latin American psyche. It is not something new, strange, unknown, and imported. It has a long history. It is the older *Yo el rey* (I the King), except that the new, often self-appointed monarch has no symbolic seal with which to cover himself with legitimacy. That is the real difficulty. The mass of the people, however, regardless of whether they support him or not, expect him to govern. *Él que manda, manda.* He who rules must rule rather than reign. When one goes into a town and is looking for the person who has power, he doesn't ask for the mayor, he wants to know *"¿Quién manda acá?"*—"Who is in charge here?" And if it is clear that the governor or president does not govern, then there is little but derision and contempt. He isn't a man; he lacks guts. Someone else must have the power, as in the case of Calles and Ortíz Rubio in Mexico. Calles was *el mero jefe,* and Ortíz Rubio was only the president. One is reminded of the remark by Manuel Urrutia Lleó when he resigned as president of Cuba: "If Fidel has all the power then let him have all the responsibility." The people expect the president to rule, not just to govern. They expect him to have all the power.

How to build a representative democracy when the popular expectancies are for a strong man, strong enough to override not only popular opposition but the constitutional limitations of an independent legislature and judiciary, has remained an unanswered question. The numerous constitutions are eloquent testimony to the repeated efforts to limit the executive. The people want a leader and a father—the president has to be able to do everything—for they will even bring their personal and family affairs to him. Simón Bolívar wrote that the people asked him for advice on even the most personal matters, but he did not understand why they were so persistent in seeking it.

If one combines the unspoken popular demand that *él que manda, manda* and the cry *¡Que viva el presidente macho!* with a completely centralized administration in which the members of the cabinet are the tools of the executive to whom they take the least little item, then one must have serious doubts about the immediate prospects of an effective democracy. Another personal experience may illustrate how completely controlled the activities of the government can be, how even all petty decisions can only be made by the executive. It happened when General Benavides ruled Peru. I had received a grant and was there for the purpose of doing a book about the country, especially its rural areas and the Indian communities. It soon became clear that I could only do such a study if I traveled extensively in the rural districts. Most of the travel would have to be done on muleback, because then there were many fewer roads than now. Another obstacle to my intended travel was that the Guardia Nacional would not allow a foreigner to go from mountain village to mountain village by himself. He would be suspect. The Guardia Nacional literally ran the country. They stopped buses on the highways and forced everybody to identify himself; they required all newcomers to go to the police station to register; they took travelers off public vehicles and put others in their place. If I was to do a study of the rural districts of Peru, I would have to be accompanied by some official who could vouch for me and protect me against the exuberant activities of the police.

Fortunately, I located an office of Indian affairs in the Department of Agriculture. After introducing myself to the head of the office—and being a professor of history at Columbia University was a great help—I explained that I had come a long way to write a book about rural Peru and found that under the present circumstances I could not go out into the field to do any research. He agreed and was sympathetic. It would be a pity not to have such a book on Peru, he said. It would be a useful thing for Peru to have such a book. It was a pity. But what was to be done? "I cannot go alone," I said, "and you agree the book needs to be written, and you are the head of the Indian Bureau. It seems to me that you are the logical person to go with me." After some discussion he agreed to come along, but added that "I will have to ask the minister of agriculture. Come back next Wednesday." When I returned the next week, my friend in the Indian affairs office said that the minister was agreeable to his going with me but the minister wanted to see me the next Thursday. The minister of agriculture had a medical degree from the University of Michigan and understood the meaning of field research. He was charming and pleased with the project. "Before I give my consent, I will have to ask the president. Come back a week from today." A week later the minister told me, "Yes, the president agreed to your going and being accompanied but asked that you wait three weeks." "But why?" "There is going to be a military parade in the president's honor and he wants you to see it."

Finally, we got off and traveled a good many weeks over wide areas unmolested by the police. One evening we reached Junín and stayed in a comfortable little hotel that kept us out of the cold. The hotel had a radio and at six in the evening, the state radio, among many other items, announced that on this day Professor Frank Tannenbaum, accompanied by the Chief of the Indian Section, had reached Junín on their journey of investigation. It went on to say how important this trip was for Peru. I then learned that every day over the radio my trip had been reported step by step. Of course, anything can be turned to political fence-building. The point, however, is that the smallest detail, even a trip by an American scholar, is something that only the president can authorize.

The ideas of the nation, democracy, and representative government are beyond the ken of the vast majority of the people. We do not really have a good word to characterize the political, social, economic situation in Latin America, at the beginning of the Independence. The notion of feudalism will not do. A feudal society presumes a contractual relationship between the king and his lords, between them and their vassals—each with rights and obligations within the law. In Latin America, with the king gone, the society became at best seignorial, where the large landowner had power over his *peones*, Indians and Negroes, imposed obligations upon them, but where they had *no rights* in law—except such as custom and tradition had woven into the social body. It was in fact an arbitrary social system in the sense that each large landowner and *cacique* enforced his own capricious will upon his dependents, applied punishments, and had his own jail. The government in the capital was far away, insecure, in danger of being overthrown at any time, or in the hands of a tyrant who had the skill and good luck to stay in office—without the law or against the law, perhaps with a constitution promulgated to serve his own particular interests that did not put any real restraints on him. The constitution was a personal and temporary document, contrived largely by the executive. The problem, both politically and psychologically, is how fast can a society of this type, complicated by racial and cultural divisions, grow into a modern nation. The customs and the traditions, the loyalties and the local ways were and are obstacles to nationhood.

[1968]

traits of such a political culture. The issue is a simple one. How long will it take the excessively nationalistic leaders of Argentina to reconcile themselves to the fact that man lives in a recalcitrant universe, that there are limits to the possible expansion of an agricultural economy dependent upon exports for its international exchange, and that wisdom would dictate the cultivation of the marvelous garden that is Argentina rather than hungering for seemingly greener pastures beyond its borders?

It would seem from the examples given that the seeds of social discord, instability, and violence are widely scattered. The extensions of illiteracy, poverty, racial discrimination, and political corruption are all there for anyone to see. It is equally easy to tag the strident nationalism, the resentment against foreign investment, the opposition to "colonialism" as causes of both the revolutions and the dictatorships and to suggest that if any or all of these difficulties were resolved, *if* they are resolvable, then a new leaf would be turned in the Latin American story.

Unfortunately, the "causes" are beneath the surface and are woven into the social fabric itself. There are, for instance, no universally accepted symbols of authority. Nothing has replaced the king, in whose name all things were done and to whom all gave obedience and obeisance. The two possible alternatives, the nation and the constitution, have not developed the reach or the firmness possessed previously by the royal will. This really means that there is no sufficient principle of legitimacy in Latin American political life. There is no universally accepted theory of government which can be symbolized. The ideas of the French Revolution with their emphasis upon individual rights are outside the experience of Latin Americans. This is also true of the constitutionalism derived chiefly from the United States. The notion that authority can be divided is probably meaningless to the mass of the people. Authority can be delegated, but an authority that is divided so that the president's will can be thwarted by a legislature or a judiciary is inconceivable to most Latin Americans—even to most of their intellectuals. They can admire it in the United States, but they cannot understand it—that is, accept it as a functioning procedure. The president must have all power or he can have no power. He must be able to do everything or else he is unable to do anything.

Then why do the authors of the constitutions write them that way? Because the political theorists and constitutional lawyers are preoccupied with ideas of perfection; they are possessed by notions of absolute justice and harmony. The constitutional document must itemize man's highest aspirations. It must be the best constitution rather than a workable one. There can be no compromise with the ideal. It is the old story of Don Quixote in constitutional form. The ideal and the real must go their own ways. The constitution-maker knows that his is an exercise of the imagination with little bearing upon practical politics. That is why he need not compromise. The document is not an instrument of government; it is a justification for the exercise of power by the executive. Furthermore, the constitutional design is largely a foreign document depending for its effectiveness upon systems of party government and honest suffrage, and neither of these is available. More than that, the conditions out of which they might be derived are nonexistent— at least at present. It is misleading to assume that the cycle of political turbulence and dictatorships is accidental. It has now lasted for 150 years, and the end is a long way off. These years have seen important changes in the economic and social life of the Latin American people. What has not changed is the proclivity for revolution and dictatorship.

As we have seen, peaceful political government requires as a minimum a universally recognized legitimate authority. In Latin America that does not exist. There is, therefore, no way of giving it symbolic form. This, in turn, makes competitive claims to power equally "right." Once the power has been seized it can be given formal sanction by an "election," required by the constitution. This competitive striving for power is personal because there are no political parties in any meaningful sense of the word. There may be numerous personal followings that, in keeping with the current fashion, call themselves parties. But that is make-believe. General Odría in Peru was not brought to power by a political party, nor were General Rojas Pinilla in Colombia, Colonel Pérez Jiménez in Venezuela, Juan Perón in Argentina, Trujillo in Santo Domingo, Batista and Castro in Cuba, Osorio in Salvador, and Somoza in Nicaragua. But why extend the list?

The political phenomenon we are dealing with is not describable in terms of European democratic political theory or United States practice. Both presume the existence of a mass of individuals competent to search their conscience for the purposes of making a personal political choice. They both assume that the choice can be freely made and registered. They also assume that these individuals may group themselves in political parties representing the interests, objectives, and purposes they have in common. They assume effective political communication among individuals, groups, and interests. They assume that political leaders talk a language meaningful to the mass of the voters, and that there is something the two have in common. They assume the existence of a tradition of local government where the habits of democracy can be acquired and its meaning discerned. European democratic political theory and United States practice assume the existence of political parties not only as the means of acquiring power but as a basis upon which government can rest; they assume a body of tradition that defines the role of the opposition, the acceptance of the opposition as a government-in-being. The assumption is further made that a government can fall without destroying the party; that political opposition is not defined as conspiracy; that the law applies equally to the party in or out of power; and that the courts will not fear the executive and will enforce the law without an eye to their own safety. But, above all, they assume that the political parties are bearers of the consensus of the communities in which they have their roots.

In the United States and Western Europe, the local party club or committee exists more for political purposes than as a gathering of individuals. It provides virtual representation to the other groups in the community. The membership of the local party club is composed of people who are often active participants in other organizations—the Red Cross, the women's church society, the athletic association, the trade union, the Chamber of Commerce, and many others. The local party club is therefore in some degree the effective bearer of the consensus of opinion and interest not merely of its members but of other organizations in the community that find virtual representation in it. This is what gives a political party its vitality and its effectiveness. It is the political link in a chain of many organizations for which the party speaks and which it virtually, even if not consciously, represents, and whose different views have been merged in the continuing debates over policy that the local party club carries on at regular intervals throughout the year. Little of this exists in Latin America. There is no effective local, regional, or national organization. The countless societies so characteristic of the English village, town, and city, with their links across the nation, have no counterparts in Latin America. And without them a political party is a meaningless and hollow frame. That is why the political party in Latin America is ephemeral and why it can only have the power given it by the leader, why it has to be personal, and why it ordinarily passes away with the leader.

These generalizations apply differently to varying parts of Latin American society. In the rural areas, where the vast majority of people live, political party organization has been least effective. The urban and rural are even further apart today than they were in the past. Industrialization and radio and television have widened the gap between them. But the rural world, especially the Indian rural community, often has a unity and identity that the city does not possess. It has a local culture, a local ethos, independent of and perhaps consciously indifferent to what the city has to offer. There are thousands of these relatively autonomous local communities that do not share the urban values, do not understand them, and seemingly do not want to understand them. The political party in Latin America has not tried and does not know how to attract these communities, or how to create a consensus upon a policy that would bridge the gap between the urban and these small, stubborn social units that know how to suffer and survive but have no ambition to project themselves beyond their own parochial horizon. Between these rural communities and the city-oriented political leaders, there can be under present circumstances no meaningful communication. They abide in the same national territory, but live in different worlds. In areas where traditional folk society exists, the political party finds itself excluded because it has no means of establishing an identity between its own objectives and those of the rural community.

Something of the same order holds for the communities confined within plantations. The individual family farm is not typical of Latin America. There are isolated places such as Costa Rica, the mountain districts in Venezuela, parts of Colombia and of Northern Mexico where the *ranchero* dominates the scene. In the greater part of Latin America, however, the large plantation is the representative unit. It embraces most of the land under cultivation, contains half or more of the rural population and perhaps more than half of the rural communities.

These plantation villages have no political life of their own. They are governed by the *hacendado* or his administrator. There is nothing here comparable to the older English manorial court to which the freeholder and tenant alike owed suit and in which they shared in local administration. Though most such communities are small, having perhaps less than 300 inhabitants on an average, there are some that are large. The country officers are employees of the *hacienda*. It is on this score that the plantation system hampers the development of political parties requisite for a stable democratic government. The criticism of the large plantation is not primarily on economic but on political and social grounds. It makes for political isolation, perpetuates social stratification and submissiveness incompatible with the growth of competent party government. The people on a plantation are as much outside the political party as those in the self-contained Indian communities.

Under these circumstances, political power derives from other sources. Neither the middle class, the trade unions, the hierarchy, nor even the church have the kind of independent cohesive organization that makes for effective political power. One or another may be used as a "front" or appealed to for support, but the decision as to who will govern is not theirs to make. That decision is made by the army and, in diminishing degree, by the traditional families that for generations have been the natural leaders of local regions. The leader may be one of the local *caudillos* who has the support of the military or an important faction of it. Or he may be an ambitious military leader who can gather sufficient support for his purposes. He may have plotted and planned, cajoled and promised, used his family or military connections, and, if his luck holds, the uprising succeeds. Peru's Luis Sánchez Cerro in Arequipa against Leguía in 1930 is a good example of a local *caudillo* leading a successful uprising.

Criticism, to a Latin American, is the mother of conspiracy, and every dubious supporter is an implicit opponent. The new president surrounds himself with unconditional followers. The members of congress, the senate, the government departments, from doormen to secretaries, are handpicked with an eye to their absolute loyalty. Elections may be held for public office, but only those who are friends of the president can be chosen. Even in Mexico, it is inconceivable that a governor of a state be elected who is not approved of by the president. If a man were strong enough to become governor against the will of the president, he would be strong enough to overthrow the central government. Power, therefore, is monolithic, it descends downwards from the leader and is reflected in all public and in many seemingly private affairs. Every activity derives its immediate legitimacy from this central source.

In most of Latin America no citizen attends a foreign congress of even the most innocent character without the consent and the financial support of the president. No trade union leader takes any action without consultation, no law is passed, no policy adopted, no road built, no foreign business established without his prior approval. An election to office is equivalent to a reward by the president of a loyal follower. And in cases where someone from the "opposition" is allowed a seat, that too has been arranged and agreed upon. The will of the president is complete, and when it fails in any instance it fails fatally. The populace is so conditioned that it expects him to be all-powerful. That is one reason why dictatorships are numerous and long-lived. The dictator is overthrown not because he denies the citizens their political liberties or because he is arbitrary, but because he fails to play the role of the omnipotent and fatherly ruler. Cruelty is not sufficient to bring a regime to an end and the case of Juan Vicente Gómez in Venezuela illustrates this. It is when the president is both cruel and weak, like Machado in Cuba, that he stirs up sufficient resistance to make his place untenable.

The people of Latin America have accepted violence as a "normal," habitual way to effectuate political change. The "revolution" or the "dictatorship," and they go together, are independent of the policy to be pursued by the government. The government may use any slogans: liberal or conservative, radical or reactionary, nationalist or cosmopolitan, federal or centralist. Its rise to power and its fall from power are destined to be by violence—a rebellion of the "people," the "oligarchy," or the "army"; and the form of the government will be "tyrannical"—that is, personal—and not subject to constitutional limitation, unless the executive through some idiosyncrasy prefers it that way. The transfer of power from one executive to his successor will be either by open revolution or by a simulated "election" that will merely sanction a decision already made. This political form has nothing to do with legality, with constitutionalism, with representative government, with democracy, with good or bad administration, with broad or narrow social policies, with reform or reaction. A government may be classified within any of those denominations, or opposing and contradictory ones at different times, and yet the manner of its coming to power, and the way the power will be transmitted, will be the same—by revolution or dictatorship or both. Revolution and dictatorship have a life of their own. Nor are there any good prospects that different ways will soon be adopted, or that they can be. For it is not a matter of education—that is, classroom schooling. It is a matter of habituation to a way in politics. To change this way calls for a metamorphosis in implicit value and attitude towards the nature, role, and place of public power—and that cannot be predicted, directed, or controlled. Many things can happen that ought to modify the basic commitment of a people, but somehow fail to do so. For instance, the Russian Revolution should have abolished police government, but it did not; the French Revolution ought to have decentralized French administration, but it did not. We must grow accustomed to the idea that revolution and dictatorship are Latin America's political style; it is "natural" and it will continue for a long, long time. The conditions for its change are absent, and cannot be improvised.

A significant shift in political power has, however, become increasingly visible in recent years. Participation by the military, and especially the army, in politics is traditional and expected. Until a few years ago it was an army close to the people. It had few professional standards, it was poorly armed, and different sections were under the control of local leaders. No single officer, no central government, had full control of all the armed forces in the nation, and many local political *caudillos* were also "colonels" or "generals" who had an important military following. The president of the country was ever aware of his dependence upon the support of regional leaders, and a certain unofficial distribution of power prevailed. The local leader had a local following because he defended and represented the locality against the center. To that extent it was true that the revolutions were expressions of the popular will. It was possible to change an unacceptable government by "popular" rebellion under local leadership.

This has now become much more difficult and in many places perhaps impossible. The army has been given a professional character. It has been motorized, equipped with machine guns, tanks, aircraft, and has become mobile and easy to concentrate through the use of the radio and wireless telephone. Only the government has the means to acquire these new arms, and only the professional army is trained to use them. The equalizing and democratic impact of the antiquated musket has disappeared, and with it the prospects of "popular" and "democratic" revolutions. No one except the army can now hope to organize a successful revolution against the government, and no one can defeat the army except the army. The overthrow of Perón in Argentina in 1955 is a case in point. Only by dissension within the armed forces could the ten-year dictatorship be brought to an end. The professional army is now invincible against an unarmed populace, and the government itself is at the mercy of its own armed forces. The results of this change are fully visible.

The army now rules the state in Latin America—either directly or through some acceptable agent. If the army leaders can agree among themselves, or if the commanding officer can control all of the armed services, he can remain in office for life, and be replaced by a government of "colonels" or by another general. The army, just because it has become professionalized, just because modern arms are expensive, and just because it is omnipotent, has replaced the older, more regional, more "democratic" ruling *caudillos* with their traditional family and regional obligations. This change is perhaps more significant for the immediate future than movements of social reform or nationalism, about which so much has been written. The army has the advantage of being a relatively small, compact, and disciplined body. It can take from the public treasury whatever it needs for its own purposes. The army is the new oligarchy, the privileged class; its officers have certain access to wealth, power, and prestige, and the noncommissioned personnel and soldiers can aspire to a higher standard of living than is possible in any other career. The character of the government and its policies is dictated by the will and whim of the army chieftain, who also may be president of the country by force of occupancy without any legal sanction. The military has become an occupying force—an army of occupation that is most difficult to dislodge except by a division within its ranks, and that does not necessarily lead to the reconquest of the government by the civilian population. Viewed even in the most favorable light, the army has replaced the older ruling groups in Latin America. It is the new "governing family."

[1956]

Politics and Government
in Latin America

United States relations with Latin America are deeply influenced by the continuing political instability of its governments. If one takes the last fifteen years, few governments have escaped one or more political upheavals. Some of these sudden turnovers deeply affect the internal policy of the government and in consequence its external affairs as well. One can say continuing political instability is the most immediate and most serious barrier the United States has in developing and preserving a consistent policy with our southern neighbors.

In spite of the great emphasis placed upon the theme of economic development, Latin America's most sensitive difficulties are political and social. Unless and until there is some visible change in the political and social environment, even the best plans for economic betterment will falter. Furthermore, deliberate efforts to change social and political institutions are beset with greater hazards and deeper subtleties than mere changes in the economy. At least the economist believes that given sufficient investment he can predict the rate of growth and, given a certain rate of growth, he can, or thinks he can, predict human felicity. But how does the political scientist prevent a Rojas Pinilla from coming to power, or a Perón, or a Trujillo? How does he eliminate the local *caudillo?* How does he give the Indian a vivid sense of the political process and convert him into a responsible citizen aware of the nation? How does the sociologist make the *señorito* feel like an ordinary citizen? How does he convert a strong attachment to the extended family to a loyalty for the nation as a whole?

When speaking of Latin American politics and government in general, and recognizing the great differences that exist between the different countries, one can still identify some persistent problems they have in common. One of these, among many others, is how does one first create a nation in which all elements feel equally at home and to which they are equally loyal? Does the Quechua Indian in Peru identify psychologically with the nation and not necessarily the government? How does one endow the eighteen or more Indian tribal groups in Guatemala with a sense of Guatemalan nationality? What element speaks for the nation as a whole in Guatemala—is it the *criollo,* the *mestizo,* the Indian, the church, the army, the political party, or the *caudillo?* If one were to ask the illiterate masses in most of Latin America, whose involvement in the modern world is minimal, what their political role is, they would probably stand dumbfounded by the very idea of the question.

To raise these issues is disturbing to the complacency of those of us who play with the magic of general theories as a way of explaining particular difficulties. The social and political *ambiente,* it seems to me, is the determining influence that makes or mars any governmental administrative system.

Before raising the question of efficiency in public administration, one might first inquire, what is the government and whose government is it? Is it Trujillo's, Perón's, or that of Pérez Jiménez or Batista or Castro? The question is a serious one, and no one interested in the problem of government in Latin America can escape it. It reaches beyond these specific individuals to a historical process, a tradition of centralized government identified with an individual, or with a party headed by an individual, who behaves like the head of an extended family. The head of this family may also be the president of the country. The violent and tyrannical *caudillo* is only an extreme version of a traditional expectancy that the executive has all the power, attends to all the details, and governs on behalf of the party (i.e., the political family). The answer to the question of whose government it is depends upon whom you ask. It is *our* government if *our* party is in power and it is *their* government if *our* party is not in power. It is our government or their government. It is rarely a government that rests upon a general consensus. There is a great deal of historical experience behind this political fact.

In Spain to this day the Basques do not feel that the Franco government belongs to them, nor for that matter do the Catalonians. This has been so for a long time, and the troubled history of Spain is, in part, just this inability of all residents within the Spanish domain to recognize the government as belonging to those who make up the nation. In Latin America during the colonial period, the government was the king's, or it belonged to the *peninsulares*. The *criollo* did not always feel that it was his government. The *mestizos,* the *castas,* the Negroes, the Indians were even less identified with the government than the *criollos.* Matters did not improve much after the Independence. The civil wars in Argentina, Colombia, Venezuela, Mexico, and elsewhere were joined on this question that *your* government was not *our* government. There was no universal political symbol to which all could appeal. There was no satisfactory basis for a general consensus; the new governments were not legitimate beyond question, and unless a government is absolutely legitimate, it lives on borrowed time.

The agreement between the conservative and liberal parties that brought an end to the tyranny of Rojas Pinilla in Colombia was an extraordinary feat and Alberto Lleras Camargo, who contrived it, will be remembered by the people of Colombia as a beneficent and heroic figure. But even here, *la violencia* reminds us that there are sections of the country and elements in the population that insist that this is *your* government and *not ours.* So, too, in Venezuela, in Argentina, in Peru, and in how many other places? In certain Latin American countries, large sections of the population do not accept the government as their government, no matter which party is in power. In others, the opposition party refuses to recognize the existing government as legitimate and accuses it of having come to power by violence or fraud.

The problem of legitimacy remains unresolved. The

question of how to come to power without a revolution and how to transmit the presidency without violence or the threat of violence remains on the whole unanswered. There are governments, such as those of Chile, Uruguay, Costa Rica, and Mexico, that seem to have evolved beyond this constant threat. How long is the list of exceptions? Surely, there will be no agreement on any list that could be drawn up; and if the past record is considered, it may prove temporary. In other cases, the transmission of political power is always fraught with the prospect of violence; one might almost say that if violence is to be avoided, it may be at the cost of imposition. The case of Trujillo reelecting himself for thirty years in peaceful elections and always receiving one hundred percent of all the votes—not one less, even if no one voted—is the classic example. A completely peaceful election is not necessarily always evidence that it was democratic or that it was based upon a general consensus. In fact, one could generalize that where the executive can control the election of his successor the election is likely to be a peaceful one. And this is evidenced in some recent instances where the opposition party refused to go to the polls. Knowing they would lose the election, they chose not to give the forthcoming government moral sanction by participating in the vote. The government, it was openly declared, belonged to them and not to us. The opposition would remain what political opposition in Latin America tends to be—a continuing challenge to the government's *power* rather than to its policies. The right of the government to survive is therefore under continuing challenge.

In these circumstances the question of political survival for the administration is the primary concern. It should be very clear that this is the basic difference between governments in Latin America and the United States. In the United States, the policies of the administration may be under constant and bitter attack, but no one challenges its right to survive to the end of its term and no one doubts the peaceful transfer of political power after the next election. In Latin America, with some exceptions, the government's right and ability to survive to the end of its term in office is constantly questioned. Where there is little prospect of political survival to the end of the elected period, there is even less certainty of a peaceful transmission of power.

These two considerations make centralization of government inevitable. They also make personal government unavoidable. The president is always building his political fences, always watching out for a possible conspiracy, always concerned about the loyalty, the *absoluta confianza,* of his collaborators. The history of Latin America is replete with the need for just this caution and vigilance on the part of the chief executive. What this does to administration is place every decision, even the smallest, in the president's hands. He needs all of the power he has to keep himself in office and all of the vigilance to prevent a successful challenge to his survival. An equitable division of power among the executive, the legislative, and the judiciary is an unrealizable dream. The office of the executive must first be protected against a sudden *golpe de estado, cuartelazo,* or *pronunciamiento,* before the division of power can emerge as a feasible way of government. But if centralization must, for traditional reasons as well as for those of political insecurity, take the form of personal government, then all things, including administration, become subordinated to political survival.

What are the conditions of political security? That this is the major political question will become evident if one asks how many of the governments now in power have had to face smaller or greater rebellions aimed at their overthrow. Better still, how many successful and unsuccessful attempts at the violent overthrow of government in Latin America have taken place during the last fifteen years? A detailed answer to this question would explain why the president can only govern by surrounding himself with people of *absoluta confianza.* Their loyalty to him takes precedence over every other consideration. Loyalty becomes more important than skill, efficiency, training, public concern, or personal honesty. Any school of public administration in Latin America has a primary responsibility for the study of the conditions under which political security may be achieved.

We have, so far, considered the nation itself: is it something with which all the people identify or is the idea of the nation merely in the minds of special groups? We have also raised the question of whose government it is, of the universal acceptance of the government as belonging to all of the people, the feeling that it is "their government," an imposition or a threat, or the government as something to be grasped for and taken away from those who have it now so that it might belong to "us." Finally, we have looked at how this bears upon the question of political stability and have concluded that in the absence of political stability, the idea of a division of power is an impossible dream. We have also suggested that the constant threat to the executive makes for personal government in a most detailed sense and reinforces a traditional predilection for centralization. Inevitably, if the primary virtue in government service is personal loyalty to the chief of state, then loyalty is placed above integrity, efficiency, or public concern.

One of the reasons why the president has to attend to all things is that he holds the purse strings of the nation. The central government receives the greater part of the taxable income, leaving the states, provinces, cities, and counties with a pittance. The proportion in some instances runs as high as 80 percent and more to the central government and the other 20 percent has to be divided among all other political entities. The mayors of towns and cities, the governors of the states and provinces have to stand with hat in hand if they want money, sometimes even for the most essential things. And it is not an exception when the mayor of a city tells you that he saw the president and "got" two hundred and fifty thousand pesos from him, or if a labor leader says something similar. There is nowhere else to go and no one else could or would give the money. The results are obvious. The president is more powerful, government is more personal, and the mayor and the labor leaders are more beholden and more obsequious. By the same token, the causes for discontent are always more wide-spread and more prevalent; there are always many individuals who either have no access to the chief executive or receive less than they think they require.

If the central government is the chief repository of income from taxes and the president the major distributor of government funds, the possibility for a revolution against him is always present. If he has no security because he lacks absolute legitimacy, he cannot trust anyone else either to dispense the government funds or to look to the grievances that people bring to the government.

If the concentration of finances in the central government is conducive to political insecurity, so too is the fact that the military in Latin America have no true professional function. The Latin American armies have no military reason for being. It is unlikely that Venezuela will go to war with Colombia, or Colombia with Ecuador. Only Peru and Ecuador have had border frictions between them that might lead again to the use of the army. Otherwise, Latin America is one of the world's more peaceful areas and is likely to remain so. The days when Argentina might have gone to war to unite the southern part of South America are past, and so is the likelihood of a war between Argentina and Brazil. Much the same can be said of Mexico. The United States is not going to attack Mexico, nor is Mexico going to attack either the United States or Guatemala. Only in Central America is it possible now to imagine invasion by the military from a neighboring country and even there the prospect does not seem imminent or war a likelihood. Latin America does not have the memory of centuries of war between neighbors, such as France and Germany, or Poland and Russia, and lacks the manner and the way of peoples inured to conquest, invasion, defeat, and victory.

Latin American armies have mainly a police function. They are trained to defend a nation that is in no danger from the outside. They are an institutionalized force, not disciplined by the ever-present prospect of a struggle to the death to save the nation. Therefore, if the military cannot defend the nation, then at least it can guide it. The army takes on the role of protector, adviser, and manipulator. The president finds himself subject to the armed forces whom he nominally commands. No government is certain of survival if its military disapproves of what it does or fails to do, and no chief executive can be certain that he has the absolute loyalty of the armed forces upon whose good will he has become dependent.

The role of the professional army has been distorted. Once responsible for defending the nation against the threat of invasion from abroad, it has become the major potential or actual enemy of the government. Political insecurity has now been institutionalized. The glory the military cannot win in war it pretends to achieve by forcing the civil government to bow to the dictates of its generals and colonels. For all practical purposes, Latin American governments live on the sufferance of their armed forces, and when the political parties, or groupings, will not tolerate each other, the armies turn politics into an appendix of barracks-room rivalries.

These, however, are only a few of the conditions influencing the *ambiente* within which public administration must operate. There are others of equal importance to the prospect of good administration even if of lesser direct political significance. The first of these is the persistent wandering from job to job and from ministry to ministry. This is perhaps best illustrated by a personal experience. Some years ago I asked a friend of mine in Mexico, now a highly placed person, "Where will you be next time I come to Mexico? Every time I visit the country you are somewhere else. One time you were head of the land division in the Census Office, then in the railroad administration, then in the tax division of the Treasury, then *oficial mayor* in the Ministry of Education. Now, where will you be when I return?" We had been walking. He stopped and said very gravely: "Either in the cabinet or in jail, and one or the other will be a complete accident."

Making the rounds of the ministries has been a normal way

for a bureaucrat in more than one country. This phenomenon may have its advantages as an educational device, though a rather expensive one. It can hardly be recommended in the name of administrative efficiency. There are various explanations for it, but in some ways it ties in with the element of instability and continuing shifts in the cabinet. The president in his search for political security finds himself driven to seek new support in each crisis, or threat of crisis. He reshuffles the cabinet. Each incoming minister brings in his own band of loyal followers, for the minister, like the president, has to fall back upon absolute loyalty. And, as I have seen when a minister of agriculture moved to Foreign Relations, everyone—in one case even the doorman—moved with him. The extended family, the *compadre,* the school friend, whoever makes up this kind of fellowship, gang, or bureaucratic clique, travel together and where one goes the others go. If one of them becomes a minister, they all join his department. If, as often happens, the post of the ministry terminates rather unexpectedly and some other member of this special group of public servants is given an important public office, then they all follow, including the former member of the cabinet.

The group will somehow manage to find jobs for each other and survive the changing administration, providing usually that the same party stays in office. If the party changes, then the government is no longer "ours" and another gang will fill the posts and shift about from one ministry to another. The political party which makes up the government consists of a great leader and a number of lesser ones, each with his own following. It will represent the family, the region, and it will satisfy the special traditions which place the group in this party and assure them their role in the government. In these circumstances, loyalty and friendship take precedence over efficiency, training, and public service.

The family interest takes precedence over the public interest, or, if you prefer, they are identical. It would be inconceivable to leave a needy relative out of a job. The family is the source and the base of any career and of any social security. It is the only certain relationship in an uncertain world. When the government has been lost, when the present job is no longer, when there is danger and life itself may be in jeopardy, the family and its dependents and associates are the only certain bulwark. In an authoritarian society ruled by small groups of tightly knit families, this is inevitable. Where public employment is almost the only source of ready money income and where government employment is a prerogative, privilege, and expectancy for members of the successful party, there the family takes on the role of controlling the civil service. Outsiders may call this nepotism and whatever else, but for the people involved, it is the essential of government, good or bad, because, in fact, in the circumstances there are no other acceptable choices.

The lesser members of the bureaucracy are so poorly paid that they require more than one job at a time to cover their growing needs. It is generally accepted that a university professor should have additional sources of income. The professor may practice law or medicine, be an accountant, a civil engineer, or have some government post. He is not, in most cases, a full-time professor. Clearly, the problem of the university is complicated by its dependence upon part-time teachers and it will be a good day when the university can afford a well-paid teaching staff. Something like this, only worse, occurs in public employment. Many officials have to find two and three jobs, and sometimes more, to earn enough to make ends meet. They go during the day from a job in one ministry to a job in another, then rush to meet a class in some school, then back to a government office or to some private enterprise. Obviously, better pay, greater security in the job, better professional training and pride in the service might help. However, I am not sure that these changes would be sufficient to alter the pattern.

There is probably an element of personal friendship in most of these instances where the special job is not only a favor received but a favor given. There is probably also a matter of prestige and an element of social expectancy. There may be something of a desire to have many roles, be engaged in many different kinds of activities, have contacts and friends in many different places. It is not certain that the elimination of multiple roles would necessarily improve government service. It may be that concentration in a narrow bureaucratic job for a whole lifetime should not be promoted with much enthusiasm.

Finally, we are brought to a consideration of the matter of graft—or *mordida,* as it is called in Mexico. This is a painful subject with a long and well-nigh universal history. The United States had some unsavory scandals during the Harding administration involving at least one member of the cabinet, who was sent to prison. Anyone who reads the American press with attention will recall investigations involving the misuse of public trust for personal gain as recurring phenomena. There is one saving grace in this situation in the United States: people can be and are sent to prison if charges of graft can be proven against them.

In Latin America, there are some countries where dishonesty in public office is practically unknown and others where it is rare. But the case of Cuba since Independence, the corruption of the Grau San Martín and Prio Socorrás governments, not to speak of that of Batista (where members of the cabinet are said to have taken millions out of the country in satchels and bought hotels in Miami), is notorious. The stories about the administrations under Perón, Rojas Pinilla, and Pérez Jiménez are further illustrations of this point. If one were to take them literally, one would have to believe that the pilfering of public funds is endemic in some countries, from the president down to the janitors.

I once talked about this problem with the president of one of the republics in Latin America. We both agreed that it existed, was widely prevalent, and the question was what could be done about it. The president gave me the following explanation: "All those working for the government know that, if they lost their jobs, it would be long before they would get another one. So, '¡*Hay que aprovecharse de la oportunidad!*' If I dismissed them all, the new people would have even less security and would steal even more. So the only thing that I can do is to ask them, '¡*Que roben con conciencia!*'" Public inquiries into graft in Latin America are rare. On the whole, the matter is not brought before the courts. Everyone may know about it, comment on what is going on, but no one challenges the practice legally through the legislature or the judiciary. The answer, I think, lies in the fact that the president can only govern with the support of his friends and that he cannot risk the alienation of his own friends or even members of his own family—for his power rests on their loyalty, and they are part of his party.

These explanations for pilfering in public office are insufficient. It is not that the laws are inadequate, but rather that the machinery of the law functions with a bent on behalf of friends and members of the government. Notorious are the examples of the perversion of the law under Trujillo, Batista, Perón, Pérez Jiménez, Rojas Pinilla, and others. Those are obvious cases where the law was weighted on behalf of the friends and supporters of the regime. But the law is bent to favor those in power, and their friends as well, in some countries with "democratic" governments. The police are not always impartial instruments of law enforcement. Not infrequently, they are identified as part of a general governmental operation geared to protect the favored and the select, those in office, their families and friends.

The point illustrated by this discussion of political traits in Latin America is moral and psychological. Deep down in their inner being, Latin Americans object to being governed by anyone. They want no human being to impose upon them and order them about. There is an inherent repugnance to submission, to the acceptance of orders. The old adage that every Spaniard carries a letter in his pocket signed by the king saying "This Spaniard is authorized to do whatever he pleases" is somehow a way of defining one's place in the world and one's attitude towards government. If he has to be governed, then the governor must be a member of the family, a *compadre,* someone so close that one can really feel that this is my government, that I am really being governed by my own. This attitude is antecedent to almost all else in Latin American politics and no one can do anything about it—at least not in a hurry and perhaps not deliberately. In spite of all the constitutions that have been written in the last 150 years, government here is by men and not by laws, and the constitution remains an excuse for, rather than an instrument of, government.

[1963]

The Spanish Conquest and Forjando Patria

The Spanish tradition in the Americas is in part the story of the Conquest and in part the molding impact of Spanish culture. Within something more than half a century a relatively small group of Spanish adventurers bestrode the American continent from Chile to California. Armed with the Bible and the sword, missionary and soldier impressed upon the mind of the Indian peoples a European culture: a Spanish version of European religion, government, law, administration, ethics, and outlook. Politically and spiritually, the Conquest and the imposition of Spanish culture seemed complete.

The Conquest gave to the vast area between Chile and California a common government replacing thousands of tribal political units. With a common government, it provided a single system of law, judicial tribunals, and formal procedures with ultimate appeal to the Council of the Indies. It provided a common language for a land in which hundreds of separate tongues were spoken. The Conquest gave the Americas a common religion and thousands of churches where priests preached the true faith to the heathen on a larger scale than at any time or any place before. It gave the Americas their universities and schools. The *conquistadores* brought with them many material European culture traits such as the horse, the cow, the sheep, the plow, the oxcart and draft animals, and a great variety of European vegetables and fruits.

Perhaps the most important contribution of the Spaniards was the interconnection between the system of law and the symbols of God and King. All things were done in the name of God and King. *Yo el Rey* marked out the bounds of the church, the rights of the bishop or priest, the place of the *hidalgo* and the *peón*. All of life from birth to death took place within the ruling shadow of the King. God and King were a joint symbol for all occasions. Every man knew that he was the King's subject and that all he had in the world came from the King, even as all his hopes for the next world depended upon God. Universal acceptance of these symbols provided a sense of direction and fulfillment to all men.

On close scrutiny, however, the Spanish Conquest and its cultural and political consequences were not as complete as they first seemed. The Spaniards were most successful in those areas where the Indian withered away. The measure of success is a specific one: the transplanting of a culture and its accommodation into a new environment. By that standard, Spanish culture found an easy habitat wherever it escaped the competition and resiliency of native mores. In those circumstances, the conqueror compromised only with the physical environment, and if his European institutions became Americanized, it was because the plains of Argentina and the semi-tropical climate of Cuba made demands and opened opportunities unknown in the Iberian peninsula. These two instances, and others that might be mentioned, such as the settlement of the coastal areas of Peru, have some remote analogy to English colonization in what is now the United States. The native population, if not sparse, proved only a temporary barrier to the reproduction of Spanish ways in the American setting.

It is true, of course, that the introduction of the Negro into areas where the Indian disappeared distorted the purely Spanish cultural pattern, but it did not keep it from being Spanish, because, surprisingly, the Negro proved himself susceptible to ready conversion to the Christian faith and easy accommodation to Spanish culture. He learned the Spanish language, he fitted into the Spanish family, he took on Spanish ways, and, even if not completely, he became psychologically and, in a curiously subtle manner, spiritually an insider within the scheme of Spanish-European culture in this hemisphere. The large number of freedmen—in many instances exceeding the number of slaves—testifies eloquently both to the acceptability of the Negro within the social organization and to the Negro's acceptance of it.

The relationship of the Negro to the white man can be dramatized by saying that the Negro became, culturally speaking, a European. He became predisposed to the American scene through the specific cultural framework of the family to which he belonged. He became a European in fact—not merely an instrument, but a participant in the Europeans' colonization efforts. In broad historical terms his was a partnership with the Spanish colonists in the shaping of a common destiny in this hemisphere.

Equally dramatic has been the Indian's failure to accommodate himself to European culture. The contrast between Ayacucho and Lima is the contrast between unsuccessful and successful transfer of Spanish culture to the American environment. In Lima, all is Spanish. In Ayacucho, or in Cuzco, or in a hundred other places in Peru and in Spanish America, the rim of Spanish culture embraces only one element in the population—the *mestizo;* the Indians who live on the outskirts of these communities have taken so little from their masters that it cannot be said, as it can be with the Negro, that they have become culturally European. The Spanish and Indian cultures have proved opaque and impenetrable to each other. Tradition and fashion have habituated us to speaking of Peru, of Bolivia, of Ecuador, of Guatemala, and of Mexico as nations, as if we were speaking of unified cultures. The tradition and the fashion are easily understandable. The Spaniard and the *mestizo,* who has so largely become the carrier of Spanish culture in this hemisphere, are vocal. They write the books and make the laws and deliver the speeches. The large capital cities, with their modern buildings, theaters, newspapers, universities, public schools, electric lights, and paved streets, have had a pervasive influence upon the spirit of both the native city-dweller and the foreign visitor. To them Mexico City stands for Mexico and Lima for Peru, La Paz for Bolivia, Quito for Ecuador, and Guatemala

City for Guatemala. This predisposition to universalize is easy and natural, but it is also misleading; it is too inclusive. It is perhaps no more accurate to think of Guatemala as Guatemala City than it is to think of it as Chichicastenango, or to think of Peru not as Lima but as Pisac.

The increase of the *mestizo* has tended to give the impression that European culture has proved more pervasive than it really has. A detailed examination, however, will reveal that, on the whole, the *mestizos* have filled in areas which were sparsely settled before the Conquest, or have grown in numbers about mining centers that were previously nonexistent, or occupy the larger administrative communities in heavily populated Indian areas. Mexico is a good illustration of the point. Northern states like Chihuahua, Nuevo León, Tamaulipas, Zacatecas, and San Luis Potosí are mainly *mestizo*. And great mining centers like Pachuca are also *mestizo*. But outside of Pachuca, the little towns throughout the states of Hidalgo and Mexico are largely Indian. Oaxaca City is largely *mestizo;* so is Cuernavaca. But when one gets away from the capital of the state and from the more important administrative centers in Oaxaca and Morelos, one quickly discovers one is in Indian country. Progreso and Mérida may be *mestizo,* but the little towns in Yucatán are Indian. The same is true in Chiapas. It can be generalized that where the Indian lived in organized agricultural communities before the Conquest, he has more or less effectively managed to remain, and the European and *mestizo* have penetrated only into the larger towns important commercially and administratively. Many exceptions can be found to this general statement, but they merely prove the rule.

The relative size of the Indian population varies from country to country, and statistical accuracy is impossible. The difficulty lies partly in the definition of Indian for the purpose of record, and partly in an unwillingness or inability to count the Indian population. The Indians are always hard to count, because they are widely scattered in the mountains and suspicious of outsiders. Statistical accuracy apart, what we have in a number of the countries are two racial blocs encompassed within a single state, two cultures that have lived side by side for over four hundred years in uneasy tolerance. The Conquest has remained incomplete, and Spanish culture has yet to win its major victory—that of converting the Indian into a good European. It has done so with the Negro, and the *mestizo* has proved not merely a physical but a spiritual offspring of the European conqueror. But the Indian, especially where congregated in self-sufficient communities, or hidden in isolated mountains or jungle forests, has remained more or less immune to the cultural, even if not to the political, domination of his contemporary superiors.

Anyone who has traveled widely in remote parts of Mexico, or Central and South America, will testify to numerous instances of towns—like Amatanango in Chiapas, Mexico— where the only *mestizo* was the *secretario* representing the *municipio,* or where the only *mestizo* was the teacher, if there was a school; or he will remember plantations in the central part of Peru and the northern part of Ecuador or in the mountains of Bolivia where the only representative of European culture was the owner or the administrator, and where all the rest of the people—and they might be counted by the hundreds—were as distant from European culture as they would have been had the discovery of America not taken place. This last statement is probably an exaggeration, because at least *aguardiente* or *pisco* will have found its way among the Indians. There are undoubtedly other elements too, but in the sum they weigh little, and the sudden disappearance of Lima or Guatemala City would remain largely unfelt among these people.

At the end of over four hundred years of Spanish-European influence there are millions of Indians who speak not a word of Spanish, and other millions whose knowledge of it is so elementary as to be almost useless. The Indian's resistance to linguistic inoculation makes one marvel at the cultural impenetrability of entire populations. The Otomí Indian, next door to Mexico City, the Maya Indian outside of Mérida, the Indians around Cuzco and about Lake Titicaca are examples where the contact with the European has been close and the knowledge of Spanish is at a minimum. In other places—such as plantations or isolated villages—one often finds that practically no one speaks Spanish. On one Peruvian plantation near Ayacucho in 1938 all of the orders had to be given in Quechua. In 1572, Francisco de Toledo wrote to the King that the Aymará tongue was so barbarous and difficult that it was hopeless to attempt to preach the Gospel to the Aymará in their own language, and that he had, therefore, given orders that within six months all the people should learn Quechua, which was an easy and eloquent tongue, and feasible for the preaching of the Gospel. The fourteen years of Toledo's governorship of Peru were not sufficient to achieve the ends that he had ordered accomplished in six months. And the four hundred years that have passed since his tutelage have proved no more effective with either the Quechua or the Aymará.

After four hundred years of European-Indian contacts and European political administration, the basic implement of cultural communication and understanding has failed to become a universal tool among the peoples that now make up Latin America. What is the use of the poetry and the literature, the newspapers and the books, the long discourses and elaborate laws, when in many instances at least half of the population is beyond the reach of even the simplest words in which these intellectual efforts manifest themselves? They do not speak a common tongue, and do not understand each other. Their conceptual universes are a thousand miles apart. They are all strangers within the nation. After a visit to the Yaqui country in 1937, Lázaro Cárdenas remarked wistfully as we were leaving, *"Somos extranjeros aquí."*

What has been said about the Spanish language can also be said, with a somewhat different emphasis, about the church. The reach of the church is undoubtedly greater than that of the language. There are many Indian groups who do not speak Spanish, but who are members of the church. It is true, of course, that many small tribes high up in the mountains or deep in the jungle forests have remained pagan to this day. They either have never been reached by the church at all, or, with the passing of the missions, have reverted to paganism. But of more significance is the detailed influence of the church upon the life of the rural folk, which, in some ways, seems to follow the pattern of the spread of Spanish culture.

The church is obviously Spanish and European in the large cities, where the European, the *criollo,* and the literate *mestizo* elements predominate. It is still recognizably European in the larger population centers, where the *mestizos* are important for commercial and administrative reasons. But as one moves from these larger communities to the smaller villages, where Spanish as a language declines and the Indian tongues prevail, then the church as an institution reflects the persistence of pre-Columbian traits in a thousand and one subtle ways. For instance, marriage in accordance with old custom preceding marriage in the church, sometimes by a number of years; the survival of polygamy, as among the Chamula Indians (on the part of those who can afford it); the carrying-over into the church of older Indian dances; and the continuance of ritual—all are evidence that even in matters of the Faith, the transplanting of Spanish-European culture has fallen short of its objectives, in spite of the many efforts made throughout the colonial period to suppress idolatry and extirpate paganism. The Peruvian Indian still drops a little stone when he gets over the top of the mountain in gratitude to his gods for helping him up, just as he did in the days of old. Native culture, even if distorted, has persisted within the Christian pattern, and the striving for a purity of the Faith has been defeated.

It was, however, in its introduction of the principle of private property that the Spanish Conquest precipitated the most serious conflict between European and Indian culture. To the European conqueror, private ownership was a natural extension of the personality; and the right to own, inherit, sell, mortgage, or transfer land was part and parcel of the sum of all

"natural" prerogatives of the individual. It was part of the air he
breathed, and the transplanting of Spanish culture to this
hemisphere would have been inconceivable without it. To the
Indian, however, it was a completely revolutionary, incompre-
hensible attitude. Private ownership of land in the European
sense probably never existed among the Indians. And the
revolution precipitated by this principle became from the
beginning the most serious cause of attrition between the two
races, and has persisted in being the major issue of conflict
between the European and the Indian.

It must always be remembered that Indian agriculture was
largely hoe agriculture; it was intensive in character, communal
in organization, and executed with elementary tools. Apart from
tribute—where tribute was paid—agriculture was for local
consumption. It did not produce for the market and had no
commercial objectives. Spanish agriculture was extensive rather
than intensive, and depended upon the horse, the ox, and the
plow. On a more or less extensive scale, the Spaniard also
developed ranching almost everywhere—from Cuba to Chile.
Gaining control of the government, the early settlers distributed
lands among themselves, taking them from the natives, quite
without regard for the needs of the Indian community. In the
early days the *cabildos* possessed the right to distribute lands to
the local Spaniards, and when these powers of the *cabildos* were
transferred to the viceroy because of the evil that the practice
had given rise to, much of the damage had already been done,
and the repeated attempts to protect the Indians in their
landholdings proved ineffectual. By one method or another, by
pressure, by forced sale, by taking advantage of the Indian's
ignorance of the written law, of his inability to understand the
nature of private property, the *hacienda* or the large plantation
came to be the characteristic feature of rural organization; and
such it has remained. With the exception of Mexico, the
innumerable conflicts between Indian and Spanish landowners
have brought scant change.

There are two things that impressed the Spanish administrator very deeply. One was the unending lawsuits, petitions, reclamations, and complaints that Indian communities doggedly brought against the landowners. No decision ever seemed to settle the matter. The Indians would always return to try again. And there are numerous cases where these lawsuits went on generation after generation, regardless of the outcome. The other thing that impressed the Spanish administrator was the fact that it was always the community rather than the individual that instituted and persisted in these futile efforts to recover the lost patrimony. Such was the case in Mexico, such is still the case in Peru, where the continuous, even if isolated, rebellions of the Indians against their neighboring landowners have forced the government to give the community a legal personality and to attempt to circumscribe and register the boundaries of the plantation and the village land, in the hope that a halt could be called to the constant incursion by one or the other on their neighbors' lands.

There can be no adequate understanding of the problem in its contemporary setting unless it is realized that the growth of the plantation system has sharply divided the rural community into two distinct patterns, the large plantation and the little village. The *hacienda,* varying in size, frequently embracing many thousands of acres, has tended to become a self-sufficient economic unit. It ordinarily has its own laboring force living within the confines of the plantation, sometimes including a hundred or more families, and operating largely on what might be described as a nonmonetary economy. It pays its people in kind, or allows them a couple of acres which they till for themselves as part of their compensation, and the prototype of the Mexican *tienda de raya,* in one form or another, is almost a universal institution. There are instances where plantation money, circulated only on the plantation and acceptable only at the plantation store, has been used for cash payments. As an economic unit, the plantation has a tendency to operate with a minimum expenditure of money, and at a minimum risk. Its first objective is to become self-sufficient. In part, self-sufficiency is achieved by expansion. If the *hacienda* is large enough, it includes good forest and pasture lands, the headwaters of its own irrigation system, and has varying kinds of soil for different kinds of crops; it is possible in the tropics to grow on the same plantation at different altitudes tropical, semi-tropical, and temperate-zone crops. There are plantations in Peru that seem to have achieved the ideal of growing sugarcane, bananas and coffee, rye, barley, and potatoes—not to speak of oranges and apples—within the same property.

This drive towards self-sufficiency gives the *hacienda* a large appetite and a restless eye for its neighbors' land, especially if the neighbors are weak and helpless. And what can be more tempting than the lands of the neighboring Indian village just across the boundary? The *hacienda*'s second objective is to transfer to the sharecroppers and tenants that part of the agricultural enterprise which is subject to drought or other loss. For itself it reserves those crops that can be grown under irrigation, or cyclical or perennial crops that require little annual investment and carry a minimum risk. Such plantations are frequently overburdened by debt, underequipped, and run by owners who often lack the capital to operate so large an area efficiently. As a continuing enterprise the plantation fulfills its purpose if it manages to keep its owners in customary comfort in some distant city.

The *hacienda*, however, is not merely an economic enterprise—it is also a social and political one. Its laboring population occupies what is probably the lowest rung on the social ladder. It is confined within the limits of the plantation and is often encumbered by debt that may be passed on from generation to generation. A kind of personal dependence develops between the *peón, roto, pongo,* and the master or the *patrón* that is describable only in terms unacceptable to a free society. It is an institutional structure rather than a merely personal relationship. As a political institution, it tends to dominate the local government, and the temporary officeholder in the neighborhood either begins or ends by being beholden to the local grandees.

On the rim of these plantations, sometimes squeezed very

tightly on all sides by the same *hacienda*, is the little village. The history of no two villages is alike. *Mestizo* or Indian, the little village has lived, sometimes for centuries, in constant conflict with its dominant neighbors. In many instances, it has lost practically all of its lands, and its inhabitants make their living by working as temporary laborers or as tenants on the neighboring plantations. Sometimes the village has land, but not enough land for all of its needs. In other cases, fortune has been kind to it, frequently because it was driven high into the mountains, or for some other special reasons it has been able to defend what lands were left to it. These villages vary infinitely one from the other—in size, in internal structure, in peculiar customs and tradition, and even in the manner of landholding.

Until the Independence, the villages' lands were almost always held in common. The individualistic doctrines that crept in with the Independence tended in different places, especially in Peru, Bolivia, and Mexico, to produce sporadic efforts on the part of the government to break up the communal lands. Where successful, these sometimes led to an all-too-easy transfer of the individualized Indian holding to the neighboring plantation. The illiterate recipient of a property deed sold the paper to his solicitous neighbor for a good drink. Not endowed with a sense of the meaning of private property, and unable to read or understand Spanish, he looked upon a deed (to a part of what had traditionally belonged to the community) as an irrelevant offering that "made no sense." And he who received a drink for it considered himself well paid—and then went on behaving as if the land still belonged to him and to the community.

Where the village survived, especially if it was an Indian village, it held on to its communal lands as of old. In any case, the pasture and forest lands remained communal. Even on the *hacienda* the Indian laborers who "belonged" to it behaved as if the plantation belonged to them. There is a persistent current of feeling and understanding in the mountains of Ecuador, Peru, and Bolivia that the Indian community on a plantation is in some traditional sense a corporate community. The landowner may

come and go, the plantation may be sold or transferred, but the
land continues "belonging" to the Indians upon it, and they to
it. It is not slavery or serfdom or peonage; it is a survival of the
older tradition of the Indian community in its relation to the soil,
which antedates the Conquest. The re-creation by the Mexican
Revolution of the *ejido* is a symbolic recognition of that
tradition. The personal titles to private parcels within the *ejido*
carry the limitation that these theoretically privately owned
lands cannot be sold and must be worked, or they will revert to
the community. The forest and pasture lands continue to be
communal possessions. The concept of private property, so
deeply ingrained in European culture that the very texture of
European life is unthinkable without it, has failed of complete
acceptance in its new habitat.

Thus we see that in the three facets of Spanish culture we
have examined—language, the church, and private property—
accommodation has proved difficult in that part of Spanish
America where Indian mores have survived. If a successful
conquest is to be measured by the degree of the transfer of the
conqueror's culture to the new territory, then the Spanish
Conquest remains incomplete. It may boast of successful
political dominion, but in things of the spirit and in the basic
traits of a culture—language, faith, and possession—the achievement, to say the least, has been only partial. These matters fall
within the realm of the spirit, because even private property is
an idea, a concept, a legal formula.

Can it be said that the Spanish transfer of elements of
European material culture has been more successful? How much
of the material culture brought to him by the Spaniards has the
Indian taken? What basic tools, animals, foods, and skills has he
adopted? How much has the Quechua, the Aymará, the Otomí,
the Maya, or any one of a hundred other Indian groups taken
over from Europe? The European brought wheat, but the
Indians eat a *tortilla* made out of maize, or in Bolivia, *chuño,* a
desiccated potato. The European brought his elaborate architecture, but the Indian still lives in a *choza* made out of adobe or

reeds as he did before the Spaniard arrived. The Spaniard brought shoes and boots, but the Indian is still either barefoot or wears his *huaraches* made out of materials used in olden times. The Spaniard may have brought a coat, but the Indian still wears his *poncho,* woven out of the same materials and on much the same patterns as it was before the Conquest. It would be easy to exaggerate and overstate this theme, because the material elements of the conqueror's culture have found acceptance here and there in varying degrees depending on nearness to market, on available purchasing power, on the special adaptability of a particular item.

The Indians of Spanish America, who in many of the countries represent half or more of the total population, have what is in essence a culture different from that of the rest of the population. Socially and economically, they occupy the lowest level in the society. Politically, they carry no weight. One might speak of this population as existing below the surface, and if it were not for the few *mestizo, criollo,* and foreign champions of the Indian and the occasional uprisings here 'and there that break into the papers or require the calling-out of the militia, most literate people, both in Latin America and out of it, would go on thinking and feeling as if the Indian did not exist at all.

The Mexican Indian represents a sub-class in the rural community and in the nation. Not only his material equipment but his configuration of the universe is on a different level from that of the rest of the population. All attempts at "incorporation" of the Indian have, on the whole, failed in their objectives. Much emotion and literary exercise has in recent years been poured into the term *Indigenismo.* There are those who would incorporate the Indian into the body politic because that is the way to make a nation. Manuel Gamio's expressive phrase *Forjando Patria* illuminates the inner drive of *Indigenismo.* To them *Indigenismo* is a means towards nationalism. There are others with the creed of *Indigenismo* who would save the Indian culturally, and preserve him as a symbol of the past.

The advocates of *Indigenismo,* whose interest is not just

anthropological, would give the Indians the tools of contemporary civilization, incorporate them into the state, and make good citizens of them. But there is some likelihood that they will defeat their objectives in the degree to which they are successful. They will certainly evoke nationalist feeling by endowing the Indians with literacy and self-consciousness. But it may prove a dissident Indian nationalism. The conflict between the European and the Indian cultures may be raised to a new level, where the contenders will be more equally equipped. When one recalls the resiliency of Indian cultures, the almost incredible survival of Indian groups like the Yaquis, or the persistence of our own Pueblo Indian cultures, the issue ceases to be an academic one. In 1923, at the time of Felipe Carrillo Puerta, I heard talk of a Maya federation, including all the Mayas in Yucatán, Mexico, and the neighboring countries. Even the *mestizos* in Yucatán are Yucatecan nationalists first and Mexicans second. In Michoacán, I once heard a speech made by an army officer to a group of new volunteers. In his speech he played upon the phrase *muy Michoacano,* and the talk dealt with the glory of the old Tarascan empire and civilization. In Bolivia, I heard lengthy discourses by Indians on the needs and rights of the Quechua and Aymará races and the injustices they have suffered. In Guatemala, I heard a semi-literate Indian remark that he hoped some "foreign nation" would come and save the Indians there. An effective educational system with its complement of modern tools of communication might precipitate a whole series of dissident nationalist movements. We may yet see reproduced in this hemisphere some of the political factionalism of the Iberian peninsula.

This discussion is intended to point to the implicit contradiction between *Indigenismo* and *nacionalismo.* The wisdom that might lead to an accommodation between them—a cultural and linguistic autonomy within a common political unity—is probably not to be expected. It is well within the realm of possibility that the next four hundred and fifty years will witness the reemergence in the Andean mountains of a

Quechua nationalism in modern dress. If education will give these people the tools, their own self-interest, their historical antagonism to the European, and what memory may still linger of their ancient glories will do the rest. What the Irish and the Basques have demonstrated may not be beyond the reach of the American Indian. The objective implied in Gamio's phrase *Forjando Patria* may prove a self-defeating ideal. But the route in either direction is long and the task difficult. It can be achieved only by reshaping the rural economy, which is now based upon the plantation. *La reforma agraria*, which may seem a simple matter of dividing up the estates, is really destructive of the roots of European cultural dominion in the Indian areas. If successful, it will wipe out in such places as the mountains of Peru, Bolivia, and Ecuador the only persistent source of European cultural authority, because the *hacendado* has proved the most authoritative missionary of European culture. No political agency created by the modern state has carried either the authority or the prestige that the *hacendado* and the *gamonal* have had and still have in the rural districts.

La *reforma agraria* is therefore more than land distribution, more than the distribution of wealth, more than the equalization of the rural classes. It is the most fundamental implement in what would be radical *Indigenismo*. With the passing of the plantation system would disappear also the surest, the most tenacious, even if fallible, representative of European culture with which the Indian has come in close contact. The deep internal divisions within such countries as Peru, Guatemala, Bolivia, and Ecuador are such that no national culture can be built and no political stability can be achieved without some means of encompassing the total population within the framework of the state. That has not been done in the past, and the attempt to do it in the future may well increase rather than lessen internal division.

The place and future of the Indian raises again the whole question of the meaning of the Spanish Conquest. National unity has not been achieved in many areas and may not be achievable. The long-range outcome of the Spanish impact on the American Indian may well turn out to be a more vigorous and self-conscious Indian cultural nationalism than existed before the Conquest. The evidence is, I think, clear that where the *mestizo* is immersed in an Indian community he takes on the color of what for lack of a better word might be called Indian nationalism. Military conquest of a foreign people is obviously a temporary achievement. Spiritual and cultural conquest and social incorporation are more difficult and longer-lasting. And in the end, where the original population survives in large numbers the Conquest may well prove to have been the beginning rather than the end of a self-conscious people.

[1943, 1968]

An American Commonwealth of Nations

The future historian will note, when he deals with America's participation in World War II, that for most purposes it was in effect a hemispheric undertaking. True, the brunt of the effort of necessity fell upon the United States, but given the distribution of effective power and interests in the Western world, this is neither surprising nor unexpected. Of the twenty republics south of the Rio Grande, only one—Argentina—remained seemingly indifferent to the issues involved or even in some measure friendly to our enemies. But even in this case, the Argentine government, however belatedly, broke off relations with the Axis powers and their satellites; and there is evidence that the majority of the people had from the beginning been on the side of the Allies.

This remarkable moral, political, and, in a sense, military alignment of the Western world on the same side in a great war has illumined an accepted assumption—the unity of this hemisphere. The idea is old, as old at least as Bolívar; but it was the visible threat of a German victory in Europe that at last gave it unmistakable expression. In spite of Latin American fear of the United States, so well and so long fostered by agents of Hitler and before him by others (including Latin Americans like Vasconcelos, Ugarte, Fombona, and Pereyra), it became evident that the link that tied North and South America together was more than physical—it was political and spiritual as well. There had been, before the storm clouds gathered, in an age that now seems far-off and a little unreal, much discursive and eloquent writing and preaching upon the sharp differences between the peoples and cultures of the United States and Latin America. One was Anglo-Saxon, the other Latin; one was Protestant, the other Catholic; one was material, the other spiritual; the culture of the United States was, as the tale was told, crass, coarse, and corrupted by an unholy zeal for moneymaking. We had not only a "dollar diplomacy," but also a dollar-seeking way of life. Every item in the life of the United States that could be made to brand our culture as barbarous, uncouth, and grasping was emphasized and exaggerated—a Southern lynching, a New York speakeasy, a Chicago gangster, the seventh divorce of a movie star, a corrupt political machine, all and more were used to prove that we were a gullible, godless, and greedy people, a Caliban among nations and a constant threat to the very life and independence of Latin America. "Ideological warfare" was in full swing before its name had been invented.

And yet, when the crisis came, the discord so busily sown in previous decades was largely washed away and an essential identity in attitude and community of interest quickly prevailed. This "revelation," for so it might be described, reflected the fact that the people of this hemisphere, when looking out upon the world, had a common view of the universe. For it is true that the familiar list of differences between the United States and Latin American peoples is only partially descriptive and denies the imprint of their experience in this hemisphere. The conquest and settlement of the Americas has molded all of the peoples on this side of the Atlantic into a recognizable folk in a way not shown by the ordinary catalogue of their varying characteristics. This uniqueness of outlook and attitude, of feeling and philosophy, is a by-product of the sharing by Americans everywhere of certain profound experiences in their common history in this hemisphere that have left their residue in attitude, notion, belief, practice, values, habit, language, and mannerism. More than four centuries of a common heritage have implanted in all of us a "something" that is American rather than European. It is discernible in our prose and poetry, politics and polity, in our

popular heroes and folk tales, in the stories told to children, and
in the moral issues that burden the grown-ups.

That "something" is a by-product of the essentially
universal American experience with the Indian, the Negro, the
open spaces and wide horizon, the unfilled areas, the peculiar use
of the horse (the cowboy, the *gaucho,* the *llanero,* the *vaquero* are
brothers under the skin), and the peculiar American experience
with ranching: of driving cattle a thousand miles as is still done
in Brazil, for instance. It is the persistent tradition of a culture
uprooted in the Old World and replanted and developed in the
New; the common experience of the mixture of races and
peoples in their varying degrees; the constant flow of immigrants and their amazingly rapid metamorphosis into something
essentially different from what they were; the evidence of social
and physical mobility, and the pride and self-assurance born in a
world easily molded and changed. It stems from the common
belief in progress, from the common notion that government is a
human and malleable instrument subject to pressure and open to
change by political "revolt" at the ballot box or by a "revolution," from the fact that all of the nations in the hemisphere
achieved their independence by revolution and that their
greatest heroes are all successful "rebels" against Old World
"tyranny." There is an American belief in democracy that is
ingrained even in areas where the *caudillo* and the "political
boss" are persistent and sometimes sinister figures, and that all
political upheavals have—with very few exceptions indeed—
been generated at least in the name of democracy. These
influences under varying forms and in different degrees have
given Americans a common psychological and spiritual heritage
deeper than the traditional, obvious differences that separate
them. This identity of experience extends even to the feeling of
isolation, of being set apart from the rest of the world, of being
separated and protected by both the Pacific and Atlantic oceans.
When they speak from the depths, Americans talk about the
same things and say essentially the same things about them.
Even a cursory knowledge of the truly national literature of this
hemisphere will make this clear.

It was consistent with the basic experience of the folk in the Western world that, when faced with the greatest moral and political conflagration of modern times, they reacted to it in very much the same way. Psychologically and morally, the American people everywhere responded to the alternative offered by Hitler by almost spontaneous opposition. This was what their common experience dictated.

The identity of north and south was enhanced by the common peril. Danger made clear the helplessness of the Latin American countries, individually and even collectively, in the face of a ruthless military power bent upon conquest. It also made evident the dependence of the United States upon both moral and material support from those countries for the defense of its own or any other part of the hemisphere against aggression from abroad. The military need to keep the Panama Canal and the passage around the Straits of Magellan open to United States shipping and closed to that of our enemies made the cooperation of the countries in Latin America essential to us. By the same token, the survival of the Latin American countries as individual nations depended upon the military strength of the United States. This military and diplomatic unity was born of necessity and made easier and more logical by the common historical experience of north and south.

The theme that runs through the description of the Americas as a commonwealth of nations is the idea of the juridical equality of states. The idea is one upon which our own nation is based. We long ago decided that Rhode Island is equal to New York, and that Idaho is equal to Texas. The belief that the small state is equal to the large one has conditioned our thinking and our politics.

The problem can perhaps be illustrated by an example from our own history. When Senator Borah inspired the foreign policy of the United States, it did not occur to anyone to suggest that he was trying to advance the interests of the state of Idaho. Many of us disagreed with his ideas about foreign policy. To many they seemed a mistaken and ill-founded description of what was the true American concern with the affairs of the world, but no one doubted that he, too, was concerned about the nation and not merely about the state that had sent him to the Senate. The spokesman from the little state spoke for the great nation with the same zeal and devotion as if he were speaking for the largest state in the Union. He spoke for the Union. That was possible only because in our system there are no invidious political differences between the states. Had a system of distinctions between the states been written into the Constitution, the organic unity of the nation could not have developed. The idea of equality between the states is, therefore, the base upon which the concept of unity rests. Equality between the states makes the whole greater than any of the parts, and makes the interest of the whole the visible concern of all the members of the Union, regardless of their relative positions. We have acted on that doctrine not merely internally, but in our policy towards the nations of this hemisphere.

It is no accident that a great and powerful nation like the United States should have voluntarily and as a matter of deliberate choice made the weak and the small in this hemisphere equal with itself. The concept of the juridical equality of the states is the foundation stone upon which the Inter-American system has been built. With the juridical equality of states has gone the belief that government rests upon the consent of the governed. In a subtle and deeply ingrained way, the concept of equality embraces not merely the state, but also the individual. Government in this hemisphere means government by and with the consent of the governed. In spite of the many failures in practice, the belief in the equality of the citizen before the law has persisted. This equalitarian philosophy seems natural to the Americas. It is the continuation of the experience shared in the conquest, settlement, and development of the New World. It is part of the spiritual adventure of varied and migrant peoples carving a new physical and moral environment for themselves. It is part of the optimism of open spaces and the absence of a stratified society within which one is born and dies. The peculiar American environment—and I am using the term in a hemispheric sense—has made the idea of equality natural.

It was, therefore, logical and inevitable that the ideal of law rather than of force should become the ruling instrument in the relations between the nations of this hemisphere. All of the elements of the Inter-American system—common defense against aggression, nonintervention in the internal affairs of one state by another, and, finally, the guarantee of territorial integrity—flow easily and naturally from the original belief in the equality of the small and the large in this hemisphere. That, in essence, is the peculiarly American doctrine. In 1916, Woodrow Wilson, speaking before the Second Scientific Pan-American Congress, said that one of the ways America will come into her own will be by "the states of America uniting and guaranteeing to each other absolute political independence and territorial integrity."

The 1945 Chapultepec Declaration is, therefore, only a formal acceptance of an older doctrine, and, in fact, the idea goes back even before 1916. Joaquín Nabuco, of Brazil, speaking at the laying of the cornerstone of the Pan-American Union Building, said: "These countries, with all possible differences between them, in size and in population, have established their union on the basis of the most absolute equality. Here, the vote of the smallest balances the vote of the greatest." There is a pervasive sense of interdependence and mutual interest in relation to the outside world.

The sense of common destiny and unity in this hemisphere is represented by the equal voting power of all states in the Inter-American system. This equality is symbolic of the unity. No one is misled into believing that all of the American states are equal in strength. The relative positions of the various members are not at issue. What is at issue is the common interest of the small and the great in the unity of the hemisphere for those purposes common to all.

It would, however, be unrealistic and misleading to gloss over the persistent stress and strain that prevails between the United States and the countries of Latin America. The talk in the nations to the south about the differences, the emphasis upon the cultural and spiritual divergence, the warnings of danger have a basis in the bigness, power, organized energy, wealth, and military strength of the United States. We are the great nation in this hemisphere. Our mere size and power are like a permanent shadow, protective or threatening, as you will, but inescapable and unavoidable. Our protestations of affection and concern are, in spite of our best diplomatic efforts, the protestations of the big brother; our very manner if not mannerism reflects that. This is the fact and no one can conceal it—not even by studiously avoiding mention of it. So, too, the protestations of the Latin Americans that they love us, admire us, respect us—or the opposite—are in effect the behavior of a little brother, and nothing can hide the fact, neither humility, nor bravado, nor even studious indifference. Anyone who has attended any Pan-American conference will readily identify the attitudes, speeches, disclaimers and protestations, the deference and implicit jealousy or fear that reflect the simple fact of our bigness. The overflow of American energy in the past and its possible overflow in the future are a constant theme song, accompanying every political argument, every projection into the future.

Diplomatically, this gulf between the one great power and a number of small ones has been bridged by the doctrine of equal sovereignty, a doctrine that makes Haiti and Santo Domingo—to use just two instances—equal entities with the United States in a diplomatic argument, if in nothing else. This doctrine has its numerous corollaries, the most important of which is the principle of nonintervention in the internal and external affairs of any one of the Latin American republics. Equal sovereignty as a theory and nonintervention as a policy are really deliberate attempts to redress the balance in this hemisphere between one very powerful nation and a number of weak nations. And, as a matter of fact, they do redress the balance in a certain way and within certain limits; they tend to defend the dignity and justify the confidence of the weaker political units in their dealings with the United States. They also tend to give Pan-Americanism a kind of moral basis, which it lacked until these policies were fully acquiesced in by the United States. The effect is to provide a basis of security, especially as we have actually implemented these measures in various ways, such as converting the Monroe Doctrine from a unilateral to a multilateral instrument. It cannot be denied that these changes in attitude and practice have been effective in deflecting the preoccupation of the Latin Americans with the "bigness" of the United States, for the time being. But perhaps their most important immediate consequence has been their influence upon the United States, where they have led to the writing and acceptance of a "self-denying ordinance." These changes have led us to behave as if the theory of sovereign equality were true and not merely an operational formula.

The doctrines and the conventions based upon them, useful as they may be as operational tools in a very complex and ill-balanced international structure, are nevertheless pure fictions. The theory of the equality of sovereignty, the nonintervention policy, the Monroe Doctrine and its various corollaries, the policy of recognition, whatever it may be at the moment, and even the Good Neighbor Policy are in effect intervention. In the nature of the case, given the difference of power and the inner lack of political balance in most of the countries in Latin America, whatever we do or fail to do has the force of intervention. Our policy, whatever it is, our attitude, whatever it is, has a significant influence, in many instances a decisive one, upon both the internal and the external policy of most, perhaps all, the countries in Latin America. Our power is such that we are a party to every transaction, even against our will. We are a weight in every balance. We are an influence in every political judgment, every decision. When we refuse to intervene, we merely intervene on the other side. When we do not support our friends, we in effect support our enemies; when we will not intervene on the side we believe in, we intervene on the side we do not believe in. We cannot escape the consequence of our power; we may refuse to exercise our responsibility, but in doing so we merely exercise it on the wrong side.

In a political world so unstable as Latin America, where government in most cases rests upon a slender and tentative alignment of political groups and personalities, and where the individual factor plays so large and significant a role, any move that appears to favor those in power strengthens them in their hold upon public office and tends to perpetuate it. Conversely, every move that looks like indifference on our part carries an implication of censure, weakening those who hold political power, strengthening the opposition, and hastening the day of revolution. The one thing we cannot achieve in Latin America is neutrality; our very declaration of a policy of "hands off" has the effect of lending support to one or another group contending for place and position. The Good Neighbor Policy, effective as it has been, and so valuable in promoting a moral alignment against aggression at the time when the alignment had to be made, was in effect intervention on the side of the governments in power. Any favor extended, any courtesy shown, increased the prestige and hold of the personalities in office and tended to perpetuate them.

To say this is not to suggest that any other policy would have been more desirable or that any other policy would have made us less interventionist. It is merely to point out, for the sake of "realism" and practical politics, that the doctrine of nonintervention has a much more limited meaning than it implies. Both the internal and the external policies of the countries of Latin America are sharply responsive to our mere presence; anything we do or say—even if we say or do nothing at all—has the effect of intervention. It is no accident that in many Latin American countries the American ambassador is the most important political personage in the country, even if he does his best to be the least important one.

It need only be added that our failure to admit, or our refusal to exercise, the inevitable influence that stems from our position may become a contributing cause of political chaos and disillusionment. Our moral responsibility equals our power, and the awareness of that reality is, or ought to be, the first thought in shaping our Latin American policies.

Though much has been written on the subject, we perhaps do not yet realize how greatly the Latin American countries have contributed to the fulfillment of our wartime objectives in this hemisphere. As a background for examining some of the concrete evidence of this cooperation we might first remind ourselves what our policy was in the days when our danger of becoming involved in World War II was growing. In sum, our objectives then were: (1) to organize and arm the hemisphere for defense; (2) to destroy any attempt to use any part of it for direct or indirect military operations such as espionage, the construction of submarine bases, propaganda, sabotage, or for the supply of valuable raw materials to the enemy; (3) to obtain bases for our military and naval forces; (4) to acquire as rapidly as possible the available raw materials for our own needs; (5) to achieve hemispheric unity for both political and military ends; (6) to obtain military aid from Latin America by the organization, arming, and training of local troops for use in actual combat if and when need and opportunity arose; (7) to maintain peace in the area as an essential means of achieving some or all of these objectives.

First and perhaps most important, we should note what may be called the spiritual preparation of the Latin American countries. Long before we were involved in the war they evidenced a growing sympathy for the cause of the Allies, an increasing shift towards cooperation with the United States, and at the same time a growing fear and repudiation of the doctrines and aspirations of Nazi Germany. Fully a year before December 7, 1941, there were many signs that the various nations in the Western Hemisphere were forging a common policy. Even an incomplete citation of the available material provides impressive testimony that in the face of the gathering storm the peoples of the New World were banding together for a common effort. A ground swell in favor of cooperation with the United States had been developing in Latin America before Pearl Harbor. The fatal events of that day produced a unity of action and policy in this hemisphere barely equaled and certainly not exceeded by the British Commonwealth of Nations. Even more significant, perhaps, is the fact that without the formal political unity of the British Commonwealth, and without the common background of language and culture, the nations in the Western Hemisphere in a moment of crisis behaved in fact as if they belonged together, as indeed they did, in the face of a common danger.

That this is no overstatement may be seen from the immediate response of the countries to the south of the United States after the news of Pearl Harbor was flashed to the world. The Latin American nations accepted and reacted to the attack against the United States as an attack against themselves, and with amazing speed and thoroughness they united against the aggressors. By the end of January 1942—that is to say, within six weeks of Pearl Harbor—all of the nations except Chile and Argentina had either declared war on or broken relations with the Axis, and eventually even these two countries followed suit. In the end, there was not a single nation in the hemisphere that did not cut its official contacts with the Axis powers.

This moral cooperation was accompanied by a military effort that must be judged by its potential importance. Save for naval battles, the actual conflict did not extend to this hemisphere; the war did not reach either the Pacific or the Atlantic coasts of any of the Latin American nations. But it was clear from the evidence at hand that both preceding Pearl Harbor and immediately following it, the American nations were preparing for such a possibility; and it may be assumed that they would have accepted the physical challenge of the Axis powers as in fact they accepted the moral challenge. Everywhere the moral support extended to the United States was bolstered by military effort, and it was perfectly clear that if the war had reached this hemisphere the effort would have been very much greater and would have formed a more significant part of our undertaking.

Our own aid to the military rearming of Latin America was extensive. Every country except Argentina received a certain amount of modern military equipment. But the amounts expended under lend-lease were after all only a part of the total sum of money either loaned, invested, or given to the different countries for a great variety of purposes, all of them designed to increase hemispheric solidarity, to develop and make available the raw materials needed for the war effort, and to increase the effectiveness of the Latin American nations in the general enterprise of winning both the war and the peace.

The economic and military contributions by the United States have increased the prestige of the governments in power. There is, however, no reason to assume that they have materially affected political habits in Latin America or even the basic instability there. Nothing that happened during the war has lessened the personal emphasis upon honor and prestige, the extreme individualism that borders on the anarchic, and the importance of the *personaje*. Nor has it seriously broken down the isolation of the various classes from each other, and the roles of the Indian, the *roto*, the *peón* remain substantially unchanged; so, too, those of the *gamonal*, the *hacendado*, the *amo*, and the *señor*; and the prestige of the military has, if anything, increased. We in effect armed the continent as it had never been armed before. In the sphere of domestic affairs, ambitious generals have better means at their disposal for playing the game of "revolution," and the governments have more effective tools at their disposal for the suppression of "popular" uprisings. We may have made the "normal" dictatorships more permanent, and therefore less palatable, and in consequence more tyrannical and efficient.

Perhaps more serious than the predictable stirrings of domestic political ambitions as a result of the military equipment we placed in the hands of local army chieftains is the very real danger, if not the likelihood, that these new tools may be used in older quarrels among Latin American nations. It must always be remembered that international quarrels in Latin America have all too frequently served internal political ends. What assurance was there that the arming of Peru and Ecuador would not lead to a renewal of the old animosity settled under duress after Pearl Harbor? What certainty was there that the arming of Bolivia and Chile would not lead to an attempt to satisfy an old ambition and to rectify an essentially unstable boundary situation? What, further, was the assurance that the arming of Brazil would not lead to that country's military embroilment with Argentina? To raise these questions is not to say that any such consequences were inevitable; but it is important to repeat here that unless the United States shows a sense of responsibility proportionate to its power in this hemisphere, the arming of Latin American countries may, and in all probability will, have consequences other than those intended by the United States.

It must be remembered that there is no reason to assume that political attitudes, and the persistent feeling that a government in power is a usurper, have been in any important way modified. Political practices will remain as they were before World War II; so will the essential instability of the political structure; so will the artificial character of political parties. Revolution will still be the one sure means of changing government; suppression of opposition by more or less drastic means will still continue to be a favorite political technique. The source of the difficulty lies beyond immediate cure, and certainly beyond cure from the outside. The political form is a function of the structure of society in all its ramifications, and the things that can be added by an outside paternalism will have no serious effect upon the system as it exists.

If there is a "solution" for the political instability, it must come from a better balancing of the inner forces, a greater evening-up of incomes within the different countries, a more general identification of the governments with the people, a larger participation in effective politics by the mass of the community, and a greater responsibility of political parties both in and out of government. But such a course, if it comes at all, will take a long time, a very long time. What we have done is to strengthen the governments in power. These governments came to power in most places—we need not specify—by arbitrary means, by revolutions, by pronouncements, by the suppression of the legislature, by "unanimous elections," by plebiscites, by every means except that of the accurate counting of votes freely given. The question of democracy is really irrelevant to the point. If the governments in power had not thus come to office, others in their place would have achieved public control by the same sort of "democratic" means. Democracy in our sense is not at issue. The simple point is that we have become identified with strengthening, favoring, and maintaining the present governments. We are being held responsible for saddling the present "tyrannies" upon the people. The words "present tyrannies" are used advisedly, for in their place other tyrannies would have been equally "good" or equally "bad," and they would have come to office by the "natural" process of substitution. But we have impeded this natural process of Latin American "democracy," have dammed the process; and when the dam breaks, as it will, we shall be blamed for the revolutions as we are now blamed for the tyrannies. The democratic groups accuse us of maintaining the dictatorships in office. They would equally blame us if we interfered against them.

The difficulties and perplexities are numerous. One that most Americans, official and unofficial alike, will not recognize is that our influence, our democratic influence, is essentially revolutionary in Latin America. If we really mean what we say, if the preaching of the Four Freedoms is to be taken literally, then we are vehicles of social revolution in most, perhaps all, of the Latin American countries. Revolution, bloody conflict, and prolonged social chaos: there is at present no other road to achieve the Four Freedoms. If we do not mean what we say, then we are going to be accused—are already being accused—of hypocrisy, of supporting the "evil powers," of conniving at the suppression of democracy, of saddling arbitrary and antidemocratic governments upon the people. For it is true that the Four

Freedoms, if they are ever to be achieved, involve a basic change in the land structure of Latin America, everywhere except in Mexico and Costa Rica; and this means prolonged social strife and at least temporary agricultural depression, and involves the transfer of political power and prestige from the present small and divided upper class to the large mass of the people. There is no assurance that anything that can be done will, within any reasonable time, have that effect; it might even prove to have the opposite effect. But the doing of it, whatever that implies, is a task beyond the means, purpose, or ken of what we can either propose or execute.

[1944, 1945]

Technology and Race
in Mexico

Mexico is a nation of villages. The official record for 1939 cites over 100,000 of them. We know that they are small, isolated, and poor. But what do we mean by poverty and isolation? There are some things about poverty, isolation, and cultural variation among the races in Mexico that are not subject to measurement. Much of what relates to the conceptual universe men live in—their values, their ethical biases, their notions of right and wrong, their artistic sense, their ideas of the good life, their notions of evil, their special sense of design, beauty, and art—is beyond the skill of the statistician, and beyond wholesale enumeration. A wide area of human competencies, possessions, and beliefs lies beyond the easy reach of the sociologist and economist. But there remain numerous observable and countable "things" that can be used to give substance to the definition of "poverty," "isolation," and cultural differentiation in rural Mexico.

In the attempt to secure some sense of the structure and pattern of the rural community, the author had the cooperation of the Mexican Department of Education and the Federal Census Office and with their help secured a description in considerable detail of 3611 rural villages, representing every state and territory, and one half of all the counties (*municipios*) of Mexico. Before being sent out, the questionnaire was gone over and coded by the Census Office and when the returns came in they were tabulated and checked by that office. It required over two years to complete the job.

These 3611 villages had a population of 1,877,313, or 17

percent of the total rural population of Mexico in 1930. As they stand, these villages are not typical in two important respects. They are larger, having an average of 520 people per village, whereas for the country as a whole it is much closer to 300. We are, therefore, describing communities that have greater material resources. They are also unusual in that all of these communities have the services of a teacher. Most of the Mexican villages have no teacher and no school. These communities are, therefore, closer to the larger world, are more in contact with it, are nearer to the urban centers, and have a greater measure of identity with modern Mexico. They are the richer and more "modern" rural towns in the country.

This study was commenced in 1931 and completed in 1933; but the rural picture drawn here is substantially unchanged, has remained so for the last century, and will, in the nature of the case, change but slowly in the future. Rural ways and traditions yield very slowly. What we have is a description of the Mexico the Revolution was fought to improve and modernize; how great and how difficult the task is the reader will discover for himself. This study will not and cannot give the subtle variations in Mexico from village to village, from racial group to racial group. Each Mexican community has a personality of its own, and only a great artist could do proper justice to it.

The Mexican census of 1930 abandoned the effort to count the Indians and confined itself to enumerating the number of people who spoke Indian languages. In this study each teacher was asked to state whether the population of his village was predominantly Indian, *mestizo,* or white. No teacher in a Miji, Zapotec, or Maya community could possibly miss the point. It is therefore of considerable interest to see the result of this report on the 3611 villages, and, it ought to be recalled that these are the larger communities of Mexico. The returns may be compared with the census figures for 1921. The following table shows that in 1931, on the basis of the personal testimony of the resident teachers, 36.2 percent of the communities were Indian.

If we remember that the census figures refer to the total population and the questionnaire to only the rural villages, the slightly higher proportion of Indian communities is not surprising.

RACIAL DISTRIBUTION

| | 1921 *CENSUS* | *VILLAGES IN* 1931 | |
RACE	*Percent of Population*	*Number*	*Percent*
Mestizo (Mixed)	59.33	2,035	56.3
Indian	29.16	1,306	36.2
White	9.80	270	7.5
Others	1.71	—	—
	100.00	3,611	100.0

When we turn from race to language, our questionnaire shows 77.1 percent of the villages as Spanish-speaking, and 22.9 percent speaking Indian languages. The ratio of Indian- to Spanish-speaking Mexicans is considerably higher than the record shown by the census of 1930, but the census figures are in all likelihood an understatement.*

Looked at geographically, the 3611 villages here confirm the general impression from other sources of the predominantly *mestizo* character of the northern, and the strong Indian element in the southern, part of the country. Northern states like Nuevo León and Tamaulipas gave 1.3 and 3.1 percent Indian villages, respectively, while in Yucatán the Indian villages ran as high as 93.2, and in Oaxaca 77.3 percent. Our material also confirms

* Robert Redfield, "The Indian in Mexico," *Annals of the American Academy of Political and Social Science*, March 1940, p. 134. "The tendency is to record as Spanish-speaking many persons who do not have effective control of the language. The [1930] census reports, for example, that 47 percent of the Tarahumara speak also [*sic*] Spanish. Dr. Wendell C. Bennett, who has studied these Indians, gives his impression that not more than 10 percent of the mountain Tarahumara (the largest group) can speak Spanish."

the general impression that the "white" communities in Mexico are chiefly located in the north. Of the 270 villages classed as white out of the 3611, two northern states, Nuevo León and Tamaulipas, had 101 and six northern states had 160.

The contrasts between north and south may be seen from the following comparison. Nuevo León, a northern state with 150 villages, in our study has 58 "white," whereas Puebla, a central state with 301 villages represented, shows only 3 such villages. The picture is clear. The north is white and *mestizo,* the central and southern part of the country is *mestizo* and Indian.

This is not the place to enter into a detailed discussion of the Mexican land problem, and we do not therefore wish to burden the reader with much material bearing upon that issue. But on one point we pause, because it illumines the communal character of the Mexican rural village. It is to be recalled that this information was gathered in 1931, when comparatively few villages had benefited from the agrarian program, and only 866 out of the 3611 in our sample had received land. And yet in answer to the question: "Do the pastures and forest lands belong to the community in general?" 2101 or 58.2 percent reported in the affirmative. Well over one half of even the larger villages had retained this traditional use of woodlots and pastures.

It is interesting to observe that the teachers report that in one half (49.3 percent) of the villages the land was equitably divided. If this means anything at all, it means that at least 50 percent of the communities in Mexico (the larger communities) have retained some of their communal holdings, and this is certainly true in such states as Oaxaca, Puebla, and Guerrero. But here it is in the mountains and not in the plains that the villages survived.

Equally revealing is the fact that only a few of the villages report the population renting lands from their neighbors or from the *haciendas.* On the plantations in 1931, almost every worker was both a renter (cropper) and wage laborer, generally maintaining both relationships at the same time. The worker would be a cropper in raising corn and beans, and a wageworker for such crops as wheat, barley, coffee, and *pulque.* That is, he was likely to be a sharecropper while working on subsistence crops, and a wageworker on the cash crop. Twelve and four tenths percent of the villages contained people who rented lands from their neighbors. Only a very small number, a little less than 6 percent (5.9), are given as renters on plantations.

The rental systems reveal how small a part money plays in the village economy. Only 18 percent of the villages, 649 out of 3611, pay cash for their land. The Mexican renter is known widely as an *aparcero,* or renter on shares, usually by halves. The contracts differ greatly and depend on the relative contribution made by the landowner and the cropper—especially whether the landowner provides, in addition to the land, animals, seed, and tools. Nearly 40 percent of the villages report "fourths." Money rentals are, therefore, much less general than crop-sharing systems; and rental by "halves," the *mediero,* is by far the most widely spread practice in land rentals in the villages. The ordinary sharecropper who has to depend upon his patch of corn for an income for the year must raise double what he requires for his own needs: one-half for himself, the other for the landowner.

While these figures make it clear that only a small number of the people living in villages rent lands from their neighbors and still fewer from the neighboring plantations, they show what one expects: that a considerable number of them go outside their villages during certain seasons of the year and seek employment in other places. There are many mountain communities where it is customary for a proportion of the male population, occasionally with their wives and children, to depart for lower altitudes and seek work as laborers. The coffee plantations, the sugar plantations, the mines depend to a large extent upon this migratory labor that comes down from the mountains. The Yaqui Indians in Sonora and the Chamulas in Chiapas are famous as laborers in these regions. Over 41 percent of the villages report migration to labor on plantations, 1478 out of 3611. Less than one-fifth report migration of laborers to the mines (18.6 percent of the total) and fewer than one-fourth, chiefly in the north, report migration to foreign parts—that is, mainly the United States.

Rural wages in Mexico have had a tendency to remain stationary. For a hundred years and more, the nominal wage (from two to three *reales*, that is, from 25 to 37.5 centavos) constituted the prevailing daily wage in large sections of the country. This wage in certain areas still continued in 1931. In an attempt to survey the wage situation, we secured and tabulated answers to two questions bearing on wage payments. One dealt with the maximum daily wage in the community, the other with the minimum daily wage. As was to be expected, many communities had but one wage, which served as a maximum as well as a minimum. In others there was a clear distinction between the two. Ninety percent of all the villages answered the question pertaining to the maximum wage.

MAXIMUM DAILY WAGES OF 3,250 VILLAGES, 1931

Wages in Pesos	Number	Percent
Less than 1	2,819	86.7
1 to 1.50	289	8.9
Over 1.50	142	4.4
	3,250	100.0

As illustrated, the maximum daily wage for the greater part of the country and for 86.7 percent of the villages reporting was one peso or less, usually less. Eight and nine-tenths percent reported between one peso and a peso and a half, and only some 4.4 percent of the communities reported wages above that, most of these being mining communities or communities on the American border, particularly in Lower California. At the most generous estimate, therefore, one peso, or less than fifty cents in

American money, was the standard maximum daily wage that rural labor received in Mexico.

The minimum wage was reported for 3054 villages. As we said before, the wages of a hundred years ago still persist. Of these villages, 23 report a minimum wage of 10 centavos a day, 7 report 15 centavos a day, 33 report 20 centavos a day, and 353 or 11.6 percent of the total report 25 centavos a day. More than a third of the villages report 50 centavos a day. Taking all of the villages that report 50 centavos or less per day as the minimum wage, we have 1973 or 64.6 percent of the total villages reporting. The next important group is that reporting 80 centavos, 487 villages or 15.7 percent. An almost equal number, 15.9 percent, report a minimum of one peso or more. These are the same villages that report a maximum of one peso or more. The maximum wage, therefore, for the rural laborer tends to be one peso or more, and the minimum 50 centavos or less. This wage, in 1931, was an advance of about a third over the standard wage before 1910, but the decline in the value of the peso had practically wiped out the gain that the changed wage represented.

MINIMUM DAILY WAGES OF
3,054 VILLAGES, 1931

Wages in Centavos	Number	Percent
10–50	1,973	65
51–80	594	19
Over 80	487	16
	3,054	100

One of the great complaints before the Revolution was that wages were not paid in money but in kind. In fact, the system of the *tienda de raya* (plantation store), with token coins, was so widespread as to be almost universal. One of the first decrees issued by Carranza, after settling in Vera Cruz in the early part of 1914, was the abolition of the *tienda de raya*. This abolition was later incorporated into the Constitution of 1917; it has also been repeated in every state and federal labor law issued since. It is worthy of note, therefore, that the *tienda de raya* still persisted as means of compensation for the workers of villages large enough and progressive enough to have federal schools. At least fifty villages whose residents worked on a plantation reported the continuance of a *tienda de raya*. Equally objectionable was the payment of wages in kind; but in 1931, more than twenty years after the Revolution began, the villages here under discussion reported the following details of the kind of wages received by their inhabitants:

SYSTEMS OF PAYMENT

Method of Payment	*Number of Villages*	*Percent of Total*
In money	3,064	85
In money and in kind	547	15
	3,611	100

Mexican agriculture is still in many places a hoe agriculture. The greater part of the Mexican crop is raised with primitive tools. These tools are often hand tools, or wooden plows drawn by oxen. In these circumstances each family could till but a small acreage. If we classify our 3611 villages according to the average number of acres tilled by an individual peasant (including his family), we find that 20.6 percent report one hectare (2.47 acres) as the average area tilled. Another 20.4 percent report two hectares, while 14.6 percent report three hectares. That is, 55.6 percent, or well over half, of all the larger villages report three hectares or less as the average area tilled by each individual farmer. Only 16.2 percent report a tillage of six hectares.

AVERAGE NUMBER OF HECTARES CULTIVATED

Hectares	Number of Villages	Percent of Total
1	743	20.6
2	736	20.4
3	526	14.6
4	404	11.2
5	345	9.5
6	584	16.2
Not given	273	7.5
	3,611	100.0

The tilling of these small fields still depends upon direct human energy. In many places the use of the plow—even a wooden plow—is not customary. In part this may be attributed to the nature of the terrain; it may be very rocky, as in Yucatán; it may be so steep, as in parts of Guerrero, that a plow is difficult if not impossible to manage; or, as is the case along the coasts, the heavy forests make it easier to burn down the trees and to plant between the stumps with the use of a pointed stick. Thus, "fire agriculture" is still prevalent in many parts of the country. All of these factors, and many others, tend to explain why the use of modern tools in the agriculture of Mexico has been so limited.

Of our 3611 communities, more than 96 percent have no tractors. What is true for tractors is true for cultivators and for planting, threshing, and shelling machines. Only 5.8 percent of the communities have sowing machines; only 7.9 percent use cultivators; only 4 percent of the villages have a threshing machine; and only 9.5 percent have shelling machines, this somewhat larger percentage being accounted for by the fact that corn (*maíz*) is grown everywhere. In recent years there has been an obvious increase in the use of steel plows; 45.7 percent of the communities report their use, while the wooden plow with one handle, drawn by oxen, is reported for 70 percent of the villages. There are many communities using both wooden and iron plows, but 30 percent use no plows at all. The following table gives a summary of the distribution of agricultural implements in the communities under discussion:

AGRICULTURAL IMPLEMENTS IN 3,611 VILLAGES

Villages Lacking:	Number	Percent
Tractors	3,484	96.5
Planting machines	3,303	91.4
Cultivators	3,323	92.0
Threshing machines	3,465	96.0
Shelling machines	3,267	90.5
Steel plows	1,962	54.3
Wooden plows	1,070	29.6

What proportions of the villages in Mexico lack certain kinds of domestic animals? For the 3611 villages, 5.4 out of every hundred have no cows, 13.5 have no oxen, 7.3 have no horses, 26.4 have no mules, 10.7 have no burros, nearly one-third or 31.0 have no goats, and 38.1 out of every hundred have no sheep. When it comes to pigs and chickens, the number of the villages that have them rises markedly. All but 2.1 out of every hundred of the villages have pigs and all but 1.1 out of a hundred have chickens. Taking the villages separately and by areas, we find marked differences: differences between villages that are Indian and non-Indian, differences between those that have *ejidos* and those that do not, and especially marked differences among regions. There are villages so poor that they have neither horses, nor mules, nor burros, nor cows, nor oxen. There are some that have considerable numbers of one and none of others. But it may be said that, on the average, meat and draft animals are to be found in most, even if not in all, of the villages of rural Mexico. The following table indicates the number and percent of villages that lack certain kinds of animals.

SPECIFIED DOMESTIC ANIMALS IN 3,611 VILLAGES

Villages Lacking:	Number	Percent
Cows	196	5.4
Oxen	489	13.5
Horses	265	7.3
Mules	954	26.4
Burros	385	10.7
Goats	1,118	31.0
Sheep	1,377	38.1
Pigs	76	2.1
Chickens	38	1.1

This description of the rural Mexican community must, for the purposes of drawing the picture in fuller detail, be further itemized. Out of 3611 villages, 765 or 21.2 percent are reported as still using barter, and only 260 or 7.2 percent have a local market. That means that 3351 must market their goods and do their purchasing outside their own borders. The distance between the town and the market is therefore an important consideration. Over 116 villages report that their nearest market is 80 kilometers distant, 237 villages are 20 kilometers from their market, and nearly 500 are 15 kilometers from their market town.

The following table shows the distribution of the 3611 villages according to the distances from their nearest market:

Distances	Number of Villages	Percent of Villages
Between 1 and 10 kilometers	1,984	54.9
From 11 to 40	938	26.0
From 41 to 80	308	8.5
Distance not given	121	3.4
Market in village	260	7.2
	3,611	100.0

Of the villages under consideration, 1964, or 54.4 percent, had no stores (*tiendas*).

Furthermore, the Mexican village lacks easy communication. It generally has neither train nor automobile. It has neither telegraph nor telephone; it has no post office. In addition to having—as is frequently the case—a different language, it has, even where Spanish is a common bond, no means of keeping in touch with the world beyond its own borders. The people read no newspapers, and for news from the outside depend upon the stray rumors that come from irregular contacts, through visits to markets or from itinerant passers-by. But the mere fact that the 3611 villages we are describing have a school gives them a contact with the world that smaller communities lack. The school community is in closer contact with the world than the one that has no school. In spite of that, 93.1 percent of all villages have no train communication.

It has frequently been said that the Mexican railroads have not opened up the country, that they were built for communication with the outside world rather than to satisfy internal needs. Whatever the reasons that justified the construction of the railroads through the northern and less populated areas, it is obvious that the great majority of even the larger rural communities are not served by the existing railroads.

This lack of railroad contact is partially made up for by other means of communication. Since 1924 a vigorous program of road building has been pushed by the federal and state governments. That program, as measured by the school communities in 1931, has been successful to the extent of placing automobiles in 8.2 percent of the school villages. In other words, 91.8 percent of the communities under discussion are without automobiles. In part, this is an overstatement, as 13.2 percent of the villages report bus travel. But anyone who knows Mexico knows that buses in Mexico travel where almost no roads exist. At least during the rainy season, no driver from the United States would venture his bus on roads that are utilized in Mexico. But even so, over 86 percent of all villages have neither bus nor automobile transportation. Over 28 percent of the villages report the use of oxcarts as a means of carrying their products to market. A great majority of the villages (72 percent) still depend upon mule and horse for their means of conveyance.

These figures are partially overlapping. A village that has a good road may still use the older and more traditional mode of transport, at least in part. The old method may seem less expensive, as no money value is placed upon time in the rural community. A man who has pottery to take to the market loads it on his little horse, burro, or mule, and leads it for days down mountain paths to the market, as has been the custom for centuries. He may continue doing that even if the tourist or outside merchant has found a way of reaching that particular village by automobile or by bus. With the use of the horse, burro, and mule has gone the habit of carrying one's wares on one's shoulders. Anyone who has made the trip from Mexico City to Toluca over a new and excellent road will recall seeing numerous Indians plodding along with heavy loads on their backs, carrying pottery, baskets, blankets, all of the wares that they manufacture in their little villages. The road has only made travel a little more difficult because macadam roads are hard on one's feet, and because speeding automobiles are dangerous. Nearly one half of all the villages (45.8 percent) report that the system of people carrying goods to the markets on their own backs is still the common practice.

Here we have a Mexico in which a few of the villages have trains, a few have automobiles; a few more are reached by buses; 70 percent enjoy the privilege of carrying their goods by cart, horse, mule, and burro; and nearly one-half still practice the precolonial system, reminiscent of the days when there were no draft animals in the country, when people carried their burdens upon their backs, and did ten, fifteen, and twenty miles a day with them.

What is true of transportation methods is equally true of communication by telephone, telegraph, and post office. These communities report that 11.6 percent are served by telephones. But to some extent the telephones are directly a result of the activities of the schools, which have often been responsible for bringing telephones to the communities. There are such regions as the Miji area in Oaxaca where, through the cooperation of the federal school directors, telephones have been brought into the region, connected with the schools, the teachers acting as the telephone operators. Even so, more than 85 percent of the rural villages are without telephone communication with the outside world. What is true of telephone communication is still more obvious with regard to the telegraph. In spite of the fact that the schools have on their own initiative organized post offices, 80 percent of even the larger communities have no postal connections. This gives us a picture of the isolation in statistical terms that confirms the impressions of travelers and observers in Mexico, and it makes evident the fact that all of the modern means of communication—train, automobile, telephone, telegraph, and post office—are items of minor significance in the lives of the rural folk of Mexico.

MEANS OF COMMUNICATION OF 3,611 VILLAGES

Villages Lacking:	Number	Percent
Trains	3,363	92.9
Automobiles	3,305	91.5
Buses	3,123	86.5
Oxcarts	2,585	71.6
Animals	996	27.5
Human carriers	1,958	54.2
Telephones	3,192	88.4
Telegraph	3,451	95.6
Post offices	2,923	80.9

This general physical isolation is even more marked professionally. The following table gives the number of villages that had no doctor, lawyer, engineer, druggist, midwife, herb doctor, or priest. They all had teachers.

SPECIFIED PROFESSIONALS IN 3,611 VILLAGES

Villages Lacking:	Number	Percent
Doctor	3,530	97.8
Lawyer	3,581	99.2
Engineer	3,570	98.9
Druggist	3,501	97.0
Midwife	3,011	83.4
Herb doctor	2,622	72.6
Priest	3,384	93.7

Striking as is this lack of professional service in the rural community, it is even more surprising to find how poor the rural community is in terms of skilled artisans. The following table will tell its own story:

SKILLED ARTISANS IN 3,611 VILLAGES

Villages Lacking:	Number	Percent
Carpenter	1,845	51.0
Mason	1,892	52.4
Plumber	3,477	96.3
Blacksmith	2,854	79.0
Tinsmith	3,254	90.1
Shoemaker	3,012	83.4
Harness maker	3,241	89.7
Tanner	3,082	85.4
Tailor	3,224	89.3
Weaver	3,039	84.2
Potter	3,007	83.3

There is one item of modern equipment that most of the villages can almost always boast of, and that is the sewing machine. Of all the villages, 3286, or 90.5 percent, had one. It would be possible and interesting to follow this story in even greater detail and show the differences between various parts of Mexico, but space will not permit.

There is, however, one feature that must be included, and that is the difference between the Indian and the *mestizo* and white communities. It is an important fact that in all items here considered—in wages, distance from town, the amount of land an individual can work, the possession of tools, the presence of professionals or skilled artisans—the Indian communities are visibly poorer than the others. There is, in fact, a striking difference in cultural equipment and possessions between these two elements in the population that helps reveal the two Mexicos; and the record here is of things symbolic of the greater spiritual and moral difference that cannot be measured.

It is impossible to compare the position of the Indian community with that of the *mestizo* and white communities in these moral and spiritual terms. While about the same proportions of Indian and *mestizo* communities report persons seeking work on neighboring plantations (40.7 percent as against 41.1 percent), as many as 25.9 percent of the *mestizo* villages have residents seeking work in the mines, and only 5.7 percent of the Indian villages. Even more notable is the Indian tendency to stay at home; only 5.2 percent of the Indian villages report that their inhabitants migrate abroad, as against 33.7 percent of the *mestizo* communities. This sharp divergence is reflected in the fact that many of the *mestizo* communities are located in the north.

Of the villages that report maximum wages of 1.25 pesos per day or over, only 8.7 percent are Indian, 29.4 percent *mestizo*. In the case of minimum wages of between ten centavos and one peso, 2 percent Indian as against .05 percent *mestizo* report ten centavos, 2.3 percent Indian as against .04 percent *mestizo* report twenty centavos. Exactly 20 percent of the Indian villages report twenty-five centavos per day as against 6.8 percent of the *mestizo*. Altogether, 77.4 percent of the Indian communities report up to fifty centavos as against 57.3 percent of the *mestizo* communities. When we come up to eighty centavos and one peso, then there is a sharp reversal. In the first case, the figures stand 9.4 percent as against 19.4 percent, and in the second, 7.9 percent as against 20.5 percent, for Indian and *mestizo*, respectively. The overall figures for wages between fifty centavos and one peso show 22.6 percent for Indians and 47.7 percent for *mestizos*.

This contrast in wages is substantiated by another revealing economic measurement: "How many hectares can one individual work with the customary tools used in your village?"

With a tillage of one hectare, the villages answer: Indian, 30.8 percent, *mestizo,* 14.8 percent; with two hectares: Indian, 26.7 percent, *mestizo,* 16.8 percent. When it comes to an acreage between four and six hectares, then one gets 22.5 percent for Indian villages, and 45.1 percent for *mestizo* communities.

Another question concerned itself with the means of communication with the outside world, and the answers tend to show the same contrast between Indian and *mestizo* communities. In twice as many *mestizo* communities people carry their goods to market by train; in three times as many, by auto and bus; and in twice as many, by oxcarts (*carretas*)—whereas in 66.5 percent of the Indian villages, as against 34 percent *mestizo,* people carry their goods on their own backs.

As in the factors discussed above, the relative position of the Indian communities remains inferior to that of the *mestizo* villages in the matter of tools. *Mestizo* communities have three times as many tractors (4.6 percent as against 1.5 percent), twice as many iron plows, three times as many cultivators, five times as many planters, three times as many threshing machines, and four times as many corn huskers. In the distribution of animals there seems, for the towns under consideration, greater equality; but it still remains true that of all types of animals Indian communities report fewer than *mestizo* communities. Similar tendencies are evident in other comparisons. For example, more Indian than *mestizo* villages are farther than fifteen kilometers from the nearest market town, and more *mestizo* villages have local stores (*tiendas de abarrotes*). Only 37.4 percent of the Indian villages have roads (*carreteras*) leading to them, as against 63.9 percent *mestizo* villages.

In the distribution of professional services the contrast is sharp indeed. The rural districts in their entirety are poor in professional services, but poorest of all are the Indian communities. Only .08 percent report the presence of a doctor, .05 percent a lawyer, .03 percent an engineer. (The *ejido* must have provided even these, for the *ejido* communities report a higher percentage of professional services than the non-*ejido* communities.) We can draw the contrast in the following terms. There is one doctor to every 48,270 Indians; one lawyer and one engineer to every 77,232; one druggist to every 20,873; one priest to every 8045. The *mestizo* communities are about four times as well off; they have one doctor to every 10,231 inhabitants, and so on down the line. A similar contrast can be drawn for skilled artisans. There is one carpenter for every 422 Indians, one mason for every 307, one plumber for every 11,882, one shoemaker for every 2060, one tailor for every 1766. The *mestizo* communities show a higher percentage in all the skilled services, except in the case of weavers. The same holds true for the possession of sewing machines—82.5 percent Indian villages as against 95 percent *mestizo;* and for phonographs, 46.2 percent Indian villages report possession, as against 58.5 percent *mestizo* communities.

[1946]

The Continuing Revolution

How different is Mexico now from what it was in 1910? How much of the visible change can be ascribed to the upheaval that began in 1910 and, according to political spokesmen, still continues? The "Revolution" has come to mean that new things are being done, that they are being undertaken by the government. From one point of view, the current belief in change is an assertion that the "Continuing Revolution" is the government's responsibility. The government is the beneficent instrument of the popular will, the protector of the national interest, the promoter of "progress," and the visible means of fulfilling widespread aspirations for the good life. This gives Mexican political institutions a new role. For the populace in 1910 the government was the "oppressor," something to fear and hide from. The police and the army belonged "to them," and not "to us." Few Mexicans thought of the government as "our" government. It was not "ours" in the sense at least that "we" lacked easy access to it and placed little faith in it. Political institutions were alien and something to avoid and escape from.

Today, the situation is very different. There may be criticism of public policies, of a cabinet member, governor, or politician, but the government is "ours." The people feel it belongs to them; they can approach it, influence it, use it. It is not their enemy. On the contrary, they hold it as their most important, perhaps their only, friend. Psychologically, this is a measure of the difference between 1910 and 1964. People are loyal to the government because they consider it their own and expect it to satisfy their needs. This is what is meant by the

"Revolution which still continues," i.e., the government is to bring about the changes that will meet the needs of the people. There may be differences of opinion on the speed and efficacy of changes political institutions are promoting, but almost no one, except the very few who belong to the extreme right, are saying that this government is "our" enemy, that it does not belong to us. This is a profound change in attitude on the part of the populace and marks the most important single difference between 1910 and 1964.

How unexpected this attitude is may be seen by comparing it to the views the people of Central and South America exhibit towards their governments. It is obvious that in most of these countries, there is either active hostility to the government, as in Guatemala, Ecuador, and Colombia during the years of *la violencia,* or passive denial that it is "ours," as by the Peronistas in Argentina, who represent one third of the voting population, and the Indians in Peru who are invading the highland *haciendas.* The populace of the other Latin American countries in its vast majority does not believe that the government will work in "our" behalf, nor that "we" can influence it to make changes "we" think desirable. It is the government of the "oligarchy"— "theirs."

As a result of these new attitudes, Mexico has achieved political stability and the president is a species of popular hero even if he is a political accident and no great personage before he is elected to office. Once elected, he becomes the agent of the "Continuing Revolution." He is allowed no other role. This is what the presidency has come to mean. The president is the embodiment of "progress," and progress means so much land distributed, so many kilometers of road built, so many schools constructed, so many villages given easy access to drinking water, and so many gestures affirming Mexican nationalism. It is inconceivable that, at the present stage of the "Continuing Revolution," a president of Mexico would confine his efforts to the efficient administration of government. He must be visibly carrying the "Revolution" forward or risk alienation from his supporters. But the "Revolution" now means "good works," active identification with the masses, playing the role of the big protective brother, or, better perhaps, the all-understanding and protective "father"; most necessary in this image-fulfillment is the evidence of "activity," "works," almost daily inauguration of new projects, and the continuing promise of more to come. Gone is the earlier revolutionary dream of a stronger federalism, of a *"municipio libre."* Somehow the Revolution has meant the increasing absorption by the presidency of state and municipal powers. It has, of course, long been true in Mexico that the president was the big chief, the leader, the great power, the one that inspired fear; under Díaz, the president was almost invincible. But never has the presence of the central figure been so overshadowing. There is practically no image of an independent state governor.

Now the presidency is more powerful than it has ever been because constitutionally and by law the central government controls a larger area of economic activities, and, above all, because it embodies the spirit of the "Continuing Revolution." Not only does the federal government control the banking system, the railroads, and the petroleum industry, supervise mining, run the electrical industry, oversee steel plants and petrochemical factories, build the national roads, regulate industrial relations and control the trade unions, manipulate the sugar industry, keep an eye on the *ejidos,* and supervise agricultural credit, but it carries forward a far-reaching social program. The thousands of rural schools, and many urban primary and secondary schools, the expanding program of rural sanitation and village improvement projects, the operation of the motion-picture industry, the active promotion of social security, the vast plan of housing construction, the provision of water to rural villages, the active development of art centers, all are promoted, subsidized, or operated by the central government. And all of these undertakings barely outline the multitude of activities engaged in by the federal government.

In Mexico, the federal government means the president.

Everything is done in his name, with his consent, and by his order. Every dispute, every difficulty, every election of a governor must somehow come before him for his decision, and no one from the governor down to the members of the Congress can come to office against his will or at least without his implied acquiescence. Even the mayor of the large industrial city of Monterrey, or of the small city of Celaya serving a rural area, can only be elected by the consent of the official party, which the president controls. And the candidate for the next presidential election (*el tapado*) will remain hidden until he is unveiled with the consent of the present chief executive.

In Mexico, therefore, what we are seeing is the "Continuing Revolution" embodied in a leader who must represent it in all its phases and who must carry the image of accessibility, of being one of the "people," of being a revolutionary, and of belonging to "us." The role of the government is not only to "make progress," but to be a beneficent agency headed by a "father," concerned about the welfare of his people, jealous of the dignity of the nation, and a pillar of strength against all foreign influence and interference, especially from the United States. From one point of view, the "Continuing Revolution" has eliminated politics because there is now only one politician —the president. This is more evident than it has ever been in the history of Mexico. The president has always had potential competitors—even Díaz did. But now, for the period that he is in office, the president has no competitors, there are no threats against him, and he not only rules but "reigns" almost absolutely—only, however, as long as he is the embodiment of the "Continuing Revolution."

The extent of this process is, for Mexico with its history of rebellion, quite remarkable. In the past, it would have been inconceivable that, on the eve of the gathering of the nominating convention, there should be no known candidates for the presidency. Traditionally, the aspirants for the highest office in the land were well-defined political figures. One of them would ultimately come to the presidential office because no one would be able to stop him. The careers of Porfirio Díaz, Madero, Obregón, Calles, to give only a few easily recognized names, exemplify the historical process. In each of these instances, the contenders were known long before the nomination or election; the opposition party or parties played a bold and vigorous role and the successful candidate "won" because his opponents were completely defeated. The political game was played out in public; people knew who the candidates were and could support the one they favored. More important perhaps, the occasion called for a choice between candidates who were established leaders, who had a "party," a following, and a public personality. The president could support one or another of the candidates, or might even have the power of determining who would be "elected" to succeed him. His choice, however, was a public figure and a known aspirant for the presidential office. The favored candidate had a "political" personality and he would ultimately climb up the presidential palace stairs with a victorious "army" behind him.

The "Continuing Revolution" has greatly modified this traditional political method. The P.R.I. (*Partido Revolucionario Institucional*), by grouping the political family of the "Continuing Revolution" into a single body, has killed off the political leader formerly so typical of the Mexican scene. For the first time in Mexican history, there are no political leaders except the president. There is General Cárdenas, of course. He, however, is not a political leader in the traditional sense. He is not an aspirant to the presidency and has deliberately avoided political activity. He has influence because he was an outstanding president and popular figure. But that is in the past. At present, he is an elder statesman. Alemán and Ruiz Cortines are past presidents rather than contemporary political leaders. There is no visible candidate for nomination by a convention because there are no outstanding political leaders known to the public except the president himself. The name of whoever will be nominated, *el tapado,* is a secret to be revealed in due course. The nominating convention will dutifully and unanimously confirm the choice made by the president and his advisers. All politics has been surrendered into the hands of the president. His choice of the next chief executive, *el tapado,* will not only receive a unanimous nomination but will be "elected" by an overwhelming majority. He will enter the election campaign as an almost unknown figure, without a following of his own, without a party that is his, without possessing a political personality before the Mexican public, without, in fact, being a leader.

During the campaign he will have to create for himself the stature of the successful candidate. He will do it by promising to increase the scope of the "Continuing Revolution," and after the election he will play the role of the "great father." This is the inescapable role of the president. If he failed to fulfill that role, he would be accused of having betrayed the "Continuing Revolution" and of having undermined the legitimacy of his claim to the office. The "Continuing Revolution" has legiti- mized the presidency in Mexico as it has not been legitimized in any other Latin American country. The effect has been to eliminate political activity and, in consequence, submerge political leadership. It is no exaggeration to say that the P.R.I. on the one side and the "Continuing Revolution" on the other have eliminated the *caudillo* from Mexican politics. The presidency is now so dominant that it overshadows all other political offices. The local leader has become a dependent person. He can only live within the shadow of the "great father" in the presidential palace.

The country's political stability derives from these changes. There has been no successful revolution since 1923. And no uprising since Saturnino Cedillo's petty rebellion against Cárde- nas in 1938. The turning point in the recent political history of Mexico was the election of 1928. The assassination of Obregón after his reelection precipitated a profound crisis in the Revolu- tion. In the end, the issues raised by the crisis were met by the formation of a single party that grouped the many anarchic political elements into a single body. This was foreshadowed in

President Calles' memorable message to the nation on September 1, 1928, when he declared that it was necessary for Mexico to make political transition a matter of institutional and legal rule rather than individual choice. A single political party was established on March 4, 1929. Calles and his advisers were so inexperienced in political party organization that he instructed the Mexican ambassador in Washington to secure copies of the by-laws of the Republican and Democratic parties so that they could be studied as models for party organization. (I know this because the Mexican ambassador himself asked me where he could find the "constitutions" of these two American political parties.)

I do not suppose that anyone then foresaw the effect of a single party system controlled by the president upon the political life of the nation. It probably did not occur to anyone that it would destroy a species of Mexican political leadership. The results were not to become immediately evident. It required more than a generation of single party politics, and the peaceful transfer of the presidency after repeated elections, before the old-time politicos disappeared. The president has come to office without violence since 1934. To be sure, this was made possible by the single party, but chiefly, perhaps, by the attitude of Lázaro Cárdenas, who declared, when still in office, that *"este pueblo tiene que aprender la legalidad."* And he told me that he would support a bad government for its legal term rather than a revolution against it. Neither Mexicans nor Americans have given him full credit for this position, and for maintaining it through the years. Obviously, Ávila Camacho was Cárdenas' choice as his successor for the presidency. He was *"hombre de bien"* and would make a good executive. Alemán's peaceful election to office to succeed Ávila Camacho was only possible because Cárdenas would not support a military uprising by General Henríquez Guzmán, who had looked forward to the presidency and who for a long time was spoken of as a Cárdenas protégé.

Military discontent with the Alemán administration nearly

broke out in open rebellion on two separate occasions. It was only prevented by Cárdenas' refusal to support any military uprising against a legally elected government. The peaceful transfer of power by Alemán to Ruiz Cortines was again only possible because Cárdenas stood in the path of a military uprising by Henríquez Guzmán, in his second try for the presidency. The fourth election since Cárdenas' retirement, that of Adolfo López Mateos, was unquestioned. Perhaps the Mexican people have now learned *"la legalidad."* Calles and Cárdenas will be credited by historians with having ended military rebellion and with having made possible the peaceful transfer of the presidency. The effect of this accomplishment has been to eliminate political activity, to destroy political leadership, and to so greatly enhance the power of the president as to make everyone ambitious for a public career dependent upon the will of the chief executive. Whether the elimination of political activity is a good and desirable state of affairs for a great and populous nation with a long tradition of political turmoil, partisanship, passion, and violence, only time can tell; however, I would doubt it.

In dramatic contrast to this enhancement of the powers of the central government and the elaboration of the personality of the president has been the growth not only of personal security but of a sense of freedom, independence, pride, and individualism among the people of Mexico. One might speak of two opposing currents arising from the Revolution: one that enhances the power of the president and of the central government; the other that increases the sense of self, of independence, of the *"Yo"* among the Mexican people.

When one remembers such books as the letters of Madame Calderón de la Barca, *Viva Mexico* by C. M. Flandrau, John Kenneth Turner's *Barbarous Mexico,* or even Martín Luis Guzmán's novels on the Revolution, the transformation from a *pelado,* a *peón,* a soldier serving at the whim of some illiterate adventurer like Pancho Villa, this change is truly remarkable. The Mexican people are different from what they were in 1910.

They are still quiet and polite, but they are no longer humble or afraid. They are instead self-confident, and possessed of unobtrusive pride in being Mexican.

Presumably the years of the Revolution, with their heroism, barbarism, wanderings over the land, defeats, and successes, had their influence in individualizing the Mexican, and the peasant especially. He survived as a self-confident human being with a rifle in hand, whether as hero or bandit. He was no longer a *peón* with bowed head, bullied and harassed by the *amo*. The Revolution destroyed the halo of the landowner, the European, the white man, the Spaniard. The little brown Indian and the *mestizo* somehow became important. When I once asked Miguel Othon Mandizábel, the ethnologist and writer, who was one of the followers and officers of Pancho Villa, why he never became a better-known leader, he replied, "I was too white." Somehow the Mexican came into his own psychologically in the bitter struggle that cost a million lives.

[1963]

Some Reflections
on the Mexican Revolution

It is still too early to attempt a definitive evaluation of the Mexican Revolution, and it will long remain a conjectural undertaking. The movement itself is hard to describe because the Mexican milieu is full of contradictions, and the social upheaval that began in 1910 has had varied consequences. It would require great discernment to appraise even the more obvious events that have come from the armed rebellion initiated by Madero in 1910, for it unfolded in a political environment unforeseen by the handful of individuals who assumed the responsibility of overthrowing the Díaz regime. Long before the strife they precipitated quieted down, so many changes had occurred in Mexico and in the world beyond its borders that it would be difficult to isolate them and say which was due to Mexican and which to foreign forces.

Between the fall of Díaz and the settling of the upheaval into peaceful government, American politics had been churned by the New Freedom under Woodrow Wilson and the New Deal under Franklin Roosevelt. Two great wars had torn the world, and the rise of communism and fascism had affected the substance of international relations. This period also witnessed the ephemeral League of Nations, the maturing of the Pan-American system, and the founding of the United Nations. In many subtle ways Mexican fortunes were modified by all of these events, and in turn the Mexican Revolution influenced opinion and policy in the world at large.

Of great significance to Mexico has been the changed position of the United States in world politics. Since 1910, the

United States has moved from a policy of the "big stick," to become the leader of the democracies and a champion of the independence of little nations. The Revolution, among other things, has released Mexico from American tutelage, and the peaceful accommodation to that change by the United States contributed to shaping its role of champion of the democratic nations during World War I and World War II. Surely, if the United States had forced its will upon Mexico by violence, its new role would have been different indeed.

American recognition that the Mexican people were masters in their own house had one profoundly important effect upon Mexico—the passing away of its fear of the United States. Fear of the United States was an ever-present, almost tangible element in the life of the Mexican people. Their political life was dominated by the threat of "absorption" and "dissolution," of which they were constantly reminded by their leaders. As long as this was the way the Mexican people felt, they could not be free or at ease with themselves and with the rest of the world. Much of the political strife of Mexico and its feeling of inferiority are in large part explainable by the appalling fact that, for over a century, it was haunted by the belief that it lived on the verge of destruction as a nation. As long as this obsession prevailed, the country could have no tranquility at home and no real peace with its neighbors. The oppressive burden of an impending cataclysm is no more, and a sense of release and relaxation has brought a new creative enthusiasm in its wake.

While many forces have combined to bring about this change between Mexico and the United States, for Mexicans it is natural to believe that the miracle was wrought by the Revolution. For them, it was the bristling stubbornness of Carranza, who would yield to neither threat nor blandishment, who would accept no advice, and who refused every aid except on terms of absolute and sovereign equality with any other power great or small; the more subtle, urbane, and polite, but equally intransigent, refusal of Obregón to take offered recognition by the United States if he would first, by treaty, sign away the sovereign prerogative of Mexico to manage its internal affairs; the vehement nationalism of Calles, who, when Secretary of State Kellogg accused Mexico of being on trial before the world, replied that if Mexico was on trial, so was the United States. But most of all it was the expropriation of the oil industry after the companies refused to accept a decision by the Mexican Supreme Court that symbolized the Mexicans' freedom and release from their crippling obsession.

The answer that came from General Cárdenas to the oil companies' defiance of the government was as dramatic as it was unexpected. Whatever it may have meant to the rest of the world, to the Mexicans it meant that at last—at long last—they were no longer afraid of the United States. They were free to breathe in their own country, they were free and equal and unafraid. They had challenged the ever-present ogre and nothing had happened. The thrill that went through Mexico will be long remembered. The exultation that seized the Mexican people—from the humblest Indian peasant who brought a chicken and some eggs to the president to help pay for the oil wells, to the bishops and priests who permitted the faithful to take up collections in front of their church doors for the same purpose—united the nation for the first time in its history. It was the symbolic dispersion of a threatening cloud that had hung over all Mexicans, rich and poor, conservative and radical, humble Indian and aristocrat. It freed them all. That is why they rejoiced.

If one is to mark a date in Mexico when the nation felt itself in possession of its own house at last, it was the day of the expropriation of the oil wells. After that all things were different. Mexico could now feel at ease at home and secure abroad. For the first time in our relations with Mexico, there was room for friendship because now mutual respect was possible. We could differ without acrimony, agree without fawning or cajoling. Mexico and the United States could now behave toward each other as equals.

It has followed from this change in mood and attitude that

Mexicans have ceased to be afraid of each other, of the big or the little *caciques,* and of the government. Anyone who has watched Mexico during the last thirty-five years is aware that something subtle and difficult to describe has come over the spirit of the people. They feel differently about things, and no longer walk with their eyes on the ground and in stealth. As long as they were afraid of us they were afraid of each other.

But now, since 1935 at least, a new feeling pervades the country. Political persecution has stopped. Troublesome opponents are not done away with. There are no political prisoners. People are not afraid to say what they think, whatever it is. They can criticize the government, speak badly of the president himself, and express the most extravagant political ideas. They can attend what meetings they like, and associate with whom they will. Not so long ago it was difficult to be a practicing Catholic in Mexico and dangerous to receive a priest in one's house, because anyone who did so ran the risk of having his house confiscated, the informer receiving half its value. But that too passed away, and one may now practice whatever faith one wishes.

This new mood, the discovery of the nation as something Mexican that belongs to all the people, the growing sensitivity to the dignity of the individual, the disappearance of that attitude that made it possible to divide the world between the *pelado* and the *señorito,* is the most important by-product of the Revolution. All other things have meaning only in relation to this altered feeling among Mexicans as individuals and between Mexico and the outside world.

Like most, perhaps all, really important changes, these psychological and moral mutations were embodied in no program; nor were they envisaged by any revolutionary committee. The Revolution—the real revolution—has been moral and spiritual. All other changes that have occurred in Mexico since 1910, and they have been many, are relatively less important.

Practical-minded readers will protest these dicta. Perhaps

we should devote ourselves to production figures, questions of efficiency, prices, wages, standards of living, foreign trade, and such other useful and important matters. But the practical-minded people are quite wrong in this instance. The oil wells were expropriated not for economic but for political and moral reasons, and the Mexican plantation system was destroyed, not to increase the yield from the land, but to enhance the dignity of those who tilled the soil.

It is interesting from a later vantage point to look at the Mexican Revolution as an unfolding process, and to contemplate the many contradictory directions its leaders have pursued; and yet watch the somehow unifying drift that carried the movement along. If the Mexican Revolution had no philosophy, no political theory, and no official doctrine, it did give rise to a number of separate programs—those of the Flores Magón brothers in 1906, of Madero in 1908, of Zapata in 1911, of Carranza in 1912, and of Orozco in 1913. What is notable in all of the "plans" is their meager content, their limited objectives. Only one of them, that of Orozco, makes any mention of labor. None of them is socialist in ideology or weighted with its language. The programs of the Revolution were indigenous, concerned primarily with political objectives, and only second-arily with the demand for land and agrarian matters. The decree of January 6, 1915, issued by Carranza and considered a milestone in the developing program of a popular movement, was, in the light of later developments, a limited document. The broadening of these original aims came later when the movement had achieved some inner cohesion and self-assurance.

The turning point of the Mexican Revolution is the Constitution of 1917. This constitution is above all a normative document, and the Revolution has been the gradual implementa-tion of the constitutional mandate. The constitution is, however, filled with contradictions. It would preserve federalism, but enlarges the scope of the central government. It would preserve the division of powers, but increases the prerogatives of the executive. It would defend the personal liberties of the older liberalism, but establishes the right of the professional group against the individual. It would preserve private property, but avows the principle of the equitable distribution of wealth, and of national or communal (village) ownership.

In fact, the concept of property is one of the most flexible and many-sided in the entire document. The important point is that the constitution is not rigid, is ridden by no doctrine, and if one had to explain it, one could say it was an attempt to create a legal formula for the complexities of Mexico, where the primitive Indian and modern corporation abide side by side. The document is not enforcible in its entirety, and different administrations have followed varying courses while remaining within the constitutional framework. Certainly the program embodied in the constitution is neither communist, socialist, fascist, syndicalist, nor liberal. If it has to be given a name, let it be called Mexican, for it is as native as the *maguey* plant.

With this instrument in hand, Mexican governments have done certain things that have permanently changed the structure of the country. One of these was the destruction of the *hacienda* system. Americans are not in a good position to understand the *hacienda* system because their tradition of the family farm converts landownership into something very personal and individual. One would be closer to the *hacienda* if one could re-create the English manor without the manorial court, where the lord could rule unrestrained by law or tradition. If to this were added a basically Indian *peón* on the one hand, and an absentee ownership on the other, where the owner was a stranger to the land and believed himself to be different and better than the Indian and the *mestizo* who tilled his acres, then one would get nearer to the feeling about the *hacienda*. It was destroyed because it was hated, and it was hated because it was so dominant, so oppressive, so arrogant. Less than a thousand families owned most of the land, less than two hundred owned a quarter of it, and the rest of the people of Mexico were landless, lived in little villages where they could only survive by the tolerance of the large *hacienda*, or lived in debt inside the plantation.

The plantation was not just a large farm. It was, in its own way, a state, a society, with its own stocks, its own jail, its own arbitrary power of life and death when the occasion seemed to call for it, with its own control over local justice, local police, and local militia. The Mexican Revolution was an attempt to break the hold of this institution over the destinies of the Mexican people. The owners and managers of these large plantations, with their military cliques and *caudillos,* were the government of Mexico, and the Díaz regime represented all of this at its fullest flowering. For the policy of the Díaz government seemed to be to enlarge the hold of this institution upon the Mexican nation, and squeeze the little *rancheros* and poor Indian communities out of existence.

The Díaz government invited foreign capital and yearned for foreign immigration to help remake Mexico on a new plan—a plan dictated by the ideals of order and progress. The people who pursued this ideal of order and progress, tied in with foreign investment and European migration, were pursuing a basically false notion. They persuaded themselves and others that Mexico is, will, or must be a white man's country. They tried to escape from Mexico, they sought to hide the Indian. The Indian was, they thought, a *lastre,* a burden. How wonderful Mexico would be if the Indian would only pass away—and the *mestizo,* too, because the hybrid, the halfbreed, they believed, had the vices of both races and virtues of neither. Escape, they had been taught, could be found in the workings of nature itself, in the "survival of the fittest." The future belonged to the strong and the competent, and the rest would disappear as the law of nature dictated. The sooner the better, and the natural process could be hastened by encouraging European immigration and the influx of foreign capital. The nation had to be *blanqueada* (whitened). The good people of that day were ashamed of being Mexicans. They would hide the Indian by keeping him off the main streets, they persuaded themselves that by opening the doors to the foreigners and closing them to the natives, they were working in the right direction, in the direction of order and progress. And the foreigner, delighted with the hospitality, with the easy avenues to good fortune in land and minerals, joined his hosts in an alliance against the natives, against the Mexicans, against the non-Europeans, in the belief that they were not only serving themselves but the ends of progress in Mexico as well.

Foreign capital identified itself with the *hacienda* system by acquiring enormous portions of the land, nearly one-fourth, and with the current social doctrines as well. It was not a conspiracy, it was an alliance between the foreign investor and the small ruling group of *hacendados* and their military defenders for the good of Mexico. In the end it did not work out that way because they had left the Mexican people out of the bargain. It is difficult to write of this without pointing an accusing finger, or seeming to point one, at those who ruled Mexico then, as if they were villains committed to do evil. It was, in fact, quite the opposite. They meant to do good. They wanted to develop a strong, healthy, and prosperous nation, a nation that was civilized, cultured, and progressive and that was like a European country —stable, quiet, and peaceful.

But they had wrong notions of how to accomplish these ends. They were the children of their own day; they had read or misread Darwin, and had learned their lesson from Auguste Comte and Herbert Spencer. They really believed that the law of survival of the fittest (and how could one argue with a scientific law?) would settle the matter against the Indian and the *mestizo* in favor of the European and the white man. Therefore, they were really only carrying out a policy dictated by nature itself, and if they were ashamed of Mexico and the Mexicans, they could feel satisfied in that they were working for the erasure of the weak, the incompetent, and the degraded. In time, it would be different. But there was no time, and the people objected because they were *the people.* Not that they disbelieved the theories, but they disliked the practice because the theories were worked out at their expense. Their lands were being taken away, and they were being pushed around.

One must understand this or one misses the reason for the

bitterness against the *hacienda* system, the foreigner, and the *científicos*. If the Revolution had a program, and if that program can be said to be embodied in the Mexican constitution, it was to make a nation. Almost everything good and bad that has come from the Revolution had its roots in this rebellion against being denied the human dignity claimed for the leaders, the foreigners, the Europeans. The agrarian movement, the labor movement, the opposition to foreign influence in industry, finance, and commerce, all are part of the same pattern—to establish Mexico as a real nation, its citizens equal to those of other nations, and to free Mexican culture from domination by foreign ideas and ways. That is why the discovery that Mexico need no longer be afraid of the United States was so important. If this is true, then the *real* revolution has succeeded, even if everything along the way should have failed.

But everything else has not failed. The agrarian movement is a success politically and socially, even if its economic by-products leave much to be desired. After all, there are millions of Mexicans who feel that they own the land they till, and have something to defend that is their own. And if anything is certain, no one will take their lands away from them again. It is upon this that political stability has been built. One can add to that over one million hectares placed under irrigation since 1924, the agricultural credit, the roads, and the increasing sanitation and rural health services, all of which are related to the agrarian program and the effort to increase the food supply of the nation.

The real difficulty has been with the increasing population, which is growing faster than the land can be irrigated, faster than the schools can be built. Here is an unforeseen complication for which the Revolution could make no provision. Add to this the spreading erosion of the soil that depletes the land more rapidly than all the efforts to put new land under the plow, and one sees the grave issues facing Mexico. But these problems are not attributable to the Revolution. Mexican industrialization has been part of the effort to make a nation, to make Mexico independent. Here the limits of what is feasible will be determined by available resources, possible markets, and comparative costs. Certainly, there has been much industrial development and there will be more; but in this case the effort, unless kept within the reasonable possibilities of the Mexican milieu and resource pattern, may prove self-defeating.

It is obvious that the Revolution, as embodied in the Constitution of 1917 and the policies it has given rise to, has expanded the power of the central government over such matters as land distribution, irrigation, road building, communication, banking, industrial development, the oil industry, mining, labor disputes, and many other fields. It has greatly enhanced the power of the presidency and weakened the states. To leave the matter here, however, would lead to a wrong impression of what has really happened, for Mexico today is more democratic than it was in the past.

We have already indicated that, politically, Mexico is a free country, and that the press and public opinion are relatively unrestricted. But it remains true that the program of the Mexican Revolution has not been subjected to the test of a free political election, and that it is difficult, for the time being, to see how such a test might be applied. The electoral methods are not equal to the democratic development of the country, and the purely political institutions have proven least adaptable to the changing situation. The issues here are highly complex, but it would be a mistake to assume that the lagging electoral machinery is evidence of the failure of Mexico to widen its democratic basis.

One of the difficulties is the preponderant influence of personal leadership. The leader, whether Díaz, Obregón, or Calles, is taken to be the whole government, and the people expect him to behave as if he were the whole government. If he falls below this expectancy, he may cease to be the leader; he is substituted for, not by an institution, but by another leader. How to change this psychological dependency upon leadership, so deeply ingrained, is the great riddle in the contemporary political life of the country.

It is in this sense that the political machinery fails to translate the democratic advances made by the country in the last fifty years. The base upon which the government rests has been broadened. The government is no longer a mere military dictatorship as it was under Porfirio Díaz. It needs the support of the labor movement and of the agrarian organizations, and to a lesser extent of a part of the middle class.

The fact that the labor unions and the agrarian organizations are managed, and to some extent directed, by the government merely means that they have to be managed and directed because they could get out of hand. If that were to happen, the government could not survive, relying on the army alone—at least not for long. In spite of governmental control of the electoral process, the political scene is not what it used to be. The P.R.I. (*Partido Revolucionario Institucional*) may not be an ideal political party, but it, too, has to be consulted and managed, oiled, smoothed over, and kept in working order, which means that opposing groups have to be conciliated and kept in line.

The political changes that have taken place are in the direction of more democracy. Many more interest groups have to be consulted or satisfied than previously, and the decision is not as unilateral as it was in the past. No Mexican president could at this time decide to continue himself in office without stirring up a serious upheaval. It is also probable that no president could now deal with his political opponents as Díaz, Obregón, or Calles did without bringing a swarm of hornets about his head. The decision-making processes, if not in politics then in a hundred things that are closely related to politics, have spread downward into thousands of small and large groups. Every union local, not just every national union, is a decision-making group. The same is true of thousands of *ejidos*. To make every allowance for corruption, for threat and bluster and chicanery, the mere existence of these groups and their day-to-day activities is a more continuous, and in the end more influential, political fact than all of the corrupt pressures that play about them. The electoral mechanism is not sufficiently flexible for the uninhibited consultation of all of these new decision-making instrumentalities that have arisen as a result of the Revolution. But that is not the same thing as saying that these groups do not exist, or that they have no effect upon public policy. The government is not a tyranny, nor is it uninfluenced by criticism, whether from its opponents or from groups that are allied to it.

The impact of the Revolution has given Mexico a uniquely important role in international relations. The readiness of Carranza to accept certain defeat in war rather than yield Mexico's sovereign claim to manage its own internal affairs brought the issue of relations with the United States to a climax. Carranza won the specific argument and President Wilson generalized the experience into a universal doctrine of self-determination of nations, nonintervention, and equal rights of small and great powers. The lesson we learned from our dealings with Mexico reinforced an earlier commitment to the idea of the "coordinate" state, and has served us well in two world wars. Mexico has stood by the doctrines and the policy unfolded by Carranza. In following that policy it has played a significant part in the growth of the Pan-American system. Its refusal to attend the meeting in Santiago, Chile, in 1923, because—not being recognized by the United States—it could not have its ambassador in Washington and could not participate in formulating the agenda of the conference, led to a change in the rules of the Pan-American Union. Membership and representation on the governing board became independent of recognition by the United States. Furthermore, the chairmanship of the governing board became elective, while it had hitherto been held by the United States secretary of state.

Mexico's continued pressure was an important influence in causing the United States to abandon the right of intervention at the Buenos Aires Conference in 1936. Mexico's belief in the sovereign independence of small states made it a fervent defender of Ethiopia against Mussolini, and of the Spanish

Republic against Mussolini and Hitler. It automatically aligned Mexico on the side of the United States against Germany's destruction of independent European nations. It also made Mexico an active participant in elaborating the policies that have converted the Pan-American system into the Organization of American States, embodying the principles of nonintervention, territorial integrity, and collective defense in this hemisphere. It has supported the United States in its opposition to the expansion of totalitarian influence, and if it differed with the American government in Caracas in 1954 on the Guatemalan issue, it was on the grounds of nonintervention. It was not supporting communism. Much the same could be said of the Mexican government's policy of recognition of the Castro government since the early 1960s. It was fighting for the principles it had defended in the long controversy with the Mexican oil companies. It might be added here that Mexico's nationalism in matters of natural resources and foreign invest-ment has not remained unnoticed by other nations.

The sum of the visible changes that have followed the Revolution have made Mexico a freer, more democratic, and more prosperous nation. But in spite of the optimism and the energy of these turbulent years, the country is poor, the political process clogged by *personalismo* and corruption, and political slogans suggest a growing cynicism. The earlier faith has been worn down by the stubborn recalcitrance of a difficult milieu. Both native and foreign critics have looked upon the current mood with a jaundiced eye, and have talked about crises, and even about the betrayal of the Revolution. But the critics expect what nature will not provide—a straight line of development, a visible logic in human affairs.

What may be said about these turbulent years that we call the Revolution is that they forged a new sense of identity in the people, and that the Revolution has given them a vision of freedom and a sense of growth that are more important than the accomplishments or failures in the economic or political spheres.

There is something in Mexico that was not there before. There is a renascence in matters of the spirit.

[1956]

Spontaneity and Adaptation in the Mexican Revolution

The Mexican Revolution raises many interesting and difficult questions of historical causation and transmission of ideas across time and space. Did European ideas of social change and revolution penetrate the Mexican consciousness to the point where it can be said that there was a visible impact on the minds of the early leaders of the 1910 upheaval? It seems difficult to believe that the ideas of the Enlightenment and of the French Revolution, so widely disseminated over the face of the globe, should not have had a recognizable influence on the leaders of the Mexican Revolution. It is equally difficult to believe that Marxist notions of class struggle should not have played, in 1910, a visible role in shaping both theory and policy in what was to be a deep social change. And yet the evidence for such influence is either lacking or minimal. In this sense, there is a marked contrast between the Russian and the Mexican revolutions.

The French Revolution was a unique event in the history of man. So was the Russian. It is arguable, I think, that the Russian Revolution was a lineal descendant of the French and could probably not have occurred without it. The ideas of the French *philosophes* were a necessary condition for the Russian convulsion, and the ideal of human perfectibility, so dear to the Enlightenment, was a prerequisite for a belief in the perfect state.

Marxism, with its emphasis upon economic determinism, finds its moral justification in the vision of a perfect man in a state so ideal that it no longer functions. But the Mexican

Revolution was little influenced by either Marxism or the ideas of the Enlightenment. Even the liberalism so current during the nineteenth century, with its emphasis upon individualism, played a limited role in the development of the ideas and policies of the Mexican movement.

To say that the Mexican movement was spontaneous in idea and objective would be reasonably true. It was little touched by the jargon of social revolution current at the end of the nineteenth century and the first decades of the twentieth century. Whatever influence one can trace—say, in the Flores Magón brothers—of Marxist, or better, perhaps, anarchistic ideas was marginal in the development of the program of the Mexican movement. The ideas of economic determinism, of class conflict, of proletarian revolution, of a dictatorship of the proletariat, of the expropriation of the possessing classes, of proletarian justice, of a classless society, of the withering-away of the state, of a centralized direction of the economy, of the complete control of all thought, action, and program by an all-powerful party, or the notion that the Mexican Revolution was part of a universal liberation from capitalism, imperialism, colonialism—all of these were absent from the minds of the early leaders of the movement. One can read the debates of the Constitutional Convention of 1917 and find almost no reference to the ideas that preoccupied the socialists, anarchists, and communists of Europe. The very language of convulsive revolution is missing. The words, phrases, and slogans that depict complete liberation, expressed, for example, in "Workers of the world, unite! You have nothing to lose but your chains," are absent. There is no concept of cataclysm, of complete destruction of the past, of a new birth or a new society.

What have come out of the Mexican Revolution have been many changes as adaptations to the environment, as emendations to an older society, as discoveries of new ways of doing things better and more justly than they had been done in the past. The complaints were specific. There was no general philosophical concept, no universal objective, and no claim to universal sanction. The grievances of early leaders like Madero dealt with the absence of honest elections, effective suffrage, the opportunity to run for office, and the freedom to criticize the government. The Revolution was mainly a demand by a new generation for access to power. It was revolutionary in the limited sense of demanding the abolition of corruption, self-perpetuation in office, and nepotism, and in insisting on the adherence to the Constitution of 1857.

There was little in the programs of Madero or Carranza—for example, in the so-called plans of San Luis Potosí and of Guadalupe—that can be described as social or economic. The Revolution began with Madero and was carried forward by Carranza; and, if one looks at the generals who led the armies to victory, it would be difficult to find an ideologist, in the European sense, among them.

When the movement began to specify its objectives, they were practical, limited, and immediate. The abolition of the *tienda de raya* was one of them. (It was a general store attached to a *hacienda* where purchases were compulsory for all people serving on the estate, a focal point of debt peonage.) Payment of wages in cash rather than token coin was another objective. The return of the land to the villages—which had been robbed of their legitimate holdings—was a third. Not even Zapata asked for the complete destruction of the *hacienda*. The *Plan de Ayala*, after returning the lands taken from the villages, would have taken, on the basis of prior compensation, one third of the *haciendas* for the landless. Carranza's decree of January 6, 1915, which authorized the restitution of the land to the dispossessed villages, called for applying the agrarian legislation, after the fighting was over, with a view toward maintaining an equilibrium among the different social forces. Not until 1927 was it established that all villages, even if they had no political or legal status, were eligible to receive an *ejido*. Even later, in the midst of the Cárdenas period, one of the leading agrarianists in Mexico said that the agrarian movement meant only the giving of land to the villages to supplement their income derived from working on the estates. The agrarian revolution was written into the program of the Revolution by Zapata, but it was not a revolutionary program in the European sense. It had limited objectives. It was not a plan for the absolute destruction of one social system and the creation of another. Zapata would save the landowners two thirds of their holdings and Carranza would maintain a balance of social forces.

How practical and how immediate the revolutionary idea was may be seen from the statement of objectives made by General Calles, one of the conspicuously creative leaders of the Mexican Revolution. One day in the early thirties, I asked Calles, then at the height of his power and prestige: *"¿A dónde va, mi general?"*—Where are you going?—and he replied: "We will make a village out of the *hacienda* with a school in the center [*casco*]." "And the city?" I asked. The reply was immediate, sharp, and had a note of finality to it: *"No cuenta"*—the city does not matter. The important point here is the idea of the village: a small community with a school in the middle, owning its own land and free from domination by the *hacienda*. The concept had nothing to do with class struggle, universal revolution, the ideal man, or the ideal state. It was, in fact, a non-European notion. This attitude towards the land and the village was precolonial.

In Mexico over 80 percent of the total inhabited places were located inside of plantations and were without legal status (*acasillados*). It was not until the law of 1927, seventeen years after the Revolution began, that these inhabited places were made legally competent to receive land, and it was not until the Cárdenas regime that a comprehensive land-distribution program was undertaken; but even then, Cárdenas gave the cattle ranches in the north a twenty-year guarantee of nonaffectability. And the agrarian laws provided that the landowner was entitled to keep his house and a minimum of 150 hectares of irrigated or arable land. There was also during all of these years the legal concept of the individual small holding, which was to remain unaffected by the agrarian law. None of this amounts to a universal concept of expropriation by the state suddenly enforced by a government fiat. It was, at most, an attempt to ameliorate a historically difficult situation. The program grew with the developing Revolution. More land was distributed as more villages became politically conscious; the agrarian movement is still going on.

The central element in the agrarian program has been the *ejido*. The *ejido* has both precolonial and colonial roots. As it came to fruition in the Revolution, it represented a legal concept governing real property that could not be fitted into any generalized revolutionary formula. An *ejido* is a given tract of land transferred to a village to be managed by a committee. The land does not belong to the village. It acts as custodian. It must give the land in specified extensions to the individuals within the village who are eligible to receive them. The land does not belong to the individual who receives it. He cannot sell, mortgage, or transfer it, though it can be inherited. To keep it, he must work it himself. He cannot hire labor to work it for him. If he fails to work the land, it returns to the village. But the village may not hold it; it must transfer the recovered land to someone else. The village may not sell or transfer the land away from those entitled to work it. Nor does it belong to the state. No one can condemn or expropriate the village holding. In case of unavoidable necessity, only the president, by making available an equally desirable section of land in the closest neighborhood possible, may require the village to give up its holding and accept the land offered it in the new location. Something like half of Mexico's tillable land is now in *ejidos,* the other half is mainly in small individual holdings.

I am not concerned here with the merits of this system of landownership. I am concerned with an attitude towards the land and its legal, political, and social implications; obviously, what is important here is the village. Its land is sacred, for it cannot be sold, mortgaged, or alienated in any way whatsoever. Equally significant is the meager role of the state. It neither owns nor manages the *ejido* except through credit institutions like the *Banco Ejidal.* But this is not the intent either of the original law or of those who established the bank. In fact, the state is eliminated from its operations as these are in the hands of a committee organized on the basis of law. The *ejido* assumes the form of democratic government in the small rural community. This is consistent with ancient tradition that survives to this day in villages that managed to hold on to their lands through the centuries.

If any one idea may be said to have dominated the first twenty years of the Revolution, it was this vision of a nation of self-governing villages. All other aspects of the developing society seemed secondary and unimportant, and to this day the major preoccupation of the government and of those who call themselves revolutionaries is with the land and the people who till it. Labor, industrialization, nationalism all became significant issues early in the Revolution, but they did not move to the center of the stage until after the violence had died down, until the armed peasants and soldiers had laid down their arms, and until the major battles of the Revolution had been fought and won by men of the soil, most of whom knew little of social theory or even of letters. This discussion refers to what occurred between 1910 and 1940. Since then there have developed additional features not evident in the first thirty years of the Revolution.

The attitude towards the land as something inalienable, something sacred and endowed with special significance for the well-being of man and the nation, was enshrined in Article 27 of the 1917 Constitution. The article is unique and probably could only have been written in Mexico, where the historical experience with the land has been so many-sided. After declaring that the land belongs to the nation and that subsoil rights may only be granted to private individuals or corporations for exploitation by special concession, Article 27 goes on to describe what kind of physical and moral persons may own land, what kind of land they may own, and the conditions under which they may retain it. It establishes the principle of limitation of the size of agricultural holdings, which it leaves to the states to determine. It provides for a family patrimony that cannot be alienated even by the family. It distinguishes and defines varying types of ownership of the surface by Mexicans, foreigners, churches, private or public charitable and educational institutions, commercial stock companies, banks, foreign or Mexican corporations, communal villages, and other types of permissible ownership of urban land and rural holdings, including mortgages. Finally, it establishes the right of government agencies to own and use such land as they require for their needs.

Article 27, with its many modifications embodied in the laws applying its principles to agrarian legislation, irrigation, forestry, grazing land, colonization, and other matters requiring the use of land, reflects the unique character of the Mexican Revolution. The Revolution cannot be neatly categorized as socialist, communist, nationalist, or by any other universalized formula. If we are to give a name to the concepts embodied in Article 27, we may call them the "doctrine of conditional ownership." It is meant to meet the many different kinds of needs of a society where the nomad, like the Huichol Indian, exists side by side with the modern corporation. Between these extremes, all types of land use in a society as complex as Mexico are given separate legal protection. The formula provided by Article 27 has a protean quality and is broader in scope than the law of real property. The emphasis seems generally to fall upon the use of the land. It favors the village, the small as against the large owner, the Mexican as against the foreigner, but it retains the principle of private property even if it conditions its use.

A handbill announcing a meeting of the *Confederación Nacional Agraria* in the 1920s (the printed sheet has no year) said that "Given the protean right of property, all forms of exploitation are possible," and added with pride that no country had achieved so just a notion of this right, "a concept that all the peoples are seeking and one that Russia will undoubtedly arrive at some time in the future." I suggest that this is a good case for spontaneity in ideas and form in social development.

Another aspect of the Mexican Revolution, perhaps, can be described as adaptation. I am referring to the Labor Code written into the Constitution of 1917. I say "perhaps" because I am not sure that here, as in the agrarian legislation, there was not something new, something spontaneous, that may have sprung from foreign sources, but, in fact, was converted to an original theme in modern industrial relations. It must be remembered that in 1910 or in 1917, Mexico was not an industrial nation. It had no large-scale proletariat, the workers took a minimal part in the fighting of the revolutionary battles, and labor organizations were primitive, small, and without any significant political influence. The *Casa del Obrero Mundial,* which flourished for a short period, was a platform primarily for some Spanish anarchists. It was closed down by Carranza, and in the Constitutional Convention of 1917 there were only half a dozen labor leaders, some from states like Yucatán that had no industry. And yet this convention wrote into the constitution the most elaborate code of labor's rights then in existence.

The code, unlike the agrarian one, did not come out of Mexican experience. It was compiled by a group working under Carranza from the legislation, administrative practices, and judicial decisions of the industrial nations. Here were drawn together in a single constitutional article the legal provisions taken from Germany, England, the United States, Australia, New Zealand, and other nations. This elaborate constitutional provision was offered to a country where there was neither an industrial laboring class nor a developed industrial system.

The code has had many uses. Among others, it may be said to have created the trade union movement. The right of labor to organize was sanctioned in the constitution and police powers were employed to keep a factory closed where there was a legal strike. The legality of a strike was determined by a board of arbitration in which the government had the deciding voice. In the early years of the trade union movement—and this was especially true under Obregón and Calles—the government systematically and deliberately used its powers to stimulate the organization of the trade unions. For instance, delegates to the annual national trade union conventions would receive free passes on the railroads, and labor leaders would be given jobs in the government and allowed to spend their time on trade union affairs. The trade unions became important politically to the government, especially in its difficulties with foreign companies. By an alignment with the American Federation of Labor, the Mexican trade union movement was able to secure the support of this powerful influence with the American people and government in defense of the Revolution and its policies. The point is that a constitutional provision derived from non-Mexican experience was here nationalized and put to political use in building an internal labor movement and an external labor alliance in support of a government that had come to power mainly on the shoulders of a peasant army and with objectives chiefly determined by the needs of the rural population.

All of this had little to do with socialism, communism, theoretical syndicalism, or the earlier influence of the Spanish anarchists. The C.R.O.M. (*Confederación Regional Obrera Mexicana*) was a practical labor organization, not unlike those in the United States, which directed its members to improve the conditions of labor and to support the government that had brought the trade union movement to its power and prestige. These developments might be described as an adaptation of European ideas, but it was a special kind of adaptation and it should, I think, be spoken of as the Mexicanization of the ideas inherent in a developing trade union movement. The sum of the provisions in Article 123, which deal with the rights of labor, was quite comprehensive and was obviously not immediately enforceable. The history of the last fifty years is the story of the gradual application of these provisions to the developing industrial system. It is also the history of the increasing influence of the government in the trade union movement. Given the role the government played in the development of organized labor, this was probably inevitable.

There is one feature of this development that is deeply

significant. The Labor Code, when laid before the Constitutional Convention of 1917, was defended on the grounds of reassertion of rights, of protection of the weak, of preventing monopolies, and especially of balancing the power of the worker against the employer as a means of making certain that justice would prevail. Even the provision for profit sharing was defended on the ground of harmonizing the interests of the two parties in the industrial process. It was further justified—and this in 1917—as promoting greater efficiency because it would stimulate the interest and cooperation of the workers in the establishments in which they were employed. The right to strike as developed in legislation was to be conditioned by the ability of the factory to meet the demands of the workers. The one thing the workers could not do was bankrupt their employers. The doctrine of social function apparently applied not only to land but also to industrial institutions. This brings to mind the statement of General Cárdenas to the employers in Monterrey when they threatened to shut down their factories. He told them that if they were tired of the struggle, they could surrender their industries to the state or to the workers. The one thing they could not do was close them down. We are a long way from the theme of "Workers of the world, unite! You have nothing to lose but your chains," and even further from the notion of social cataclysm and the sudden falling-away of all evil and the appearance of heaven upon earth. If the word "revolution" is to be taken in the European sense—as exemplified by the French and Russian upheavals—then some other name will have to be given to this deeply national and Mexican process of self-discovery.

It is as a form of national self-discovery that the Mexican Revolution is most significant. When Manuel Gamio wrote *Forjando Patria*, describing the forging of a nation, he was talking primarily about the internal state of Mexico. It lacked the cohesiveness of a nation. It was this lack of internal unity that made Mexico the stepmother to its own children and the mother to foreigners. There was the large Indian population that had not become identified with the Mexican nation. It was even beyond the rim of Mexican culture; for the mass of the *peones*, who were not Indians but who lived as *acasillados* inside the *hacienda* without civil rights, illiterate, and tied to the soil, were nearly as far away from the "nation" and its culture as were the Indians. The ruling elements in Mexico were largely foreign in outlook and viewed the *peones* and Indians, who were the bulk of the population, with contempt. The Indian and the *peón* were described as "noneconomic" and the hope was expressed that they could be replaced by European immigrants. All of this was being said in official journals up to the very eve of the Revolution of 1910.

The real Mexican Revolution was moral. It was the acceptance of all the people as Mexicans, as equals. It was the complete repudiation of what might be called internal colonialism. It was really the definitive repudiation of the Spanish Conquest and the rediscovery of Mexican history as a continuity, as something that was there before Cortés, and a recognition that the people of Mexico were not just the descendants of the *conquistadores*, or even of the *mestizos*. The Indian, too, was a Mexican. In fact, the history of Mexico was what had happened to the Indian. The Revolution was the recognition that the past of Mexico was in Mexico and not in Europe. This nationalism was not anti-European or anti-American. It was more a sense of indifference to the outside world. What has come with the Revolution was unplanned. For no one could know that its most significant by-product would be moral and aesthetic.

The discovery of the Mexican by the Mexican—*lo mexicano en el Mexicano,* as Leopoldo Zea put it—has changed the attitude of the people towards each other, towards Mexico, and towards the outside world. The Mexican has taken a good look at himself and likes what he sees. He no longer wishes to be a European or an American. He is proud of what he is, of what he has done, of what he is doing, and of what he hopes to do. The Mexicans of today are not unlike the Greeks in their classical period. Like the Greeks, they consider all people living beyond their border as barbarians, as somehow not well-endowed, less gifted, less worthy. How this came about is hard to say. Somehow, the Mexicans stopped being afraid of each other and of the outside world, especially of the United States. The psychological impact of the oil expropriation in 1938 was very high, but so was the carrying-through of the agrarian reform and the demonstration by Cárdenas that Mexico could be governed without violence.

[1965]

Lázaro Cárdenas

It is not at this time possible to write a completely objective and definitive estimate of the role Lázaro Cárdenas has played in Mexico, and it is doubtful that a friend should attempt to do so. General Cárdenas does not like to be praised. "It isn't good for political figures to be praised," he once said while still in the presidency, and he has continued being a political figure in spite of his desire to avoid politics after leaving office.

He once said, "The people must learn that the President of Mexico can retire." "How?" "I will go to Jiquilpán in Michoacán and have a policeman put all friends who come to see me in jail." "Will you also put me in jail if I come to visit you?" "Yes, unless you promise to talk about the Peruvian Indians and not about Mexican affairs."

This desire to avoid being involved in politics after leaving office has been hard to fulfill. "Why do you keep on traveling about so much instead of staying in your house in Mexico City?" "Because my house would be crowded with politicians to my own and to the government's embarrassment."

In part, this avoidance of the public, the effort to escape publicity, to keep out of sight, is owed to natural shyness. His political courage and political involvement are a matter of duty. His preference is for the intimacy of a few personal friends and for good talk about the world and its affairs. In part, also, this effort to stay out of the limelight is owed to the sagacity of an experienced hand in Mexican politics.

The attempt to retire and to withdraw from public consciousness stems from a desire to break with the ingrained tradition of the *caudillo*. "This people must learn the lesson of legality." For him, the only way to teach this lesson was to make himself unavailable to those who looked for a leader in opposition to the government. "I will support a bad government for its legal period rather than a revolution to establish a good government." He said this while still in the presidency and he kept his word. Surely the elections of Ávila Camacho, Miguel Alemán, Adolfo Ruiz Cortines would not have been the relatively peaceful and polite affairs they were if it had not been known that Cárdenas stood in the path of a revolution against the officially sponsored candidate, or, if one prefers, against the candidate of the officially sponsored political party.

It is interesting to note that Cárdenas is not the leader of a political party, and he is not the head of the army. Yet his influence in Mexican public affairs has been great since his retirement from office and, on occasions such as the preservation of public peace during the Alemán administration, it was decisive.

Politically, this is a phenomenon in Latin America. For the influence, it may be said, emanates from the individual rather than the office he might hold. In this sense Cárdenas reminds one of Gandhi. This comparison may seem surprising to Mexicans, who might prefer other terms. When, as an immensely popular leader, he traveled throughout the country, enthusiastic crowds would shout, "*¡Viva el presidente macho!*" However, the comparison has many points in its favor. Cárdenas is a complex and many-sided human being, but the features of simplicity, gentleness, and compassion are the most conspicuous. There are innumerable experiences that illustrate these qualities. One day, coming down the unfinished road between Popocatepetl and Ixtaccihuatl, one of the torrential rains that occur in Mexico suddenly poured down from the sky. The president saw a barefoot Indian walking along the road covering himself with a straw raincoat. Cárdenas stopped the car, made his adjutant call the drenched Indian into the automobile, and drove with him down to where he wanted to go. I felt certain that the surprised pedestrian had no idea of whose car he was riding in and, as he spoke no Spanish, he could only express his gratitude by a gesture.

Those who had occasion to travel with Cárdenas in the country will remember the simplicity and selflessness of his devotion to the people. Cárdenas would stand against the wall of a building in the hot sun for hours listening to men, women, and children who crowded to get near him and ask for favors; then the president would write down their names and what they wanted, and, sitting up half the night, he would arrange these notes so that they could be given to the proper cabinet member to satisfy the requests he had granted. I have seen him grill a member of his cabinet months later as to what he had done with those orders. His unfailing memory could prove embarrassing to an indolent official.

One day, long after he had retired from the presidency, we were driving down a steep mountain road in Michoacán near the *azufreras de San Andrés*. These are numerous sulphur springs of varying size and color, scattered over a wide mountainous area. It was raining hard when we noticed two people carrying a sick old man up a steep slippery hill. He had been brought here for treatment in the local hot springs. His middle-aged daughter was waiting for him by a truck in which he was to be transported back home again. In spite of the rain, Cárdenas got out of his car, sent his adjutant down the slippery hillside to help carry the crippled old man; then he asked the forlorn woman if she had a doctor, what town she lived in, how long her father had been ill, and, taking note of it all, promised to send his own physician to examine him and to see if some arrangements could be made for the old man to be cared for in some public institution.

Cárdenas was, during his presidency, completely identified with the people. He traveled over the country from village to village and town to town as no chief executive had ever done before and without any sense of personal danger. When once I remarked to him that he was risking his life unnecessarily by a complete disregard of personal safety, he replied in a poetic phrase that I have never forgotten, *"Es mejor morir haciendo el bien que mantenerse vivo haciendo el mal."*

One day during the height of the excitement after the oil expropriation in 1938, we visited a city in Vera Cruz where thousands of people crowded the streets and shouted themselves hoarse in cheering him. Late that afternoon we slipped out the back door of the building we were in and went to visit the local hospital in a converted monastery. It was dark inside, as the windows were high and narrow. The long hall was filled with sick people on their beds. As we walked along, the president stopped and talked to each patient. About halfway across the hall, he suddenly said to one of them, "Didn't I see you today in the crowd when I arrived this morning?" "Yes, Mr. President. I am not so sick that I am not allowed to go out during the day for a little while. Yes, I was in the crowd that welcomed you to our city." Later when we left the hospital I said, "If I had not been present, I would not have believed the story of your recognizing a patient in dim light on a day when thousands of people crowded the streets." "There is nothing strange about it. I noticed a pale man in the crowd and thought that if he asked me for help I would give him 20 pesos, but he didn't ask me." Many hours later Cárdenas was able to identify him as a patient in the hospital.

These personal experiences are so typical of the man that one could fill a volume with them, but the purpose here is mainly to assess the role of Cárdenas in Mexican history. I shall confine myself to a limited number of the things he oversaw as president—the agrarian reform, the oil expropriation, and the effort to teach the Mexican people that the president can retire.

In talking one day about the basis of Mexican politics, Cárdenas remarked, "When all the land belongs to the villages, the government will also belong to them. Now the government rests on the army." The agrarian reform was politically motivated. The government could only belong to the villages when the land belonged to them. Mexican democracy could only become a reality when the *hacienda* system would disappear. The redemption of the rural population economically and socially would express itself in the transfer of political power to the mass of the people, the *campesinos*. The carrying-out of the agrarian reform, so often promised and so often postponed, was, therefore, more than a vindication of rights, or an act of social justice. It was not merely a return of lands lost. It was an expression of faith in the *campesino* and the Indian and in the rural village. The rural folk standing on their own land, free from domination by the *hacendado*, would not only govern their own village, but collectively govern the nation.

There is something of the older, Jeffersonian Democrat in Cárdenas. For him, the big city didn't really matter. I remember one day remarking that the military who served him seemed to have more integrity and a better sense of the nation than many of his civilian followers. "It is perfectly natural," he said. "The military are raised in the country, where everything is healthy, while the civilians are raised in the city, where everything is corrupt."

A nation of independent self-governing villages, where each individual was assured a place in his own *ejido*, was free from exploitation, and became an active participant in the affairs of his community—such was his ideal. The six years of the Cárdenas administration, from 1934 to 1940, were not long enough to pattern all of Mexico; to distribute all of the land; to set all of the villages on a firm basis; to educate enough leaders; to find the finances for all of the needs of all of the villages and all of their people; and to find a sufficient number of honest, well-trained, devoted, and selfless associates who, like the missionaries of an older day, would give themselves to the task of reconstructing Mexico. It was the lack of dedication among too many of the younger leaders, the worm of self-aggrandizement and personal ambition, that undermined the attempt to remake Mexico in the short period of six years. One thing, however, is perfectly clear. Mexico will be a different country for these heroic endeavors.

The *hacienda* system is dead, and it will not be revived even though the *ejidos* have found a host of unforeseen difficulties in their path. The prospect of a Mexican government resting on the consent of the masses of the people is visibly nearer today than it was in 1934. Certainly, the industrialization and the economic growth of Mexico would not have been possible without the profound changes in the rural community that were wrought by the Cárdenas agrarian program.

If the agrarian reform was politically motivated, so too was the oil expropriation. Its aim was not primarily to transfer the oil wells from foreign to Mexican hands, but to free Mexico from the threat of the oil companies meddling in Mexican politics; it was to keep them "from deciding who the next president of Mexico was going to be" that Cárdenas expropriated the oil companies. He knew of at least one instance in which Saturnino Cedillo had been offered a half-million dollars to start a revolution against his government (and it was not made by an American company). That incident happened relatively early in the Cárdenas administration, before Cedillo had been built up by interested parties to believe that he could be president of Mexico.

The public defiance by the oil companies of the decision of the Mexican Supreme Court, favoring the wage claims of the oil workers, raised the issue of national dignity and political sovereignty. Cárdenas had little choice in the matter. Politically, the oil companies had placed the government in an extremely difficult position and themselves beyond the pale of the law. Under the circumstances, the expropriation decree was the logical reaction of the government.

Whatever the economic results of the action taken by Cárdenas, and these are certainly debatable, there can be no question about its political and psychological consequences. It electrified and united Mexico as it never had been united before, not even during the Independence period. It gave Mexico the sense of having freed itself and of no longer being afraid of the United States. Mexico had achieved political equality with its northern neighbor at one bound, and the experience was exhilarating.

The flow of creative energy and self-confidence that has filled the years since the oil expropriation is a direct result of the spiritual awakening that it precipitated. For the first time in their history, at least since the Spanish Conquest, Mexicans looked at themselves and approved of what they saw. They no longer wanted to be Europeans or North Americans. They were content with being what they were and immersed in their own values. This is where they are different from the Russians. They did not wish to imitate, rival, or surpass the Americans. They had overcome their inferiority complex as the Russians have not. In fact, they could now be quite friendly to the United States.

It is characteristic of Cárdenas that through all of this excitement he kept his head. He uttered no blasts against the American people; did not daily denounce the American government; did not insult the secretary of state or deride the president of the United States. Quite the opposite, he remained a friend of U.S. Ambassador Josephus Daniels, and once remarked, "It was my good fortune to be President of Mexico when Roosevelt was President of the United States." During the height of the diplomatic excitement, he never lost his perspective; he was quite concerned with the defense of the Western Hemisphere and was prepared for a joint policy against the threat of German aggression.

His feeling about Roosevelt was suggested by the remark "Two men of good will, if they sat down together, could settle this issue." All through the excitement, opposition, and attacks in the American press and the boycott by the oil companies, Cárdenas kept his equanimity and assumed no heroic posture. Dignity, simplicity, a quiet voice, and a friendly gesture were characteristic of his behavior throughout what must have been a trying and grueling experience.

Beyond the importance of his agrarian and oil policies lies the effort to teach the people of Mexico "that they can be governed without violence," that the Mexican nation can be ruled without the *Ley Fuga*, without brutality, without the strong hand not only of a Díaz, but also of an Obregón and a Calles. Cárdenas looked for a way to convert the nation to the ideal of legality, to the transfer of power without a *cuartelazo*, and to its assumption without a revolution.

It must be remembered that this insistence upon a peaceful transfer of the executive office was, insofar as Mexico was concerned, an innovation. If Cárdenas succeeded in banishing revolution as the expected means of transferring power, then his service to his country will be beyond measure. As long as violence is the ever-present prospect of political change, all other reforms are tentative and hang in the balance, for no one can surely predict the course of a revolution once it has been let loose.

His mere presence has kept the peace and made elections possible without too much violence and certainly without revolution, but what will happen when he is no longer on the stage no one can foretell. Here, I think, lies the greatest failure of the Mexican Revolution. It has not institutionalized the process of the transfer of power in the sense that it has not developed a political party system drawing its effective power from the thousands of communities that constitute the Mexican nation. The *Partido Revolucionario Institucional*, whatever it is, is not a political party. It is a tool of the government, or better, perhaps, a tool of the executive. Cárdenas himself recognized that the time has long since come for Mexico to have an effective two-party system. He also recognized that the time has come for the Mexican government to try to decentralize its powers and transfer some of its prerogatives to the states. It may prove impossible in a single lifetime to persuade a nation steeped in an authoritarian tradition and habituated to violence as an instrument of politics to accept instead the less dramatic but more peaceful process of political argument and party dissidence. If this is so, then Cárdenas will have failed in his most important effort.

A short essay such as this does not permit a full discussion either of the man or of all of his policies. One must, however, mention his support of Finland against Russia, of Ethiopia against Mussolini, of the Spanish Republic, and his admission to Mexico of so many Spaniards driven from their land. He opposed Nazi Germany and supported Roosevelt's policies against Hitler long before we were involved in the war. Cárdenas will be remembered for his support of trade unionism —though I think he lacked a full understanding of the nature of this institution in the modern world—his broad program of road building, and his continuation of the irrigation policy.

It always seemed to me that his greatest weakness was in the choice of some of his civilian collaborators. He had many loyal and competent men about him, but certainly not all could qualify for these terms of praise. Finally, and possibly most important of all, were his singular patience, good humor, and compassion for human frailty. He ruled Mexico for six years without killing anyone, without filling the jails with political prisoners, without driving anyone into exile, without a policy of "liquidating" his enemies, without denying the people their right of petition, without suppressing freedom of speech or assembly, without braggadocio, bombast, or theatrical postures. During his years in office, fear for the first time passed away from among the Mexican people and the humblest human being had access to the president of the country. He would listen in patience to the lowliest of his fellows and he could, as he once remarked, if all other things failed him, *"al menos la paciencia tengo para dárselos."* And that is why they have always loved and followed him.

[1960]

Latin America
as a Field of Study
for the Social Scientist

Unless what one writes about Latin America is recognized as legitimate and meaningful by Latin Americans, one has misplaced much time and effort. But how does one accomplish being accepted on the high ground of having understood, recognized, and evaluated a facet of social existence, past or present, with such acumen that those born to the culture accept what has been contrived as legitimate, "as if it had been done by one of us"? This has nothing to do with point of view or with critical judgment. It has something to do with having become an "insider" without having lost the earmarks of being an "outsider." The latter I suspect one can never quite achieve. It has something to do with "flavor," unconscious involvement, evident immersion in the culture to a point where one is no longer conscious of being immersed. This is a precondition of validity without which most work must remain faulty or just inaccurate, even if all the facts are true. I remember a distinguished Peruvian historian remarking on a two-volume *History of Latin America*, written by an American professor, *"¡Qué historia!"* To some extent this was a comment on many of the American textbook histories so widely used in American universities. There is something the matter with them. It is not an insufficiency of facts; it is a lack of involvement on the part of the author. The tone in which the material is presented is wrong. It reminds me of a statement by an American naval intelligence officer, who remarked that "we know everything about that country, the depth of the seaports, the number of people, the names of the political parties, the biographies of the leaders, the height of the mountains—in fact everything there is to know—but we do not understand what is going on."

How does one acquire understanding? That is the real question. The answer, I suspect, is that every student and scholar must find his own way to whatever light he may ultimately have. On this crucial issue no one can really help him consciously. One can facilitate access to material, bibliography, libraries, people, but all of these are incidental and may have little bearing on the insight and wisdom he will ultimately garner, and on how much light he will shed.

What follows is primarily concerned with the question of orientation and approach to the subject rather than with the subject itself. It is also principally devoted to the training of students who are going to work in the field.

Speaking primarily of American students, though it probably applies to Europeans as well, one must begin by recognizing that Latin America is *terra incognita* in the literal sense of the word. It is so much an unknown world to most American students that it is difficult for them to discover a sense of direction—or perhaps it would be truer to say that, culturally speaking, they cannot feel the ground they stand on. In their vast majority, they are oriented towards Europe. From their earliest days, a large part of their education is European. The children's stories, the fables, the fairy tales, the gossip of their parents and their grandparents, some of the early books they read are mostly European in origin or have been influenced by European experience. As they get on in years, they become acquainted with Shakespeare, Shelley, Byron, Dickens, Galsworthy, Shaw; with Goethe, Schiller, Gerhart Hauptmann, Kant, Max Weber, or Bismarck; with Voltaire, Rousseau, Anatole France, Proust, and many others. All of this is built upon a background of Greek and Roman history and literature, with Plato, Aristotle, Virgil, and Cicero, to pick names at random. Almost any American graduate student undertaking research in England, France, Germany, or Italy has his feet on the ground or has a sense of direction when he starts out on his adventure. He is already a European, Englishman, Frenchman, German, or Italian, not only because he has learned the language but because he is culturally an insider even if he has only a meager knowledge of the institutional development of the country he is going to. The inner sense of meaning is not completely beyond his ken. He is not a total stranger to the values, attitudes, *Weltanschauung* of the area he is seeking to work in. Half or more of his problem—the key to the meaning of things—is in his possession before he begins his work.

On the other hand, the average American graduate student either has no knowledge of Latin America, or what he presumably knows may well be a caricature, or he may begin with a strong prejudice against the area because of the slanted information that may have come his way. It is probably no exaggeration to say that not one in a hundred, perhaps not one in a thousand, graduate students in the United States could, off-hand, mention a dozen significant names either in literature or in politics for all of Latin America. He simply lacks contact with the area and has none of that kind of emotional and ideational background that ties him to Europe and gives him a sense of direction. He really does not know his way about. This is what I meant by Latin America being a *terra incognita*.

Even at a much less significant level of understanding, the American and, I suppose, the European student is unaware of the inner basis of political and institutional life in Latin America. I can illustrate the point by giving some American and English examples. If a foreign student who is going to do serious research in the United States is not perceptive of that strange phenomenon called the Democratic party or the special role of the supreme court, or of the very complex and personal relations that exist between the president and the Congress, then he is due to have great difficulty in making a thoughtful study of any significant American problem. Similarly, anyone planning re-search on an English problem who does not understand the historical significance of the phrase "King in Parliament," the special conditions that through the centuries have tied the justice of the peace to the House of Commons, or the personal and family ties that have so often bound the House of Lords to the House of Commons, or the special place in English history occupied by the manor and the manorial court will simply meander if he is trying seriously to deal with any important issue in English social, political, or economic history. The point is that most American students approaching Europe have a sense of the fitness of things within the culture that they lack for Latin America. And the difficulty is a major one, because what one knows about Europe one has mainly acquired unconsciously in the process of growing up rather than by formal instruction.

The question to be asked is how can this deficiency be remedied. The answer, I think, is that it cannot be fully corrected. To do so would require a complete realignment of American or European ways, which is manifestly absurd. Something will in time be done by formal education but it will be little. Those responsible for training future scholars to work in Latin America must recognize this matter as a major obstacle. There are two suggestions that occur to me. The first is that anyone proposing to work there in any of the social sciences should give himself a good grounding in the literature, especially the novels and poetry. This is where he will find access to those many undefined elements in the culture without which one cannot really "understand what is going on," to use the phrase of the naval intelligence officer cited above. And what he will find in the literature he will find nowhere else, neither in history, sociology, political science, nor economics. In one sense, the other disciplines will only become meaningful if the student has a broad knowledge of the literature. The other suggestion is that the student go to Latin America for a somewhat lengthy period. I would suggest a minimum of two years—one of which should be spent in extensive travel and in developing the widest possible personal contacts. The travel should be mainly outside the large cities. These suggestions will not initially give him what the American student possesses as a matter of course before he gets started on his study of Europe—but they will contribute to setting him on his way toward a career as a scholar in the area.

In many ways an intellectual involvement for the American and, I presume, European student with Latin America is beset with difficulties as great as those found in the study of Asia, the Middle East, and Africa. Probably European students have a greater familiarity with China, India, and Egypt than with Ecuador, Paraguay, or even Brazil and Mexico. Partly this is due to the inconclusive state of Latin American culture. The complex of Spaniard or Portuguese, Indian and Negro, has not yet worked an amalgam. One cannot speak of a mature society here as one can of Germany or France. Nor is the nation in many places, except in a legal sense, fully developed. The nation may consist of mutually antagonistic elements as, for instance, in Guatemala, Ecuador, and Peru. Who, in these countries, speaks for all of the nation—the *criollo,* the *mestizo,* the Indian, the church, the army, the government? We are dealing with a society that has not yet found its cultural design and that cannot be described in the general terms one may use when writing about Britain or France.

The intellectual, foreign and native, has tended to slight the reality, and to write about themes that are essentially biased by European experience and education. It is a matter of no mean significance that the *hacienda* should, until very recently, have received no serious attention from Latin Americans—the novelists excepted. Here is an institution that has deeply influenced the social, political, economic, and cultural life in all of Latin America and yet neither sociologist, historian, economist, nor political scientist has probed the subject with the seriousness it deserves. One might ask why this basic institution has remained so neglected. The reasons are probably numerous. I would, however, like to suggest two. Intellectuals have belonged to the limited number of oligarchical landholding families used to an authoritarian tradition, where personal rule has remained incarnate. That kind of society does not allow for self-examination or serious sociological research. An authoritarian tradition does not bring "social problems" into focus. For these same reasons, the social sciences, including history (other than political hero-dominated history), have not flourished in this cultural milieu. The gap that lies between the ideal and the practical, between theory and practice, between the constitution and the government, between the law and its application, between the promise and the fulfillment, has not allowed for social science research.

This discrepancy between the law and the performance goes back to Spanish days. It has persisted and it has pervaded almost every institution. It is easy to find many an astute gloss on the constitution but difficult to discover a realistic study of the political process in any country. The kind of analysis the political scientist takes pleasure in doing in the United States remains to be developed in Latin America. And this separation, between the dream and the reality, is part of the inner workings of the culture itself. It is not a deliberate act; in essence, it is an aspiration for perfection and an indifference to the shortcomings of recalcitrant institutions and the failings of mortal man. The proclamation of the ideal so often repeated is more satisfying and more absorbing than the effort to change a given institution. A continuing focus on the ideal inhibits detailed study of the immediate difficulty. That is why revolution is seemingly so "natural"—it will bring forth the ideal. The current passion for planning belongs to the same mood. It is the promise of fulfillment of man's desires. It is, I suspect, a substitute for facing recalcitrant realities. It is also one way of unconsciously escaping the recognition that it will take time and effort to move from where the society is now to where it will be in the next generation. But the idea that man is capable of and should make a conscious and deliberate choice in shaping the direction of his own culture is somehow ingrained in the *Weltanschauung*, and must be accepted as one of the "facts" of Latin American reality—for an attitude is a "fact" possessed of a dynamic propensity.

How to prepare students that come out of the "materialistic" environment in the United States and Western Europe to face these "real" situations is a major question. It occurs to me that no one ought to go into the field unless he has had training in cultural anthropology and social psychology, with emphasis upon the role of "myth" in social life. Unless the American and European student is prepared to accept the hankering after perfection, the ideal, the absolute as a basic fact in the intellectual and social life of the area, he will misunderstand and misinterpret even the most obvious political phenomena. I am not sure that this lesson can be taught or given its place in a program designed to train future Latin Americanists. It can only be learned on the ground.

The European and American student does not appreciate the historical isolation of Latin America from the great forces that shaped modern Europe. When one asks who the Western European and American is, how he came to be possessed of the peculiar attitudes, values, beliefs, and practices that characterize him, one has to look back to the historical processes that have influenced him and his ways. Modern Western man is the child not only of the Renaissance but of the Protestant Reformation, the Catholic Counter Reformation, the Enlightenment, the French Revolution, the Industrial Revolution, and the great transformations that shifted political power from the hands of a monarch or an aristocracy into the hands of the people. This process, from the Reformation on, was marked by more than four centuries of conflict, violence, revolution, political strife, and many wars, great and small. Latin America has not passed through the crucible of modern European experience. With the exception of a limited number of late European immigrants or exceptional individuals educated in Europe from their childhood, the "modern" attitudes are not "natural" to Latin Americans.

This point is well illustrated in a discussion about the middle class. We are told that it consists of government employees, professionals, and, as an afterthought, businessmen. But the bureaucracy does not belong to the middle class any more than the army officer or the priest. If anything, they are part of the original social structure, part of the traditional hierarchy. The same may be said of the professionals. Like the bureaucrats, they are careerists interested in promotion. The businessman, the entrepreneur, is neither a bureaucrat nor a professional. He is a child of those forces that destroyed a feudal society and does not depend upon "official" support. He uses it and perverts it to get on in the world. The entrepreneur requires a body of beliefs that places the highest value on personal ambition, on the accumulation of wealth, on material progress, on efficiency, on inventiveness, on new things and new ways. Neither the bureaucracy nor the professional is characterized by these values or ambitions. On the whole, the educated Latin American does not in outlook belong to the middle class.

Latin America does not partake of Western ways, pre-cisely because it escaped the crucible within which they were wrought. Its history has not been marked by great social movements, and it belongs in idea to the world before the Reformation. The exceptional Latin American who has shed his own culture and become a "good" European or American will not accept this diagnosis, and argues that his compatriots share his views. If they did, the area would be very different and would have lost much that it values most; it would have gained, in turn, the elements of a culture dominated by the individual who wants to get on in the world. Obviously, this is not the case. What kind of training would best prepare students to understand this world so different from their own? Certainly not modern European history, liberal economics, or the sort of political science that studies voting behavior. A good under-standing of the milieu of medieval Europe would probably be more helpful in approaching Latin America than a reading of Rousseau's *Social Contract* or the speeches by Robespierre.

These are but some of the questions that need to be raised. There are others. It is, I think, impossible to comprehend the Latin American complex without first gaining a vivid sense of its physical configuration. There is little in Europe or in the United

States so varied and so full of contrasts as, say, Bolivia, or Peru, or even Mexico. A trip by automobile from Lima to Pucallpa on the Río Ucayali, which now requires about four days, is an unforgettable experience. It begins at sea level and goes to fourteen or fifteen thousand feet and then down close to sea level again on one of the Amazonian headwaters some 3500 miles away from the Atlantic. The juxtaposition of the wet jungle and the snow-capped mountains supplies an unknown number of different ecological systems as a basis for varied cultural adaptations. In Mexico, for instance, every couple of hundred feet up or down the mountainside reveal a different agricultural setting, different ways of dealing with the natural environment, different clothing, architecture, food and work habits, and, in some places, different traditions, music, and even different language and social organization, especially in the little villages.

One who has not been on the Amazon or spent even a short time on one or more of its tributaries, touched the Wet Forest, climbed by mule-back, or in some places now by car, to the snow line and seen the way man has adapted to the incredibly varied physical environment, or gathered a sense of the natural isolation of the Latin American community locked in on all sides by steep mountains, will fall short of knowing this unique world. The physical difference and distance between Chiapas and Chihuahua or Tabasco and Sonora in Mexico are hard to put in a single formula, a single name, or to describe in their impact on the whole society. There may be other places in the world, especially in the Far East, where the physical contrasts are as sharp, but certainly they are no more dramatic. In Bolivia, Peru, and Ecuador, the snow line at sixteen to eighteen thousand feet and the wet tropics are, as the crow flies, in many places less than a hundred miles apart. And these contrasts are of major dimension. The Amazonian basin is some 2.7 million square miles and the Andean wall it touches stretches from Venezuela and Colombia to the tip of South America some 4500 miles away. On a smaller scale these sharp contrasts repeat themselves in Central America, Mexico, and even in the West Indies. He who would feel at home in the Latin American environment must somehow have touched, felt, and experienced Iquitos and Lima, Manaus and Rio, the desert of the *altiplano,* the water-soaked lands on the Beni in Bolivia, and the flat rich soil that lies outside of Buenos Aires or Rosario in Argentina.

If the student does not count these places in his experience, then he will remain basically uninformed and unenlightened about the special quality of what we call Latin American civilization. He must touch the continent literally with his own hands and absorb some of it through his pores or he will ever remain a pedestrian academician no matter how many books he has read and what dusty documents he has turned over in the archives. The living reality has a specially distinctive ecological base and it can only be comprehended by first acquiring some intimacy with the physical setting to which man has in so many different ways adapted.

This world of contrasts in the physical environment has its counterparts in the many different kinds of societies that abide within it. Europeans have nothing comparable to the diversity in social organization that one may find in most, if not all, parts of Latin America. Economists absorbed by problems of development and interested in capital savings and finances; political scientists concerned with constitutional forms, legislative practices, and political party organization; sociologists interested in the study of cities; and anthropologists engaged in community studies, all may spend much time without becoming aware of the implications of a setting where seemingly all of the variables in human culture are crowded into the same national boundary. Within it, they may find almost every intermediate form of organization, family structure, landholding system, and culture. These different systems, with their separately unique cultural variants, have their own ways, their own "common law," their own persistence, continuity, and ability to survive. The cultural systems in their variety are all part of the nation, even if the national leaders in the capital city are unaware of the fact and speak as if the capital city were the nation. He who would write meaningfully about Latin America must somehow have it in his psychological makeup that he is not writing about France, Germany, England, Denmark, or Italy. Here is a different order of things. The questions of change, growth, development, education, progress, and whatever have different dimensions in this part of the world. The government does not speak for all of the people—for some of them may not know what it is. Outside the urban centers, Latin America is a little-known complex of cultural and social varieties. I have sometimes thought that Americans, with their emphasis upon "success" and individual growth, are peculiarly unprepared to deal with or understand the complex of variables we call Latin America. I suspect that this is less true for Europeans.

We should now consider the contrasts between the city and the country. In Latin America—and in slightly varying degrees this is true everywhere—the difference between urban civilization and rural ways is one of absolutes. In Mexico, the contrast between the inhabitants of Mexico City and the Otomí Indians, who live close to the capital, may be measured by a thousand years. The Otomí do not belong to the Western world at all and have managed to remain beyond its reach in spite of four hundred years of physical contact with the modern, the Western, the civilized. This fact is dramatic—and I cite it for that reason. The point, however, applies in varying degrees everywhere. The big city has everything—from Karl Marx to Sartre, from electric lights to computers, from universities to bookstores—and the country has none of these things; sometimes, as in Guatemala and Peru, it may not even have Spanish. The point is that the rural, in most instances, belongs to the age before industrialism—before, if you like, the discovery of America. We are talking about a feudal heritage dominated by the *patrón*, or a tiny isolated village that tills its poor and often small holdings by methods that have not changed since the discovery of America or earlier. The city, factually and symbolically, has light, while there is only a fagot in the country. These are two separate cultures, two different ways of looking at the world—and, most important, the country is static while the city is dynamic, and they do not communicate with each other. With the exception of a number of community studies by anthropologists, the rural remains virgin soil unstudied and largely unknown—except for some recent work by sociologists in Colombia, Peru, and Brazil. Broadly speaking, the Latin American social scientist is not prepared to do serious work in the rural community—partly because of the kind of education he has received, partly because of the isolation in which it has to be done, and partly because of the low intellectual priority placed on detailed studies dealing with peasant society and its problems. And yet any effort either to understand or to plan for the development of that part of the world must begin by recognizing that a society so sharply differentiated, so clearly made up of urban and rural cultures, will have great difficulty in moving towards becoming an industrial state.

With improved means of travel and communication, there has been a flocking of hundreds of thousands of the rural folk to the urban centers, bringing with them rural customs and habits, crowding the surrounding hills of Caracas, Rio, Lima, untrained for urban life and the city. There is an element of catastrophe in this rapid migration to the city because the city is incapable of either absorbing, employing, or moving the newcomers. The governments have neither the resources to bring a halt to the migration nor the means to find a place for the migrants. No European or American can possibly imagine what a human and political burden this presents unless he has seen those masses of men, women, and children in Bahia, Rio, or Santiago.

Let me add two other items that need to be considered in any attempt to understand Latin America. The name we give the area is deceptive because it carries with it the notion of uniformity and similarity. The facts are quite different. The contrasts between Argentina and Peru are greater than those between Italy and Germany or than between any two European countries. Chile is sharply different from Peru, but so is Colombia from either; Venezuela is unlike any country on the east or west coast. This is equally true of Ecuador and Bolivia. Brazil, with its many sharp regional distinctions, is a universe all by itself. And this uniqueness in national style is true for Uruguay and Paraguay. Despite the many similarities in historical experience, no two countries in South America are sufficiently alike for anyone to assume that, knowing one, he may speak confidently about its neighbor.

These contrasts hold for the relatively small area of Central America. Guatemala and Costa Rica are more unlike each other than Poland and Spain, and Salvador, Honduras, and Nicaragua are each distinctive. No country is like Mexico. In fact, a number of cultures—each with a style of its own—are in process of development, and lumping them together is a matter of convenience for literary purposes rather than a methodologically permissible device for one who is interested in the way a particular nation has come to be what it is and in what trends operate within it.

The student must deeply immerse himself in two or three sharply different national cultures and, in addition, build a general acquaintance with the other countries by wide reading and extensive and frequent visits in widely separated parts of the area. Special consideration must be given to the West Indies, which differ sharply among themselves. A West Indian culture with a dominant African base is developing, something that is neither African, European, nor American—North or South—but distinctly West Indian. The marks of this cultural emergence are even now visible in the music and literature, family, and, one suspects, political organization of the West Indies.

This leads me to my final point, which is perhaps the only one I should have dealt with—the paucity of historical and other social science studies of the area. While countries differ from each other in this respect, it is true to say that, in comparison with the United States and any country in Western Europe, the scholarly production by Latin Americans about themselves or by outsiders about the area is inadequate and, with many honorable exceptions, of insufficient quality.

There are no public libraries, excepting the national library (which is not always properly arranged for a student's needs), that are comparable to similar institutions in the United States and Europe, that have gathered, classified, indexed, and made available the story of the past in many of its facets—from the private papers of an individual to the records of trade unions, churches, business firms, political movements, and so forth. In Latin America, these materials, if they exist at all, are in the hands of a private person and one can gain access to them only with the help of a well-placed friend. The ability to make and keep friends, to be genuinely interested and concerned, and to have a real involvement with the people and their cultural milieu is of primary importance. Personal friends, when one is fortunate enough to have them, will open many doors, get around bureaucratic rules, and facilitate access to what can be made useful—even the machinery of a government department in the collection of materials not otherwise available.

I should like to suggest also that it is not feasible to work on modern Latin America without the accumulation of newspaper files and large collections of pamphlets. These are hard to come by but are indispensable. For various reasons, the innumerable monographs on a thousand subjects one finds in the United States or Europe are substituted for by the signed article in a daily newspaper, a magazine, or a pamphlet. Some of the best books we have are collections of such articles compiled by their authors. Any university seriously interested in training students in the Latin American area would be well advised to collect offset copies of newspapers, magazines, and, if possible, pamphlets. Book publication until very recently was expensive, the sales small, and the authors usually too poor to finance the printing of their own manuscripts. Unless an author could secure government support for publication, he was confined to the signed newspaper article. For instance, no modern history of Peru could be written without a file of *El Comercio*.

The many difficulties posed in this paper are a challenge to the student. They are the occasion for deeper involvement, wider contacts, broader understanding. He who wants to devote a lifetime to the study of Latin America will find a hundred hospitable friends wherever he goes, ready to open every door and provide every assistance. The only condition for such friendship and cooperation is an honest devotion to disinterested scholarship and a companionable involvement with the peoples and their culture.

[1964]

Index

A Note on the Type

This book was set by computer in Janson, a recutting made direct from
type cast from matrices long thought to have been made by the Dutchman
Anton Janson, who was a practicing type founder in Leipzig during the
years 1668–87. However, it has been conclusively demonstrated that these
types are actually the work of Nicholas Kis (1650–1702), a Hungarian,
who most probably learned his trade from the master Dutch type founder
Kirk Voskens. The type is an excellent example of the influential and
sturdy Dutch types that prevailed in England up to the time William
Caslon developed his own incomparable designs from these Dutch faces.

Composed, printed, and bound by The Colonial Press Inc.,
Clinton, Massachusetts. Typography and binding design
by Susan Mitchell.